1994   1st Edi

A LONG B

Service to the Crown — Home and Abroad

A LONG BEAT:

Service to the Crown — Home and Abroad

Arthur Hughes Jenkins

GEE AND SON (DENBIGH) LTD.

ISBN 0 7074 0260 3

Published and Printed by
Gee and Son (Denbigh) Ltd., Chapel Street, Denbigh, Clwyd

Sadly our father, Arthur Hughes Jenkins died before this book was published.

We, his surviving daughters, are publishing this book in his memory, and in memory of our mother, Falmai and our younger sister, Sarah.

Hedd —

Diana and Rowena

CONTENTS

PREFACE

Seventy years since is but the flicker of memory. Each morning as the clock struck 8 a.m. and Richard Thomas, the postman-time-keeper strode resolutely into the village on his five mile trek to the hill farms and hamlets, a group of five or so teenagers set forth on our two mile trudge from Penrhyn-coch to Bow Street to catch the train *en route* for Ardwyn Grammar School, Aberystwyth. Even then Arthur Hughes Jenkins towered above us in his near six foot frame.

As the youngest and smallest of the group, I would frequently have missed my train were it not for his large helping hand, his cheerful smile, his shortened step and above all, his continuous interesting chatter. He enjoyed most subjects because they opened-up new worlds, but literature and particularly geography took pride of place. Geography taught him of other people and exotic places which fed his inquisitive mind and adventurous spirit. *A Long Beat* is a most appropriate title for his autobiography which relates the experiences of one who spent a large part of his active life maintaining law and order in the Royal Air Force, his native Cardiganshire, Hong Kong, Africa and the Falkland Islands. It is a colourful, fascinating story.

A.H.J., who was descended from a hardy stock of master stone-masons, had obviously inherited their passionate love of detail and superb craftsmanship — qualities to be found in this engrossing volume. Sadly its completion was over-shadowed by a short illness which proved fatal, so that he was deprived of the authors' ultimate pleasure of seeing his work in print. He passed away at his Anglesey home on 19 August 1994, and his ashes were interred in his parents' grave at St. John's Church, Penrhyn-coch, on his 84th birthday, 28 September 1994.

David Jenkins

9

A LONG BEAT

I was born in the Parish of Trefeurig in the County of Cardigan, the third of six children of John Daniel and Antoinette Jenkins. We lived in Penrhyncoch. In 1910, the village was separated by two or three fields into three parts. We lived in Penrhyn Canol (middle). Penrhyn Isaf (lower) at a three road junction, had the village Post Office and its shop, a smithy, a church and its school. The upper section though was known as Garth. It had two small general shops and the Baptist Chapel (Horeb). Unusually perhaps, the Baptist chapel here had been built a number of years earlier than the church.

The roads to the east led to Elerch, Brogynnin (birth place of Dafydd ap Gwilym, the famous early Welsh poet) Salem, Penybontrhydybeddau (Head of the bridge of the ford of the graves), Cwmsymlog and Cwmerfin and on through the hills to Ponterwyd and Talybont. To the west the road led to Llanbadarn and to Aberystwyth with its University College and National Library of Wales and to Bow Street on the Aberystwyth-Machynlleth Road and the railway station. Aberystwyth was some five miles distant from Penrhyncoch. Gogerddan Mansion, then the home of the Pryse Family, lay about a mile west of Penrhyn Isaf.

There were many disused lead mines (all with a long and interesting history) within a few miles of Penrhyncoch and the nearest, in a narrow valley perhaps a mile or so from my home, was known to us as Gwaith Glanrafon or Bronfloyd Mine. It became a favourite playground for my brothers and myself and our contemporaries.

Transport to Aberystwyth town in my earlier years was by horse drawn brake. The larger of these, drawn by two horses, could carry about a dozen passengers. The open, four-wheeled

11

vehicle, had three or four rows of seats, approached up a fixed stairway type of ladder at the rear. On the hills, fit passengers were required to dismount and walk, to ease the burden on the horses. In the village, the children always sought to get on to the steps for short rides. Grazed knees were a common sight. Later, John B. Morgan, a relative, started a motor bus service. I feel a twinge of nostalgia for that old bus too. It was the forerunner of what one sees as the Cwmderi Bus in that very long running Welsh TV soap, 'Pobl y Cwm' (Valley Folk). The distant view of Penrhyncoch, in the valley, is never kept on the screen long enough for me to appreciate every spot of the picture. Today's bus company, now Evans owned, carries the name Penrhyncoch not only to Aberystwyth but to most parts of Europe on its coaches.

The village school was staffed by two ladies (Miss Jane Jones and Miss Harper). Two of my brothers were not alone in being required to move to other schools where discipline was more adequately enforced. For my scholarship year, when one was prepared for the examination for entry to the secondary school (Ardwyn Grammar School at Aberystwyth) it was decided that I had to travel daily to Alexandra Road Board School at Aberystwyth. This meant a two mile walk with a short cut through part of Gogerddan grounds, to the railway station at Bow Street and return again in the evening.

The two streams — rivers to us, of course — Stewi and Seilo run through Penrhyncoch to the north side and south side of the village. The Seilo flowed past the Bronfloyd and other lead mines. The Stewi ran clear of these. The former was fishless but the Stewi was a stream of importance to the village lads. Tickling trout could be well rewarding and the river pools became our swimming pools where we soon learned to swim dog paddle fashion. A Sunday afternoon expedition to the river by two of my brothers and myself, at a time when we should have been in Sunday School, is well remembered. We had hidden our bathing costumes in the morning and in the afternoon, instead of going up the hill to Horeb, we retrieved our costumes and headed for the Stewi, where we worked a number of pools over a distance of half a mile or so.

12

Leaving suitable large stones available for the trout to escape we chased the fish from less suitable spots in the pool and then made regular visits to the stones where we could first tickle and then seize the fish with our hands. When we reached home, we were carrying between us, on bulrush strings, twenty six trout. Mother was so pleased to see such a feed of trout that I do not remember that she remembered to punish us for 'mitching' (playing truant) from Sunday School! It is a fish tale we have told many times.

The river Seilo, a little way up stream, was partly diverted to produce the power to operate a mill wheel. We sailed paper boats in the leat and paid regular visits to the mill to watch all the grinding operations. The leat was carried to a point above the mill wheel and then rejoined the river. Such mills were common in those days but rarities today. Nearby the Seilo, with simple ford, could be crossed to approach the farm known as Cwmbwa and foot passengers had the use of a simple wooden bridge. It used to be the delight of the young lads to gather at the ford on days when the visiting steam engine and threshing machine were taken to Cwmbwa to thresh the season's yield of barley, oats or other cereal crops. A steepish hill led straight from the stream for some hundred yards or so and each piece of machinery had to be hauled up in turn by using a very full team of horses. With shouts galore, the cracking of whips and the occasional use of wheel stops, success had to follow and in due course, we boys would earn a meal and some pence for helping with some of the chores such as carrying water for the machine's boiler and removing straw. Rat and mouse destruction also attracted our attention. It was near this ford that I heard of the declaration of war in 1914, although what actually was said, by who and to whom, I do not remember. We also earned pocket money for helping in stone collecting from the open fields where they surfaced and could damage hay cutting machinery.

Postal deliveries in those days were made by a postman who walked with his load from Bow Street in the morning to Cwmsymlog and who then collected the mail on his homeward trip in the afternoon. On Sundays, however, delivery of mail

13

was made only from the village Post Office, over the lower half of a stable door. I remember distinctly various post cards that were sent home during the First World War by an uncle and when on one occasion in an attempt to beat the censor, he wrote about Cwrt Farm's bull (tarw Cwrt) to indicate he was at or near Bullecourt in France.

The war years were tough in Penrhyncoch as they were everywhere else. Rationing of food was severe and official and the general poverty had its own limiting effect. School dinners had not yet been heard of but a thin soup of sorts was provided for all in school, for some time, and could not have been more appreciated.

One became aware of the departure of practically all young men as the war years dragged on. Female workers from away came to work on the local farms. One wonders how it was that such interest in the land girls was taken by lads of our tender years.

For some reason, unknown to me then but guessed at now, we had at the school quite a number of wooden, imitation rifles. I would think they were probably about two thirds actual size but to us they were very real. I can see us trying to use them in drill like movements but, best of all, of course, was when we went to mock war with them. A field on the further side of the nearby Stewi was low lying and boggy and a number of drainage ditches, in parallel lines running towards the river, became our trenches. To hold or capture these as best we might, we fought desperately, mainly with muddy, earthy clods as grenades and verbal bang bangs for rifle shots. Occasionally we sought to disarm our opponents. I can now only imagine the mess we must have been in at the conclusion of the day's fighting.

We were fascinated by the shafts and adits at the Bronfloyd mine particularly but which had their dangers, though not always apparent in our earlier years. We were for ever picking up and examining chunks of lead ore and some of the more interesting pieces would be carried home. We investigated as much as we could the water logged levels and internal workings. The mine though disused for some time, still contained

14

a lot of surface machinery including some of the ore crushers. I can remember an occasion which must have been during the latter stages of the war, when we were at some distance from the crushers, where we had left our eldest brother, and heard a most unusual roaring sound. We presumed he had succeeded in starting up some of the machinery. The sound increased though and we saw our very first aircraft approaching at a low height and pass overhead. Watching it cross the narrow valley, we then saw a man running homeward from a field some half mile distant. We had our own thoughts about what we had just heard and witnessed, so it was no surprise to hear the next day that Jack Pantdrain had indeed run home convinced the Germans were arriving. It had been a habit with us to test the depth of some of the shafts, presumably ventilating shafts, by dropping stones and waiting to hear the sound of a landing in the depths. Most of the shafts had some sort of protecting fencing around them. My brother, we felt sure, once saved the life of one of our friends when we were indulging in this practice. The lad had a very large stone balanced on top of a firm wooden fence and delayed releasing the stone, when leaning over, until he was over balancing and sliding off the fence. My brother only managed to stop him falling in when he luckily grabbed and was able to hang on to the back of his boot above the heel. Even all these years later, I see that some of these shafts have even recently been made safer.

A leaking leat from the Stewi stream once placed me in real peril. A continuing leak caused a quagmire to be formed and crossing it, as I thought in a safe place, I suddenly found myself sinking into the seemingly bottomless quicksand like earth. My two brothers were unable to free me. Then, while one held me firmly by the hand, the other ran the few hundred yards to fetch my father who was able to pull me free. We avoided that particular short cut home from the Stewi after that. The leat was most useful to us and several neighbours for it then ran in the field at the back of our gardens and by a pipe through the hedge, kept a small pool in our garden supplied with useful but not drinking water. Drinking water had to be carried quite some distance from a common source of supply at Garth. My father dowsed for water and had dug wells for others when house building in rural areas. I don't know why it took so long before my mother prevailed on him to do likewise at our home! In the event, he found ample supply of water thirteen feet down in the corner of our garden and in due course a force pump fed this to the house. In the severe drought of 1921 a number of our neighbours were also supplied at our pump which did not run dry.

It was long after dark when we heard a knock at the door that night in November 1918 and saw an uncle of mine enter. He told us the good news that the fighting had stopped. The man who was blind, had another three miles to walk to reach his home at Cwmerfin. I think that I was struck more by the fact that the blind man had already walked several miles from Aberystwyth with his news and had still to walk home the remaining miles in the dark than at his actual news. Later I was to escort him on some of his journeys around the county to tune and repair pianos. I came to dismantle pianos ready for his attention too. Nearly seventy years later I can still smell seccotine. He was the organist at his chapel in Cwmerfin and he repaired organs too.

I was never taught to play the piano but I was in the class at my Aberystwyth school where the famous Sir Walford Davies then professor of music at the College and later to become Master of the King's Music, came and tried to teach us some music and to play the tin whistle in the process. We were expected to learn and practise 'Tonic Solfa' at Horeb Band of Hope meetings. In those days, too, more children attended Sunday School than seems the case today, though at Horeb, workers still continue in their efforts and with a great deal of success.

The river Seilo was our local Jordan and Horeb Baptists used the river in which to baptise new members by total immersion in a pool usually improved for the occasion. Access to the river at this point was through a small property owned by Elias Jenkins, my father's uncle and only a few yards across the road from my home.

In October 1991 when revisiting Penrhyncoch, I went to

16

Brondderw, Penrhyncoch. My Home. Where the story began.

Leading apprentice, 1929. RAF Ruislip, Middlesex.

Jenkins family at Brondderw. Summer 1927.
Back Row. Left to Right: Tommy, Arthur, Glyn.
Front Row. Left to Right: Eileen, Mother, Eddie, Father, Bessie.

Horeb and looked again at my grandfather's grave and others and I was pointing out the grave of the minister (Rev. O. E. Williams) who had baptised me in the river nearly seventy years ago, when we were approached by his daughter who then led us into the chapel to see her husband, Dr. David Jenkins (former Librarian of the National Library of Wales) where he was supervising the final touches to some internal improvements that had become necessary. He, with the late David W. James of Y Felin (The mill) and myself for some time when we were so young, years ago, shared the opening of the Sunday School proceedings. In our turn, we would read out a selected hymn and, an impromptu prayer, give thanks for the occasion and seek God's Blessing. Dr. Jenkins confirmed that all baptisms were still carried out in the river Seilo. I remembered a man being baptised with snow falling on the scene. He was our local postman. Many other memories were revived as Dr. Jenkins pointed out where so and so and so and so used to sit in those long distant days at the normal Sunday services.

The Baptist cause in Penrhyncoch is much older than the local church, St. John's with its Gogerddan influences. In 1787, one Dafydd Hughes of Felinfoel, near Llanelli, was on a missionary journey from Harlech to Carmarthen. He was invited to stay in Gogerddan on his way south and to preach there. Shortly afterwards he baptised two young women in the river by the mansion, where the Seilo and the Stewi were now one river. Both women were from Harlech and a few months later he baptised another four. Later the Baptists formed their own church in Penrhyncoch and it became the mother church of others at Aberystwyth, Talybont, Llanrhystud and Swydd-ffynnon.

I had learned to ride a cycle at a very early age. In these days of ten gear cycles, mountain bikes and so many other varieties of specialist cycles, it is difficult to imagine that we had to learn to ride on bicycles with solid rubber tyres, for pneumatic tyres were still a rarity. The penny farthing was already a museum piece at that time.

Fox hunting by the Gogerddan pack went on for many years. As youngsters we tried to be available at certain gates to assist

17

and receive our due rewards. Packet's of five Woodbine cigarettes for 2d (about 5/6ths of today's one pence) were amongst our ensuing purchases. The hunting process is regularly described and portrayed by the pros and the antis. We youngsters did not miss much and mothers and daughters routinely wore their fox furs.

One of my twelfth birthday gifts was to be allowed to fire my first shot with a 12 bore shotgun. In some of these matters I had to take third place to my two older brothers. Generally we concentrated more on shooting rabbits than on ferretting and netting them. Each cartridge was a valuable commodity but I confess to shooting ferns on occasion instead of rabbits, as in the gloaming, hard staring to get that grazing rabbit to take home never succeeded in turning ferns into rabbits. There was one occasion when I did shoot a rabbit and its neck-attached weasel but that was in broad daylight with the poor rabbit squealing and running.

Between the World Wars, before the introduction of that dreadful disease of myxamatosis, rabbit catching in the county was a widespread industry. Trappers were employed full-time and their catches, by the hundreds, would be collected by lorries, usually for ready markets in the Midlands. Farmers gained by the sale of rabbit rights and by the reduction in losses of their crops and grazing. I do not know whether a rabbit will consume as much as a goose but by their very numbers, rabbits would present a far greater problem. In the Falkland Islands farmers were paying for each beak of the Upland goose which consumed much of the rations of their wool producing sheep.

Long before the National Health Service was dreamt about, various schemes existed to pay for specialist medical treatment. Individual medical practitioners had their private methods of ensuring that folk who could not afford their fees, could nevertheless be provided with essential treatments. For a payment of three pence per week, full hospital treatment was available to many families at the Aberystwyth Infirmary. Attention at a doctor's surgery too was billed according to the person in receipt of it rather than the quality or quantity of the attention. As a

18

young lad with a very badly swollen arm, I had to find my own way to the surgery some seven miles away at Borth, by riding there on a borrowed bicycle. In the event it proved to be a badly poisoned arm. The doctor directed me to return home and said he would be there later to treat me. This he did by lancing the swollen elbow to relieve the arm of its poisons. The after care needed twice daily visits for a short period by the district nurse. I was most appreciative of the attention. I can only guess at my age as I recollect the careful selection I used to make of those message bearing button shaped sweets which were available at that time. Messages like 'I Love You' and 'I Think You're Charming!!' These selections were given to the nurse bashfully and, hopefully, received with more interest than amusement.

But all was not yet serious. Our home made footballs were usually pig's bladders. In those days, the pig was often the mainstay of a family's home economy. Where there was room for a pig sty, people kept a pig if they could. The pig was fed mainly on left overs and almost anything would be acceptable. Usually a barrel of sorts would be kept convenient to the sty to receive cabbage leaves, potatoes and potato peelings and in fact all manner of things that would become a mix and then be fed by the tin full from the barrel to the pig's trough. I doubt whether a goose was ever fed to a Welsh pig but in the Falkland Islands, it was a common practice in the country for a shepherd to feed Upland geese to his pig. He would shoot these wild geese for they deprived his other creatures of their best pasture, and throw them, as picked up, to the pig.

In Penrhyncoch, in those days, it was DICK LLADD MOCH (Pig Killer Dick) who came avisiting to despatch and deal with the family's pig. We did not keep a pig ourselves but passed on anything useful for it to our neighbour. Dick Lladd Moch had his annual round of customers. He would arrive with his special apron, bag of knives and tools then check that all was in order — an adequate supply of boiling water, suitable board or door laid ready to receive the dying pig. A good sound line was secured around the pig's upper jaw and it was then led

19

protestingly to the appointed spot. If all went well the pig was held steady with its head held high with the line. A long knife was inserted to a depth of about six inches at the base of the neck where the arteries would be severed and the animal went to the floor as the rush of blood took its life away. I was present once when the pig broke loose with only a partial cutting effected. There were hectic and noisy minutes before the pig was caught again in the confined small yard and then properly dispatched.

Then came the scraping off of the bristles with special scrapers and the boiling water, followed by hoisting of the carcass and its cutting up in due course. There was then also the custom of taking a few choice pieces to neighbours. Home cured really meant cured at home and 'bowing to the pig' meant literally bowing your head to pass under the side of bacon or whatever as it hung suspended in various parts of the house — often on an upstairs landing. Some people used the cleaned bladder in which to store the fats rendered down into lard.

I remember being disturbed at some of our early horse riding sessions. Each season a number of ponies were brought by Benji Baker from Rhydypennau to graze a nearby field. It had become a practice of my older brothers to corner and catch some of the ponies and using a home made string bridle, to ride them round the field. So we caught them and on occasion rode them or fell off them. A particular occasion I recall is when in the moonlight, we saw a man approaching us and it behove us to depart the ponies and make our escape. My brothers disappeared quickly while I could only run in ever diminishing circles to land eventually on my back with feet in the air to avoid if I could, the man who now had all but caught me. He leaned over me and my raised feet stretched to support him by his middle until he was all but thrown over my head. It was my father! I understood later that my elder brother had spent the next two hours under his grandfather's bed in his nearby home. Glyn got home safely to his own bed. Probably on account of my youth, my father must have thought the chase and catching was enough for me. But we have remembered it all for these many years.

My grandparents kept a cow or two and a pig or two though their 'farm' was only of two fields. They had an exceptionally nice large Russet apple tree in their garden. We knew the crop was stored in the hayshed in the field next to our home. Time came when we now thought it timely to collect a supply of these apples without permission. We climbed to the top of the hay in the shed and started digging with our arms into the hay but to our great disappointment we found not the delicious ripened apples but a horrible mess of well cooked apple stew. The apples were presumably covered by hay which had become too heated and the crop was thus destroyed. We allowed Dadcu (grandfather) to find out for himself.

The long walk to and from Bow Street railway station, the ten minute train ride into Aberystwyth and then the walk of not less than a mile to and from Ardwyn School for several years from September 1922, in my case, was a necessary evil for some of us before the advent of school buses. I can remember they were hard times economically and a stop at Pain's shop on the way to Ardwyn to buy a pennyworth of broken biscuits was almost an event. Would it be countenanced today? During my last year or two in school, if the weather was cold I seem to remember that my father's overcoat was always a little on the large and heavy side. There were no lightweight and colourful anoraks then.

At school, there was very little guidance, if any, available when choice of subjects for study arose. French or Welsh started from the first year and German or Latin from the next year for example, in the Fifth Form, the School Certificate year, a further choice could be made by me to carry on with a fourth year in French or a third year in German. My choice of German rather than French was made solely for the reason that the German mistress was an infinitely better disciplinarian and teacher than the more qualified French teacher. A number of my contemporaries who chose French, failed to qualify for their Central Welsh Board School Certificate as their failure to pass in French gave them no foreign language as a pass to

21

go with some of their other excellent results. In consequence of this their studies were delayed a whole year. Some time later, I gathered that the French master had been transferred to elementary school teaching. Later in this case meant some sixty years later when I read of it in someone's autobiography.

I have other happier memories of meetings, long after school days, with former school friends. I met Willie Ellis in St. Vincent in the West Indies. He always drew pictures of beautiful sailing ships at our back table in our geography class. As captain of a Canadian bauxite carrying ship on its way from Demerara to Canada he stopped off to see me in St. Vincent a quarter of a century later. We met up again in Wales, briefly, some twenty years after that.

Ardwyn School pupils had use of the gymnasium facilities of the University College at Aberystwyth. In those days of early film making, an Aberystwyth cinema proprietor (Mr. Cheetham of the Palladium Cinema then at Market and Eastgate streets) filmed some of our outdoor physical displays on the College field. Our excitement at a showing of the film in the cinema may be imagined. This film and others taken then in the area have been made available for viewing some sixty five years later.

A school strike in the early twenties meant that Ardwyn pupils of under school leaving age had to attend their elementary schools. In my case, I attended briefly, at my fourth school, the school at Penybontrhydybeddau. This meant a walk of over two miles from my home in Penrhyncoch. The railway strike in 1926 meant a long walk from Penrhyncoch to Aberystwyth and back to attend school at Ardwyn.

My first encounter with the police was on a street in Aberystwyth, when indulging in a game of 'waiting for the train' football. Unfortunately, one of the goal posts was my father's overcoat and a hurried retreat on seeing the law approaching was out of the question for me. A verbal warning and without name taking was not unacceptable by me.

Having earned my school certificate in 1926, I returned for the first term only of the next school year and the ending of those school years was quite traumatic. Life in the in between wars years was quite hard and the securing of my first job

22

was very pleasing to myself and, I hoped, to my parents, for while I could not yet be entirely self supporting, I hoped to lessen their burden. I became a sort of apprentice bookseller cum shop assistant and general dog's body in the main bookshop in Aberystwyth. Mr. Sansbury the manager of S. V. Galloway's bookshop, became my helpful and understanding immediate boss. Time came when we suspected a certain member of the cloth of removing books unlawfully and it was suggested that on the man's next visit, I should watch him carefully and on his departure, in any event, 'tail' him to obtain his address for he was not known to belong to any local church. The tracking was successfully accomplished and the address seemed to indicate that the man was a holiday-maker and indeed nothing more was seen or heard of him at the shop.

I was unaware then that this was in fact to be the first essay on my part in the prevention of breaches of the peace during the coming years. It was thought best that I should be a lodger in Aberystwyth during the week and return home for the weekends only. My meeting and talking one evening with a young constable had nothing to do with my 'tracking' effort. From time to time, I walked his hourly beat with him and was interested to know that he had also served a short stint in the Palestine Police before becoming a member of the Cardiganshire Constabulary. These walks and talks aroused no thoughts that I can remember, that I should consider a police career. I was still only sixteen and living from home was still a most novel experience.

My mother was English and though she claimed some distant Welsh connections, life in a small almost entirely Welsh rural community was a big change for her after life in Birmingham. It was natural then that our mother spoke to us in English and our knowledge of Welsh was minimal until we went to school. We would laugh at mother's attempts on occasion to speak Welsh with callers. What I now remember is that there was little she did not understand but speaking in Welsh was always a problem for her. My brothers and sisters, like myself, then continued speaking in English to my mother but invariably spoke in Welsh with our father, even when we were all sharing in the general conversation. It could well have been that our English was improved thereby but that our Welsh was to some extent hampered.

A few months only at the booksellers found me in search of something different to do and so it was in April 1927 that I was enrolled as a Boy Apprentice Clerk General Duties in the Royal Air Force Record Office at Ruislip in Middlesex. The terms of the engagement provided for the apprenticeship to take two years and that for twelve years from the age of eighteen I should be bound to serve in the Royal Air Force.

Groups of boys were being enrolled every three months and I found I was in the Seventh Entry and that I was the eightieth such apprentice. We were paid seven shillings (35p) per week in the first year and, of course, free food, accommodation and uniform. Five shillings (25p) per week though was retained by the Service to be handed over when we went on leave, and after payment of one's share of barrack damages. The weekly pay parades were preceded by route marches through the surrounding countryside and dressed in 'best blues', breeches and puttees. When my number was called in the pay queue, I would respond with 'Sir, 080' step forward with open palm and receive a 2/- piece (10p), then salute, a smart about turn and make way for the next apprentice. Almost every week though, like other boys, I would have had bars of chocolate on credit and the seller, usually a more affluent apprentice, would be right there to collect his dues and the two shilling piece would disappear. Sixteen year olds do get hungry. We were known to leave camp, without permission, on occasion, and bring back the occasional swede from a nearby field.

Entrants were required to have earned a Senior school certificate before enrolment in each alternate Entry or to pass an RAF examination of equivalent standard for other Entries. Our training included the continuation of educational studies and attendance at religious instruction by a local minister of one's own denomination. We were taught shorthand, typing and all aspects of clerical work and R.A.F. procedures. Writing home, baths, sport and leisure activities were all well supervised. For example, the boys were only allowed to travel out of Camp in

24

company of one or more other boys; never with the men of our Station. Neither were they allowed to 'associate with females down the village'! To go on Special Pass, away from Camp, on weekend or other leave, one was allowed to travel alone. I would occasionally go to London at a weekend and visit the Welsh Baptist Church in Castle Street, where the services were, naturally, in Welsh. After the evening service, I would go with a number of the congregation on a walk to Hyde Park at Marble Arch where other Welsh people would also foregather to sing Welsh hymns. We would meet old friends and make new ones. I felt the visits were always so worthwhile.

Smoking was punishable by confinement to barracks though those who attained the age of 18 years before completion of the two years apprenticeship, could obtain a pass permitting smoking other than in camp buildings!

The passing out of the First Entry was quite an event as the most senior Royal Air Force Officer, the Chief of the Air Staff ('Boom' Trenchard, often known as the Father of the Air Force) Marshal of the Royal Air Force Viscount Trenchard came to participate in the usual passing out parade procedures. The originator of the Apprentice Clerk Scheme (the late Air Vice Marshal Sir John W. Cordingley) was the Officer Commanding the Royal Air Force Record Office. Introduced in 1925, it was continued to 1942 during which time just over 2,000 apprentice clerks were attested. The Ninth Annual Reunion of Ex-Ruislip Apprentices was scheduled for 1992.

Visits to nearby R.A.F. Northolt were often of interest, for example, seeing Ramsay Macdonald being brought back for Parliamentary business from Scotland in a then-normal open cockpit; being shown a Siskin fighter aircraft's 'ground communication system' — just a Morse-tapping key by the pilot's right hand!! As I sat astride the fuselage behind the single cockpit to be shown this, the pilot was Flight Lieutenant S. M. Webster who had just won the Schneider Trophy in Venice in 1927.

After twenty weeks, my first leave became due and that homesick-making Paddington-Aberystwyth marked train I saw passing almost daily was now to become my transport home. I had become used to seeing people working in their gardens and allotments on Sundays. Coming from Wales, I had been shocked by this when I first saw it. My fear of the use of barrack room language retreated at once when I found myself back again in my own environment. And for this I was most grateful.

Life in a barrack room was a testing time for young boys. Our dormitory held twenty one beds for our total Seventh Entry, with an instructor occupying an adjoining single room. Heating was provided in winter by two donkey stoves which had to be kept black-leaded and polished at all times. Dark brown lines covered the entire floor space and this, of course, had to be kept clean and polished. A weekly inspection demanded extra polishing and this was usually a communal effort when a half mattress (called a biscuit) was placed on a blanket with a boy to sit thereon, which two others in stocking feet, pulled from end to end of the room. Each boy then, as best he could, protected his own bed space and kept it spotless until the inspection next day. The stoves went unlit and we turned in early! The ablution room at the end of the dormitory had cold water taps only. There were no showers and the baths were away in a separate block and could not be used except when made specially available for supervised regular baths and after games.

I joined a small group of boys who acquired a crystal set (radio) and with necessary headphones and wiring, we were able to listen to those occasional broadcasts from London —2LO. The night orderly officer soon came to frown on sleeping head-phoned apprentices. Not to be outdone, another group acquired a Two Valve Set and these too were connected up for bedtime listening. The rivalry became rather intense and I can only remember now that at some fairly early stage, the 'Crystal' boys connected themselves as well to the Two Valve Set and for some time shared the better reception without the knowledge or permission of the Two Valvers. And it was only to prove the point that we were getting equally good reception that the precise wiring connections were exposed and our deception of them admitted. Our dormitory had become known as the bird-cage.

We were very fortunate in the athletics scene for being near RAF Uxbridge, where there were all the suitable facilities, we were taken there to be coached and sometimes by RAF champions who were themselves in training, in a variety of field and track events. Two or three of these were up to Olympic standard. We even had a visit and talk by Harold Abrahams, the 1924 Olympic Sprint Champion. For the respective age groups pass standards were set for a whole series of events and attainment of a standard, with more or less unlimited attempts, was credited to the individual, to his flight and to our station. On a system of percentages, a Higgins shield was thus competed for annually by the boys at the several training places in the Air Force at that time. In this way while there were only about 100 boys at Ruislip, we could perhaps win against the apprentice mechanics at RAF Halton, Bucks., where they may number as many as 3,000. This scheme introduced boys to events they might otherwise not have contemplated attempting. I still proudly keep my two certificates and two medals for which I qualified in my two years.

The end of the apprenticeship came in due course with all the examinations. One was expected to pass in one of three qualifications — Leading Aircraftman, Aircaftman First Class or Aircraftman 2nd Class, all in the trade 'Clerk, General Duties'. We were then immediately available for posting to any RAF unit but only those in the United Kingdom in the first instance.

My posting was to the office of the Officer Commanding the Officers' Engineering Course at the Home Aircraft Depot, Henlow, Bedfordshire. The pay of a Leading Aircraftman Clerk G.D. at that time was £1.11.6 (£1.56) a week.

I had been introduced to Rugby football by an Irish P.T. instructor when at Ruislip and managed to make the station's team. Now at Henlow I was able to play against teams of quite good standards. We played as far afield as London, Leamington, Cambridge, Northampton and Bedford of course. Flight Lieutenant G. R. Beamish of Ireland and Lions fame, played

27

with us in some of our service cup matches. By chance too, he was kind enough to let me ride with him in a Gipsy Moth, after trying the rear cockpit for fit with an injured shoulder, and gave me my first experience of looping the loop and inverted flying. The Gipsy Moth was one of twelve of the type provided specially to enable officers on the two year engineering course to maintain their flying standards with a minimum of forty hours flying per annum. It was not a standard RAF aircraft but I believe the Tiger Moth was produced later so that the front cockpit as well as the rear cockpit was situated aft of struts and wiring which in the Gipsy could have created extra difficulty for the front passenger/pilot in departing the aircraft in an emergency.

As applications for cross country flights were submitted through my office, I was often enabled to have flights to other RAF stations and where, usually, we would display! Trips over Twickenham on an international rugby match day and Brooklands all added to the interest of service life. On some occasions I would be invited to take over the controls. The first time this happened, I was told by the pilot, in the rear cockpit, that he would waggle the wings for me to know when to take over — no radio communications in those days — and to keep the top of the nose in line with the horizon — this before taking off of course. What I first thought was a waggle was not a waggle and I found the joystick stiff and steady but a few minutes later there was no mistaking a waggle and I took hold of the stick. After a short while I found my attempt at keeping the aircraft in level flight was not very succesful so I decided I would do a waggle and then threw my arms in the air quickly as a sign that control was all his again!

Henlow was also the home of the Parachute Packing and Repair Unit. Testing of parachutes was carried out by actual pull offs and drops. On a Vickers Vimy aircaft, a small platform was built around the two rear outer struts and a volunteer airman stood on each, with parachute ready to be deployed. He would be holding the strut and standing in front of it at take-off and at the appropriate time they would receive the signal to move around to the rear of the strut ready for the signal for each simultaneously to pull the rip cord of his parachute. The parachute would then tear him off his platform and duly land him at the planned area on the airfield below. Sometimes several aircraft flew in formation and all operated the parachutes at the same time. My name was on the List but did not appear for action before I left for RAF Hendon, so I can only say what happened to others. The advances in parachutes have been as startling as advances in most other techniques over the years.

A young Aberystwyth man heeded not my advice that to do a delayed parachute drop was not commendable practice but in a short time after his first drop, not in the service though, he held several amateur records for delayed drops

Air races to and from distant places overseas were becoming common events. I assisted with paper work for one competitor in his bid to beat the record for a flight to Australia. He was one of our course officers who had been held a prisoner of war by the Turks in the Great War and was co-author, with a Welsh Jones, of a book entitled *The Road to Endor* which was an account of their efforts to obtain their freedom. Flight Lieut. C. W. Hill had made excellent progress as far as Sourabaya, where his aircaft, in a muddy landing, sustained too much damage to attempt to continue. He had then given his collapsible boat (intended for use in case of Timor Sea crossing problems) to the following Kingsford Smith, a famous record holding pilot of those days. Was this not the first of aircraft dinghies?

29

R.101 and R.100

When I arrived at RAF Henlow in April 1929, I soon heard a lot about the R.101, for the Royal Airship Works Cardington were only some ten miles away. Most of the workmen and crews lived in the Bedford area. The airship was almost ready. Up at Howden in Yorkshire the Airship R.100, designed and built by the Airship Guarantee Company, on a private enterprise basis was expected to be completed about the same time. The R.101 was being constructed partly by the State, as represented by the Air Ministry and the Royal Airship Works with the assistance of some private firms, notably Boulton and Paul Ltd. Both airships were, of course, produced to the orders of the Air Ministry. A definite airship development policy had eventually been established back in 1924 under the Labour Government then in office. It called for two rigid airships to be built and each was to have a capacity of about five million cubic feet. This meant they would be far bigger than anything of the sort ever built before; in fact, to nearly twice the size of any previous airship. Lord Thomson who was the Air Minister in the 1924 Labour Government was most enthusiastic. His choice of title 'Thomson of Cardington' would seem to confirm this.

The R.101 was to be 732 ft. long — the length of two soccer pitches, end to end. The height including the projecting control car would be about 140 ft. She had five engine cars of which two were placed forward, a slight distance outboard, two a little abaft of midships and further out from the centre line, while the fifth was placed aft, on the centre line. The engine cars, though comparatively small, could nevertheless provide enough room for an engineer to enter by a ladder from the interior of the ship and to move about in it to attend to his engine.

The accommodation was located on two decks. The upper deck carried a large lounge with promenades on each side. The promenades had glass windows in the outer cover of the ship. A dining room to accommodate up to 50 passengers and a number of two-berth cabins were also on this deck. The lower deck carried the Captain's Control Room, with open communication between it and the projecting control car beneath. The electric kitchen too was on this deck.

Passengers entered the ship through a hinged gangway near the extreme nose and this was accessible from the circular gallery at the top of the mooring mast which could be reached both by lift and stairs.

Unfortunately, the lifting medium had to be hydrogen and not the infinitely safer helium monopolised by the U.S. While the main engines were powered by heavy oil, each had a smaller petrol engine to start it. The normal fuel tanks had a capacity of about 30 tons.

The water ballast system had a capacity of about 15 tons but this could be replenished by trapped rain.

Over the next few months, I heard more and more such detail. We knew that when actually flying or when attached to a mast, an airship can cope remarkably well with very variable weather conditions but when the ship was going to be manhandled out of her shed to the mooring mast, a flat calm was essential.

Then in early October, when it seemed we might have had the weather conditions needed, we had one or two alarms and we gathered that vast crowds were finding their way to Bedford ready to see the giant airship when she was brought out of her shed for the first time. On 11th October I was told I was to be one of some 150 airmen from RAF Henlow who were to join with a party from the Royal Airship Works and another small party from Bedford town, making some 400 in all, who would be required to do the manhandling of R.101 early the next morning. So then we were driven to Cardington. We seemed mere ants in the vastness of the shed and the airship was just too big to be seen all at once. Despite her size, however, it seems she was ballasted so precisely that in the stillness of the shed, she could be lifted or lowered by hand so to speak.

The control car was protected from contact with the ground by a moveable pad and a basket affair held in place by several transverse poles passed through the base of the car. These poles projected on each side and a number of us were detailed to handle them. Fore and aft, other men handled the ropes suspended from the ship and in due course we were given our orders to take the ship forward and all walking together, it seemed we were doing so. We all knew what a slight breeze will do to an umbrella and we feared what might happen if any breeze was more than we could cope with when the ship emerged through those gigantic doors. Doubtless there were those in charge whose fears were considerably greater than ours.

Together then we continued to walk, pull on ropes and handle the poles until we finally reached the so-far-away seen Mooring Mast. Crowds lining the roads could be heard cheering. We saw a cable from the mast being joined to the end of a cable which had been lowered from the nose of the ship. We then removed our long poles and the pad from the base of the control car and when the winches in the Mooring Mast hauled in the joined cable, the nose of R.101 was raised to the top of the Mast and secured. The cables were then separated and recovered to the ship and mast respectively. At the mast, R.101 would always turn into the wind, like a weather vane, and I remember there was also attached to the ship, at times, near the tail end, a heavy roller which moved easily with it as it swung at anchor as it were and at the same time helped to maintain the ship on an even keel.

And that is where we left the giant ship on 12th October, 1929. It was a Saturday and during the weekend the roads to Cardington were congested with traffic and it was thought that nearly a million people must have seen her. On Monday, about mid-day, she actually flew for the first time and went on to fly over London. She flew over the Midlands as well in October

P.C. 38 Jenkins.

Falmai Wyn Pugh, 1933.

but on the 21st we returned her to the shed where she remained for about a week before she was manhandled again to the Mast, before flying over Norfolk. She was flown several times in November and before the end of the month, she had carried out an endurance flight lasting about a day and a half. On November 30th though, we took her back to the shed once more. Those of us who were handling the poles at the control car, by this time knew how to cope with several shallow wet ditches between the Mast and the shed. We lifted the poles together and then hung on them by our hands until across the wet parts and our combined weight brought the ship down to our walking level again. I think the actual lift was not more than four or five feet — most of us just kept our feet off the ground and rode the poles. But the R.101 had bigger problems and she remained in her shed until 23rd June, 1930.

After her return to the Mast she was flown on trials and to the Air Display at Hendon but all was not well, so on the 29th June, R.101 had to be taken again to the shed and remained there till 1st October. I am only able to say that during this period she underwent a very major refit. Apparently it was decided that she had to be given more lift and this was done by cutting her into two parts, extending her then by adding an extra bay to accommodate more gas bags. R.101 was then some 70 feet longer. We heard a lot of criticism especially when this became more generally known and her performance compared with that of R.100. We had handled R.100 when she came to Cardington. She made a successful flight to Canada and back and appeared to be giving satisfactory results. I am not able to enter any discussion on the merits or demerits of the two ships nor express any personal opinion.

The day we brought the ship back out to the Mooring Mast, the 1st of October, 1930, she set out on what became her only trial flight with the new bay in place. The flight lasted less than 20 hours. Having returned to the Mooring Mast on 2nd October, R.101 stayed there being refuelled and prepared in every possible way for her real maiden voyage long since scheduled to India. The Air Minister, Lord Thomson came aboard with five other passengers and with six people from

33

the Royal Airship Works including Major Scott the Assistant Director (Flying) who was Officer in Charge of Flight (and who had directed our own little efforts with the aid of his megaphone). The crew for this voyage numbered 42 so there were in all 54 people on board when departure time at last became possible, though still in poor weather conditions, long after dark on Saturday, 4th October, 1930. There were still crowds there waiting to see her off.

The Captain for the flight was Flight Lieutenant H. C. Irwin. The first stop was to be in Egypt. R.101 flew over Bedford then south to London by about 8 p.m. Radio messages were being exchanged and reports on the bad weather being encountered were sent by the ship. She was fighting an adverse wind and seemed to be having problems with lift. She crossed the Channel. At midnight she reported to Cardington and all seemed to be well. Later, after radio checks, the ship was just north of Beauvais and acknowledged by R.101 to Le Bourget. Just after 2 a.m. Le Bourget asked R.101 for her speed and tried again for the answer some minutes later. No answer came from the ship but Le Bourget, in a matter of only minutes later, had the news that the R.101 had crashed some 3 miles outside Beauvais and reported to the world that the giant airship had caught fire.

One of the wireless operators and five engineers only survived.

The news came to us at Henlow early that Sunday morning.

In France, everything that could be done was apparently done. A day of mourning throughout France and its colonies was ordered by the French Cabinet. The world sent its sympathies.

The coffins lay in state in Beauvais Town Hall till Tuesday then taken in a great procession to the railway station and on by rail to Boulogne. Wreaths and flowers covered the coffins as British Navy destroyers brought them to Dover where a special train carried the coffins to London. Later, they lay-in-state in Westminster Hall. A Memorial Service was held in St. Paul's Cathedral and a Requiem Mass was said at the Westminster Cathedral for those of the dead who were Roman Catholics.

On the following Saturday, all the bodies were brought back to Cardington by train from Euston to Bedford. The procession to Euston was an overpowering spectacle. Comrades of the dead headed the procession. The third watch of the R.101 and the crew of R.100 followed their lost comrades. The nation mourned and showed it.

Bedford was a town of quiet streets, shuttered shops, of houses all with drawn blinds. All places of business were shut. The last scenes at Bedford too were unforgettable not because of any ceremonial or military tributes but because of the home-coming of these men after the splendour of the service at St. Paul's and magnificence of the lying-in-state at Westminster Hall. Only fourteen of the coffins bore names. The other thirty-four bore only the words 'To the Memory of the Unknown Airman who died on October 5th.'

They were all known to somebody and some of them were known to us at Henlow. We buried them on the 11th October 1930. On the 13th I wrote to my sister — the actual letter is in front of me now — (25 October 1991) — from RAF Henlow. It reads —

'Dear Bessie,

I have just come in from the cinema and supper and I have suddenly remembered that tomorrow is your Birthday — I am very sorry — I was thinking about it last week — I think the events of this last week end put it out of my mind . . . You will have read all about the R.101 in the papers. I expect you will have seen all about the funeral at Cardington in the papers as well. It will give you more details than I can but you will be interested to know that I was one of the coffin bearers. It was a terrible ordeal. There were six of us to a coffin. We wore greatcoats with belt and bayonet &c as you will see from the photos. Later, you will probably see it in the cinemas as Gaumonts', Fox's and Movietone people were there. We paraded on the square here at 9 a.m. and 286 of us (bearers) left for Bedford on the tenders. The roads outside Bedford were filling up at 11 o'clock. We got to the Station soon after. Before the train came in, the Escort Party, Firing Party and

35

our Band arrived by special train from Henlow soon after — and an Army Band at about 12 o'clock.

Some people fainted when the Funeral Train pulled in — including one of the Army bandsmen. Before we had started on the march out, one of our fellows in the Escort Party also fainted away. We saw him on the stretcher as we marched past.

It was terrible to see the relatives come out of the train — then the hundreds of wreaths — above 18 RAF planes flew in formation, droning to the sound of bells from the Bedford churches. It was terribly impressive.

Then, in turn, six bearers went on to the platform — brought out a coffin and carried it, draped with the Union Jack to the rows of waiting RAF six-wheel tenders. Coffin after coffin came out — the 39th was our turn — we marched slowly from our tender, lifted up the coffin — it was very heavy and bore it slowly to our tender. We pulled down the Union Jack all over it and placed wreaths on top. The next coffin lay in the tender besides ours.

Silence reigned — a sob here and there alone broke the silence. Then the church bells again and then the roar of 18 aeroplanes swooping down in formation to salute the dead. It seemed as if I moved in a dream or rather a nightmare, for I wanted to scream out every minute. My cap was tight on my forehead again. I was standing to attention by the front wheel of the tender. All the coffins were on their tenders ready for the last stage of their long journey.

I heard the Band start playing the 'Dead March' — the clash of the cymbals felt like ice down my spine. We moved slowly forward. On the bridge in the distance, I could see the Escort Party marching slowly, slowly on — behind them the Firing Party — the Band — then the first of the tenders. Slowly we moved onwards — We were out of the station and in the street — Left, right, left right — thousands of people were in front gardens, windows, balconies &c. Women crying — dreadful. On we went, over the bridge — We could see the last of the tenders and the front of the long, long row of cars bringing the relatives.

It was hot — the sun was pouring down on us — my arms

36

stiff at my sides — shoulders back — My back started aching :
— My cap tight — a dead head. Sweat ran down into my
eyes, down my face — I couldn't move my hands up! My
feet were like lead. Slowly hundreds of faces seemed to move
back from my right. The smell of the flowers came to us
mixed with the smell of the exhaust of the tender in front of
us. The Band miles ahead it seemed, died down — the band
far behind started another 'Dead March'.

Policemen saluted as we passed — Children whimpered and
women cried. I looked ahead. I tried to swallow. A Sergeant
marching just in front of me beside the tender, seemed to falter
in his stride — nearly put me out of step. I glanced down,
then, with averted face, I carried on the Slow March.
Thousands of people lined the road all the way.

My head ached — the engines revving up, made it worse.
I felt like dropping. I noticed another airman on a stretcher,
on the road side just in front of the crowd, being attended to
by some St. John Ambulance men.

Onwards under the trees, round the bend we could see
tender after tender with the flowers showing above their sides
— the two black rows of people each side of the road.

The train had arrived in as it struck a quarter-to-two. We
must have come about two miles. Another mile and a half —
slow marching all the time. The roadside thick with people.
I felt like dropping. My kingdom for a drop of water — to
take my cap off. Still onwards — we quick marched for about
two hundred yards — my legs going automatically — a pain
down the centre of my back. We halted. Over there the two
big sheds — through the trees the Church. The trees full of
people. A stand with a cameraman on it.

The church bells tolled away and women cried aloud
Another I see faints away. We move on again — a yard at a
time now. Over the cemetery wall I can see a big mound of
earth — the grave the other side of it. We halt again. We
pull back the coffin. I stoop down, put my shoulder under it,
arise and 'Slow March'! Slowly we move through the gates
—a policeman moves the Union Jack from my eyes — I see

37

the mourners, clergy, high officers — the Band, the Firing Party, yes and the survivors — below me the grave.

The sides of the grave are covered with moss and flowers — a border all round the top. At the bottom, in rows, are the 38 coffins still covered in the Union Jack. The silence is unbroken save for the clicking of the cameras and the sobs from the women. The officers salute the coffin. Someone takes my cap from my hand. I turn to my right and down, slowly, step by step we move into the grave. The coffin is heavy — an undertaker meets us half way down the ramp — he pushes against the coffin to stop it slipping. We are shown its resting place. We halt, turn inwards and lower him — Lord Thomson or my mate's brother? — to the ground. We straighten up — our bit is done. We file up the ramp to make room for the next — No. 40 — still 8 more to come.

I find my hat — fall in again by the road — our tender has moved up to the village green to make room for the others. We wait. I wipe my face. Someone asks an ambulance man for a drink of water. A crowd march up the road — they come across to our party and give us water.

The bells still toll away. It is nearly 5 o'clock! The sun dips behind the big shed — the home of R.101. A hymn — the burial service. Then three volleys fired over the grave. The 'Last Post' creeps upon us again. All is still: we hear a scream. Reveille comes to us from the distance, cheering us a little. Someone hurries past with a stretcher — they return slowly with their burden — a young widow in a dead faint — she looks like a ghost — she nearly fell in the grave.

We 'fall in', move away and unload hundreds of wreaths from the waiting special tenders. It is darkening. Women are still crying. We climb into our tenders. Someone says he saw blood coming from one of the coffins. I learn that a Flight Sergeant has some on his greatcoat. We fall quiet — a batch of policemen pass by. We start up. It is cold — the moon is coming up. Cars upon cars pass by. We are off slowly — we gather speed and 30 or more in a row, with 14 of us on each tender, we hurl away from the mournful scene.

We are hungry — we are back in Camp — it is 7.45 p.m. We had breakfast at 7.30 a.m.

We awake from our reverie. Was it real — true? We buy the *Evening News* and see photos taken earlier in the day of the Processions in London. Yes, the R.101 is done for — they have returned.

Bessie, it is five minutes past ten. Lights out at 10.15. I must close. F/Lt. Hill has arrived at Rangoon this morning — two days ahead of Hinkler. I wish him the Best of Luck. Goodnight Bessie fach. Best Love to All at Home. Your loving brother, Arthur. PS. Write soon, will you?'

In just under twelve months, R.101 had made a total of only twelve flights with a total flying time of 127 hours and 11 minutes.

About a year after the disaster, with feelings still very high against airships, it was decided that the R.100 at Cardington should be dismantled and broken up for scrap.

The two giant sheds still stand at Cardington as impressive as ever. When I visited the grave and memorial in 1990 I saw a small modern airship flying in the area.

Arguments still go on as to what and who was to be blamed for the loss of R.101. Douglas H. Robinson, an American historian of the big rigid airships who had written in detail about the German Navy's airship operations in World War I, in his book *The Airship in Combat,* has also published *Giants in the Sky,* an attempt, in one volume, to tell the story of 161 rigid airships that were built and flown between 1900 and 1940. An entire chapter is devoted to R.101 and R.100. He told me some years ago that reading Neville Shute's aviation auto- biography, *Slide Rule,* was a 'must'. Shute worked on R.100 and flew in her to Canada. Both he and Barnes Wallis were very critical of the R.101. I express no opinion.

Having attended the R.A.F. Flying Display when as a Boy Apprentice I was there as a Programme Seller, I was interested when a temporary posting came in early 1931, for me to go to Hendon for duty with the Display's Publicity Staff. For the short period I was there, some of us lived under canvas and were not very amused though I found the work very interesting. The London University Auxiliary Squadron flew there and I managed to procure a ride in a Westland Wapiti aircraft. A two-seater, with the pilot in the forward open cockpit and the bomb-dropper cum machine-gun operator sat on a little seat in the rear cockpit.

I was not to know that before the actual display in the summer, I would have moved out of the Royal Air Force.

On the national and international scene, financial strains were becoming ever heavier. The 1929 Wall Street Crash in the United States was the forerunner of others and 1931 was to become our great problem year in Britain. All the armed forces were being cut to the bone and prospects of promotion naturally reduced. Then again the chances of actual selection for training to become a pilot were more limited for service clerks, one thought, than for men with mechanical and technical qualifications. My selection as being 'Suitable for training as an airman pilot' left, I felt, still with minimal prospect of selection for actual training. It was possible for those of us who had served two years of the twelve required, from date of attaining eighteenth birthday, to be selected to become pilots but there was the condition that flying duties, as a Sergeant Pilot, would be available for five years only, after which one would be remustered into one's trade and reclassified into an appropriate rank on ability in that trade. This meant that a sergeant pilot, after five years, might return to a junior rank as Leading, First Class or Second Class Clerk General Duties, in my case, and my flying experience would be out of date after another five years as clerk and it would be almost impossible to find a flying job on re-entering civilian life at thirty years of age. There were, of course, a variety of possibilities.

I had given the matter quite some thought but I certainly did not consider that we might be at War with Germany again before my thirtieth birthday with all that that might mean.

So it was that some of us sought to leave the Service and others remained. For those who remained, and I speak of ex-Ruislip Boy Apprentices (and indeed it would be the same for other RAF boy apprentices — fitters and electricians etc.)

promotion came very rapidly for many as the Royal Air Force was expanded at the approach of and during the Second World War. Sixty two years after leaving RAF Ruislip, I met one of my former Seventh Entry friends, now retired Wing Commander Brian Morgan and we talked of many others.

I had considered trying to obtain a position in the civil police service. Some Police Forces would not consider applicants who were serving in the armed forces without proof of availability and the RAF in my case, would not consider an application for my discharge by purchase without evidence that I would be appointed to a Police Force. Fortunately, I discovered while on Easter Leave in 1931 that there was a vacancy for one constable in the Cardiganshire Constabulary and in short time, had been found suitable for the appointment and given a written promise that I would be appointed as soon as my discharge from the Royal Air Force was completed.

I was still stationed at Hendon in May 1931, when my discharge by purchase was authorised. The cost was £31.10.0 (£31.50). I returned to Henlow briefly to complete discharge arrangements but I then returned to Cardiganshire and on the 17th May, I was sworn in as a Constable in the Cardiganshire Constabulary. I was equipped with uniform, notebook, handcuffs and truncheon and found I was to share private lodgings with another constable who was still on probation. We were each being paid £3.10.0 (£3.50) per week with 2/6d (12½p) per week lodging allowance.

I was told that as it was already about the beginning of the holiday resort's season, my attendance at the Birmingham City Police Training School would be delayed till the end of the summer and in the meantime I would by carrying out normal duties and with the assistance of other police officers as required.

The strength of the Force at that time was about 40 and of these the Chief Constable and his Deputy were both at Aberystwyth with two sergeants and seven constables. One of the sergeants was the Chief Constable's Chief Clerk with the other on general duties. Both lived in quarters above the Police Station and Headquarters offices which were then located at the centre of things in Great Darkgate Street.

The Cardigan and Lampeter Divisions had their own inspector in charge. Aberaeron, in the Aberystwyth Division, had its Sergeant and constable, Talybont had its own Sergeant who was also the County's Inspector of Weights and Measures and with one or two other Sergeants and the constables in other rural areas. Later came changes of course, but at that time the ratio of police to population made Cardiganshire one of the least policed areas in the country.

Aberystwyth town for patrolling purposes was divided into two Beats. Beat 1 and Beat 2 were each of one hour duration. There was also a bicycle beat. As I remember now, Beat 1 began, on the hour, from the junction of North Parade and Terrace Road on to the railway station, left along Alexandra Road into Stanley Road, then left up Trinity Place and left along Trinity Road to the junction of Northgate Street and North Road at Coopers. Then left along Northgate Street, left along North Road to Queen's Road and right to walk round Alexandra Hall at the north end of Victoria Terrace on the Promenade. Southward then on Marine Terrace and back into Terrace Road to North Parade where the beat ended after a walk down its length as far as the Queen's Road/Northgate Street/Thespian Street junction and back to Terrace Road by the end of the hour. Along the Beat, the timed points were at five minute or ten minute intervals and a good reason would be required if a timed point was not accurately kept.

One night, the No. 1 Beatman saw an old fashioned invalid chair on Victoria Terrace pavement. He reported to Beatman No. 2 at the end of the hour who suggested that perhaps someone had committed suicide. No. 1 said that could be the case so instead of resuming their individual beats the two officers made their way on a not unpleasant night to Victoria Terrace. With almost the whole of the hour to themselves, they went down to the steeply pebbly beach. No body was found. They each smoked a cigarette at the foot of the sea wall before collecting the chair to take to the Police Station. The chair was being pulled from Terrace Road towards the Police Station when No. 1 was told by No. 2 to keep to the left of what was then the new fangled road centre white line and then the

42

sergeant was seen coming to meet them. He had searched both beats, on his bicycle, for them: where had they been? A verbal account was given of their suspicions and their fruitless search for a body on the beach. It appeared acceptable. I was No. 2. I was met by the sergeant on several occasions over the next two or three weeks and I repeated our report on being questioned. Some three weeks then after the incident, the sergeant told me that No. 1 (who had seen the invalid chair first) must have been very slow not to have realised that the 'bathchair' was not a self-propelled chair. The sergeant must have concluded something too for he never mentioned the incident to No. 1 !!

No. 2 Beat covered the area between Terrace Road to the east, Trefechan railway bridge (below Dinas Terrace) to the south and South Marine Terrace, Seaview Place, Pier Street and part of Marine Terrace on the west. As with No. 1 Beat this Beat also required five minute or ten minute points to be properly attended. They were the only two officers covering the night shift, from 9 p.m. to 6 a.m. With a shared one hour meal break and a standby period, this meant that each man normally would have walked his full beat six times during his tour of night duty.

There came a time later when more emphasis was placed on the need for 'discretionary' beats where the officer was to patrol a given area of ground rather than a timed walk along a fixed route. A danger of the time-fixed route was that would be law breakers as well as others found no trouble in discovering where the officer might be at any given time or where he might be expected. In an effort to overcome the disadvantages, I prepared three different routes on each Beat, called them 1A, 1B, 1C and 2A, 2B and 2C and for each tour of duty the sequence in which they were to be walked was varied so that one could be found by the sergeant at any given time. It would be virtually impossible for the villain to anticipate the officer's movements. Who knows — may be one day Panda-cramped policemen may again be allowed to walk these interesting beats on cold winter nights and hot summer days.

Elsewhere in the county, patrols of areas rather than fixed

beat walking was the rule although constables in adjoining rural stations would be required to meet their opposite numbers at points on the boundary of their districts at fixed times on fixed dates. In an adjoining county, a sergeant attending at one such point was surprised to meet his new chief constable waiting. Motorised sergeants were an extreme rarity then — this one happened to arrive in his own private old car and as he walked away from it to meet the chief, the chief pointed out to him that the car was on the move, — fortunately into the near hedgebank — his remark to the chief, so we heard, was 'It's alright, Sir. It has only gone to graze.'

In Aberystwyth, one night, a young constable walking Beat 1 made time to check on the door of one of a row of newly built, lock-up shops by Aberystwyth Railway Station. The door was not locked and its key was in place but on the inner side. He decided to check all the other doors as they were a 'lookalikes' lot and found the key fitted all of them. His report had produced new locks on all by the following evening.

Routine foot patrols in the same places and times could provide a reasonably good picture of what was normal and thus an abnormality was quickly spotted. A man wanted for a series of thefts from lodgings he had left without paying, as well, might have been expected to visit Aberystwyth. The Constable on Beat 2 one day was about to enter Mill Street from Chalybeate Street when on looking towards the railway station area, he saw a man in dark clothing with what was probably a bowler hat, standing at the corner of Union Street. The wanted man was described as having a Yorkshire accent and who had given his or at least a name at his lodgings, was said to be wearing a navy blue suit, patent leather shoes and a bowler hat. His hair was said to be parted in the middle. The man, as seen, was only one of a number of people moving around in that area but seemed not quite part of the normal picture — a slight abnormality in the scene! The constable felt he would be justified to leave his fixed beat and investigate a little closer. As he then started to walk towards Union Street, he saw the man turn and go in to Union Street, so decided to hurry his pace so as to obtain the closer view he needed. He was surprised to see the man was now much further away than he might have been expected to be. He therefore decided he would run the rest of the way in Union Street and in Cambrian Street then caught up with the man, both being now somewhat breathless at the junction with Chalybeate Street. It was a bowler hat, they were patent leather shoes, and it was a navy blue suit (the clothing at that time was not that much out of place as it would seem to be now in the 90s). The man gave a different name when asked for it and when asked to produce proof, did so with a driving licence in that name but the address was in Keighley, Yorkshire. He was walked to the police station in Great Darkgate Street some 250 yards away where it was seen at once on removal of the bowler hat that his hair indeed had a middle parting. He was wanted for twenty six offences and was duly handed over.

A different sort of incident on the Beat was on my night shift. I was told by a man that one of his lodgers had not yet come in and as it was already 11.15 p.m. he feared he had absconded without paying. The lodger had explained his presence in Aberystwyth by saying he was a representative of a firekindling bundle firm. I left my Beat to go to the police station and with the sergeant there searched through a number of issues of the *Police Gazette*, an official publication with a countrywide police circulation. A recent copy had a description of a man wanted by other Forces from the south of England to south Wales for false pretences who had given this story of kindling sales.

The sergeant and I then went to the bed and breakfast establishment — a private house — where we were told all was well and that the man was back and safely in bed. Although we had but a poor description of the man, we did have a detailed description of tattoo markings on one of his arms. We decided we would like to see the man and were then taken upstairs and shown his bedroom door. We entered after knocking and opening the door and after a very brief talk, asked to see his forearms. We were surprised to find that the tattoo marks he bore were entirely different to what we were expecting to see. The man's reactions, however, were such that I suggested

45

to the sergeant we should nevertheless take him to the police station for questioning with regard to the listed offences. The man had evidently been able to follow our discussion and rose, dressed and accompanied us to the station — I did hold his arm on our walk through the now darkened streets — where he admitted at once that he was indeed our man. We felt that it was probably the man's first description which was very poor that had included what had come to be accepted as a correct description of the tattooing. This then naturally had been repeated in the subsequent issues of the *Police Gazette* but fortunately his 'story' remained constant and the connection was maintained. His *modus operandi* gave him away.

One never knew quite what one might encounter on a beat. A report of suicide, road accident, sudden death? Somebody wanting to know the time? Out on the beat, the police meet all sorts of situations and people. I can sit back now and it would take hours to recall so many kinds of incidents. Have you ever been cursed? It may not have been a true member of the Romany people who cursed me once but a summer visitor to the Aberystwyth resort must have been very impressed for he came up to me to express his pleasure at seeing I had survived something he had apparently taken more seriously than I had done after an encounter the season before. I had had to deal with some minor law breaker and had been roundly cursed for my pains.

There were long dull hours too. One Sunday afternoon I had just remarked to someone that if ever I would commit suicide (what a thing to say!) it would be on a Sunday afternoon in Aberystwyth, when the sergeant came on a bicycle and told me to go as quickly as I could to Trefechan River Bridge to intercept a man driving a stolen/joy ridden car expected to be returning to town. It was not long before the car appeared. I signalled it to stop. The car slowed right down then suddenly accelerated. I was all but in its path. The running board on its offside brushed against me and left some of its dirt on the front crease of my trousers! (Most cars in those days had running boards as a sort of step for driver and passengers to enter the vehicle).

A quickly thrown truncheon and the bicycle lamp did nothing to stop the driver who a few minutes later abandoned the car on the promenade and mixed with the holiday makers. He was met though as he arrived at his home. For taking that car and others, some of which had been damaged, he was fined a most paltry fine and much to my disgust too after our too close encounter.

It was the practice, in Aberystwyth's main street, for the patrolling constable not to walk the pavement but the centre of the road where he ensured the traffic met and passed him on its correct side. This before the white line was introduced.

I had heard Lloyd George make a speech at the Queen's Hall, that long College building when it lay between the rear of Queen's Road and North Road and it had been as impressive as I had expected. It was not long afterwards, in 1933, that the building caught fire. It burned to the ground as it was of timber construction. Originally, elsewhere, it had been an aeroplane hangar. Police always assisted the volunteer fire brigades and as the heat at this fire was about to set the Catholic church roof alight. I was carrying a length of hose forward but had to be kept drenched by a hose as I crossed the intervening ground. Windows of houses on the North Road End were also becoming ignited by the intense heat.

A special routine patrol on Sundays in the summer season took one round about thirty shops where Sunday trading would be observed and reported on. The defendants would regularly be fined a nominal sum which never did deter them. Sixty years later, Sunday trading is all in the news again.

I was required to guard a prisoner at the local hospital the very first night I was on night duty. He had been arrested by the Deputy Chief Constable and the police constable driving him in a police motor cycle combination. No police car had yet been purchased! When the officers stopped the man who was wanted on a murder charge in South Wales he attempted to run away but then turned round to face them in an adjoining field, he said if they came any nearer he would cut his throat and this he did. He was taken into custody and they undoubtedly saved his life. That first night he watched me intently

47

and I felt he would get away if he could. By the second night, however, he was quite changed and responsive. Later he was sentenced to four years imprisonment for manslaughter.

I suppose most police officers have at one time or other dealt with cases of suicide. It became an understood thing that if one suicide occurred, it would almost certainly be followed by several more — there must be another two, we would say. We thought it was a case of a would-be suicide being encouraged to act when he heard someone else had — plucked up courage? succeeded.

Sudden deaths always called for some police action as we were each for the occasion a Coroner's Officer.

As a very young child I had been lifted up to see my grandfather in his coffin. I simply hated seeing the picture of a coffin which was put in an advertisement on the back page of the weekly *Carpenter and Builder* which came to our house for years. I rather dreaded then some of the special duties which would befall me as a constable and to counter this, I volunteered to be present at a post mortem examination at the first opportunity and in due course I was able to cope.

At the end of the 1931 holiday season and with winter coming on, I was sent to the Birmingham City Police Training School for my postponed Recruit's Training Course. I think it was of advantage to me on the course that I had already been 'broken in' as it were. My own Force might possibly have benefitted more had I started after some training. Being back at school with a group of trainees was quite an experience. We were schooled during the day but in the evenings accompanied the Birmingham policeman on his beat for some three or four hours. I probably found this easier too than did most of the others. I was now in plain clothes and all the responsibility devolved on my uniformed 'instructor'.

Officers were usually required in those days in Birmingham to submit their written reports before going off duty. We came in one evening in time to hear a Birmingham policeman (a bandsman too as it happened) at his report, ask, 'How do you spell chauffeur?' My tutor promptly said, 'D R I V E R' and added, 'If you can't spell a word, don't use it'.

A certain amount of boxing was considered necessary for all of us. The instructor — anybody remember Bolstridge? — would soon sort us out and matched us in likely pairs. One really big lad did not like it and went to the floor apparently wishing the instructor to believe he had been knocked out. His poor acting though deceived no one. He was helped to his feet, helped to his stool and comforted. Then after the next little bout, he was invited to his feet and asked to defend himself against another much smaller recruit and who was known to us all as quite a useful boxer. There and then the big one had to learn his lesson. I have remembered that over the years and it taught us all a lesson.

Part of our homework each evening in addition to the patrolling was to learn 'off by heart' five legal definitions until we had learned a total of one hundred and five of them. We were all required to qualify in first aid to the injured. We were certainly required to cram in a big load of information in the thirteen weeks. Most of the recruits on my course, came from other Police Forces — Flintshire, Newport Borough, Salisbury City, Isle of Ely among others. It was known that some Chief Constables (hopefully only if other things were equal) preferred sports enthusiasts of their own kind. Swimmers were favoured in Liverpool one was told, Rugby football players in Glamorgan and Isle of Ely liked good cricketers. My co-lodger (in the private home of a Greener gunsmith) in Birmingham had been a professional cricketer and his hands showed it. Some fifty years on, I happened to notice a man who seemed to shop where and when I did and for reasons you may suspect, thought for sure that he too had been a policeman. So I spoke to him. Yes, he had indeed served in the Police and in the Isle of Ely Force and he even knew Eagle my fellow lodger! He would certainly ask him if he remembered me. The answer came soon — Yes, he did and did I remember his treatment of the boil on my bum? Eagles as well as elephants?

And talking about shopping, it was the case in those early years that the Inspector of Weights and Measures, in Cardiganshire, was a police sergeant (as was the case too in one adjoining county, at least). Police would take milk samples when requested for analysis, particularly for added water and quality, from milk being distributed door to door. If standards were not reached, we would be called upon to take a special sample known as 'appeal to cow'. Then we would attend at the morning milking and take a sample of the milk as near as possible to the mix from which the first sample was taken, for comparison purposes.

Police were called on to perform various duties required of them by the Diseases of Animals Acts. Reporting of suspected TB in cattle, for instance : suspected anthrax and sheep scab. When sheep scab had been detected, orders would be given for double dipping. Normally a single dip sufficed to keep the scab at bay. We had to witness all such dipping and had to ensure that the dip was maintained at the approved strength and that the sheep were properly dipped.

In Cardiganshire, we were also inspectors under the Explosives Acts and had our own special police responsibilities as well. Was the explosive store (magazine) properly constructed and secured and was the applicant a suitable person to be granted a certificate to possess and use explosives?

Pedlars and hawkers were common in the early thirties and plain tramping tramps. The tramping fraternity were a stranger mix than one would suspect, until one checked individuals.

Alcoholics sometimes became methylated spirit drinkers as it was relatively cheap to buy. I had to collect one victim who had seemingly been 'burnt up' by the Meths drinking. The body nearer just skin and bone than could be imagined. Then there were people who had just taken to the road for the simpler life — real philosophers. They slept where they could, in farm buildings, hedgerows, in the old workhouses (before the days of DHSS) or in a 'common lodging house.' Some gave the police trouble wherever they went either because of too much alcohol or the lack of it. One such was Owen Peters, a big, strong and hard man. He had a long list of convictions for being drunk and disorderly, begging alms and assaulting the police. His round brought him regularly to Aberystwyth. It usually took two constables to arrest him wherever he was (one could not in those days radio anybody to bring transport and assistance). It so happened that on my first meeting with him, I was able to secure him with an armlock almost as if he had helped me to secure it. It was enough. I was able to walk him with no trouble to the police station. Thereafter it sufficed for me to say, 'Come on Owen', and he would accompany me without any armlock. I put this down to sheer luck on my first encounter and that he feared a repeat of the armlock. Others still had all the trouble they wanted or did NOT want!

My first posting was to Cardigan Town. It had its special interests. Many of the public houses there still sold their own home brewed beer. It was standard practice for the police to visit each public house after the night closing time which was ten o'clock there in those days, and invite all non-residents to leave. We varied the route so that our early arrival would hopefully be anticipated. Other visits, in and out of the permitted hours, were also made. I am sure this kept offences to a minimum.

The river Teifi, a noted salmon and sewin (sea trout) river, brought us extra work from time to time or, I should say, mis-users of the river. Very few coracle fishermen are on the river in the nineties compared with the thirties. We were mainly called on to protect the water bailiffs when they were likely to encounter trouble with the large net fishermen. A very common offence committed by the salmon netmen, would be when they let their net out for more than the two-thirds width of the river or failing to return the far end of the net back to its own bank without delay. If done wilfully, the intention was to improve their catch, or at least their chances, but at the same time there would be a reduction in the numbers of fish allowed to go upstream.

In these days of easier travel, Welsh programmes on television and radio, we have become accustomed to the great variety of accents, colloquialisms and just words that go to make up the Welsh language but over half a century ago, I was amazed to discover that the Cardigan area Welsh was in many respects so different from my Aberystwyth area Welsh.

Certain tithes were still payable in South Cardiganshire in the early thirties though there was considerable resistance to their collection. I shall not forget one special occasion when a

51

number of court bailiffs arranged a vast joint operation to distrain on quite a number of farmers, commencing early one morning. They were going to distrain this time by seizing cattle. Word had, however, got around and most of the farmers barricaded entrances to their farm buildings and approach lanes. Police accompanied the various parties of bailiffs and their helpers with necessary transport. In the event nothing serious occurred possibly because so many farmers had to stay at home to look after their own private interests. Later in the day though when a convoy of trucks had formed, crowds had gathered and when one of the trucks overturned going down the hill at Adpar, trouble did break out. One of the constables who at that time was rather out of favour with some of the folk became a target for stone throwers and the incident may well have developed into a major problem had not some of his colleagues succeeded in whisking him away through the back door of a property and so out of the area.

Our Inspector at Cardigan had almost reached the end of his service and must have joined the Force near the turn of the century. He was known to everyone as 'WNCWL DAFI' (Uncle David) and undoubtedly because he was everybody's sort of Uncle. It was said that on a then busy traffic day, he was standing at the top of Priory Street which runs, at the T-junction, into High Street and Pendre, and with three lesser streets immediately adjacent to the junction. He decided he had to take charge of the traffic and using his extended arms and hands signalled traffic approaching on two roads to stop but he wanted to stop a third stream as well. He must have thought quickly — he put his foot up to stop the Priory Street traffic. This never became one of the approved STOP signals.

The town's volunteer Fire Brigade's engine was known to all and sundry as ADA. She was previously in use by the Southampton Docks Fire Brigade. She was kept in the Guildhall building and was difficult to start. Fortunately, Priory Street sloped away from the Guildhall so that push starts were fairly easy if frequent. She had solid rubber tyres. At some time someone had fastened a piece of wire mesh under the entire engine base so as to catch and retain any pieces that fell away! Despite her solid tyres, she was used to answer rural calls as well as all those in the Borough. I remember being aboard her going down hill into Aberporth to a farm fire near Tresaith when poor ADA caught fire herself. We managed to confine it to one of the rear wheel brake drums though and soon continued our journey.

My first posting to Cardigan was very short really and I was then removed to Aberaeron that most delightful little holiday town which in its time had boasted of three shipyards. It was now more noted for its quite unique layout, its Alban Square, its architecture, its colours, its picturesque stone walled harbour and of course, its river and seafishing. My fellow constable at Cardigan was my first co-lodger at Aberystwyth and the former Palestine policeman with whom I had walked the Aberystwyth beat as a sixteen year old before I went to the Royal Air Force. At Aberaeron I was the only constable under a Sergeant. We had a rural area as well as the town to police. The sergeant really took me under his wing, for I still had less than four years' service and I found his cool, calm approach to all our problems of considerable help and guidance. I have remembered Sergeant Rhys Davies along these many years and not only for our police work together but for our talks on general subjects and then current affairs. I was soon moved to a rural station on my own but felt I could then cope. It was at Aberaeron I had my first road accident. I was riding an old Douglas belt driven motor cycle with poor acetylene lighting when an overtaking van caught my right sleeve and pulled me off. The driver carried me and the motor cycle back to town and I can remember my embarrassment back at 'Gorwel' when the landlady Mrs. Griffiths had to help me to undress for both my hands were by that time useless. My gauntlets had saved them from severe road grazing but my wrists and hands were so strained as to lose all their strength until the following morning.

I had already noted, when reading the *Police Review* (a bobby's weekly magazine), mainly, that a number of police officers at some time in their service or indeed at the end of their police careers on occasion, were going in for the church, in their particular Christian denomination, or preparing themselves for ordination. It seemed as if, in coping with people with all sorts of problems, they had discovered that the best law book was the Bible. And here was Sergeant Rhys Davies in Aberaeron producing a Christmas Carol, as he had done before, and indeed he did so for a number of years. They were sung in those early Christmas morning services at his church. We had, together, tried to cope with a most tragic shooting accident. A very young lad had come across a shotgun in the shed outside his home. The gun was still loaded. It was accidentally fired and the other very young lad approaching had taken the entire charge at close range. It was heart breaking then and it is heart breaking now. That was the first of many fatal shooting accidents I was to deal with along the years.

Llanfarian was my rural station and naturally I felt the responsibility. The Aberaearon-Aberystwyth road crosses the river Ystwyth here and the village is also known as Pentrebont (Bridge village) and Figure Four, southern end of the village. (Why Figure Four? Possibly descriptive of the road at its junction with the road to Llanilar to the south east and Llanychaiarn to the north west?) At that time too the railway from Aberystwyth crossed over the road at the northern end of the village but the station there was named LLANRHYSTYD ROAD STATION. The district to be policed was quite extensive — to Llanddeiniol to the south (some six miles), north to Aberystwyth and Penparcau (some 4 miles) and half way to Devil's Bridge through Capel Seion (some six miles from Penparcau). I found lodgings with Mr. and Mrs. Leech at the shop on the corner leading to Llanilar. Mr. Leech worked at Llanilar Railway station. Over thirty years later, in a Welsh church in Slough, I met Mrs. Leech again.

One night I had a call from my colleague at Llanon (his district bordered on mine) to intercept a motorist suspected of being drunk in charge of his motor car. I did so and my colleague arrived very soon after him. We both felt the man should not be driving and so took him into custody. A doctor was called to examine him. After a straight line walking test, the motorist was asked to look up a certain name and address in the telephone directory handed to him. He refused, saying he was unable to read. The doctor then drew a circle about an inch in diameter on a piece of paper and marked in a dot at the centre. He then drew another circle and invited the driver to put in a dot likewise. Something was drawn and when the doctor asked what it was supposed to be, the answer he got was 'Mickey Mouse, Sir'. The doctor was unable to certify that the man was not fit to drive. Why had they not thought of breathalyser bags then?

Parry the Post was our local postman. He had lost an arm and usually wore one of two artificial limbs. Off duty, he rode that marvellous motor cycle, a 'Brough Superior'. (Lawrence of Arabia rode one too but he died in a road crash). Parry was also an excellent shot with his 12 bore gun and an expert with rod and line.

Farmers were entitled to keep two dogs without dog licences if they were in use to assist the farmer with his livestock. We would sometime need to check and then perhaps test Sealyhams and Corgis as working dogs, for dog breeding was a sideline too on occasion.

Farmers suffered losses as well, and one morning I was called out to a Llanddeiniol farm and in the corner of a rather small field saw a pile of dead sheep. Most were covered in mud, a few showed signs of having been bitten. There were twenty two of them, just piled up as they had been worried during the early hours by dogs in what had been just a wet corner of the field. The culprits were a little Scottie and a large Alsatian. The Scottie used to leave home, travel about half a mile to collect the Alsatian and then, well away from their own homes, find sheep to worry before finding their way back home again. They had been doing this a number of times. Both were put down of course.

Dafydd Philip Roberts would have been well known to all my contemporaries. He was quite a character. He came routinely into our areas. His offences were False Pretences and Theft. His *modus operandi* never varied. His physical features were such that his description was easy and invariably accurate. He would profess to be a cattle dealer, visiting farms and would

55

set about selecting and buying some cattle. Arranging for their collection later, he would tender a cheque in payment there and then but ask for some cash as change, but not an amount to justify suspicion. To make a hurried exit from the immediate area, he would help himself at times to a bicycle.

On this particular occasion, the police had early information and he was being tracked before he had cleared the area. He was forced to retreat into the hills and before the day was out he was observed still retreating while he observed them gradually closing in. When still about a mile ahead and almost on the brow of a hill, he was seen to sit down and there he waited until the three policemen came up to him. He explained that he had seen them getting closer but he'd be damned if he was going to walk back to meet them. He was determined they should walk as far as he had done.

I had been more involved in clearing up a crime where a housekeeper had reported the theft of five one pound notes from under her pillow during the day. The money was in an envelope. No one had been seen acting suspiciously. No clue, so back to see her for a second time — yes, the money was clipped together. And yet a little later — no, not clipped but pinned together with a pin struck through them. The hunt revealed a stranger had travelled on the bus to Aberaeron. In brief, we traced this man into Aberaeron, in a pub, back to Penparcau area — found in bus conductor's takings and elsewhere four one pound notes with two pin holes in each and when put together the holes matched precisely. We found the man hiding in an outhouse at Penparcau. This man proved to be one Beadles not of our area at all and not a nice man. At the Dartmoor Prison Riots sometime before, he had been one of the ring leaders. At the Inquiry into those riots, Dafydd Philip Roberts had been found to have helped in saving the life of one of the prison warders and his four years sentence was reduced to two so he was immediately released. A lot of us always had a soft spot for Dafydd so it was just like him to behave the way he did.

56

POLICE FEDERATION

The Federation was created in order to ensure there would be no police strike again after the one in 1919. It was a sort of Police Trade Union but with no ties of any sort to any other organisation. Each Force had its own branches to serve the special interests of the various ranks and we could also act as a Joint Branch Board. It happened that I was Secretary to the Constables Branch Board in our Force and to the Joint Branch Board. We could make representations on most matters although some subjects, like individual promotions, were naturally precluded.

The lodging allowance for a single constable at that time was two shillings and sixpence a week (12½p). Police Regulations sought to ensure that a fair allowance would not be less than 80% of the average being paid generally for lodgings. The tramp's common lodging house charge was 1/- per night or 35p per week — nearly three times the amount of our lodging allowance! Ultimately we did secure an improvement.

Another sore point was that young constables were not permitted to sit the examination for promotion to sergeant until they had served for ten years. Here again the Police Regulations were being ignored. There was provision for the payment of an immediate increment in pay if the officer qualified for promotion and, in later years, if still not promoted, the payment of both long service increments would be advanced. But to qualify, it was also necessary for the examination to have been passed with under five years service. So none of us could qualify for any of these increments. Representations in writing failed even on the second attempt, so permission was sought for a deputation to be received from the Joint Branch Board. The Chairman (a Sergeant) and myself as Secretary then waited

57

upon the Chief Constable. On arrival at Headquarters, our chairman said to me 'As I'm a sergeant and it does not really concern me, you do all the talking'!! I accepted the charge without comment. The outcome was that the Chief Constable gave in — in his own way. He ordered a Sergeant's Examination to be held for constables with over ten years service — and each of them was later shown as Passed. Then he ordered another examination for the constables with under ten years service. Four of us out of eight passed. We received the special increments in pay forthwith. The older constables, of course did not now qualify for the increment but were eligible for promotion.

Another regulation that would seem to have been of local manufacture was the one that required an officer to seek permission to marry and to produce, when doing so, acceptable references for his bride to be. My wife Falmai Wyn was vouched for by the Chief Constable of an adjoining county and the minister of her church. Had permission been refused, I can imagine that I would have sought the support of the Police Federation in making representations to have the rule set aside.

It was the practice that free married quarters were found and so it was in November 1935 when I was married we were found temporary accommodation in part of a private house at Penparcau, while I continued to police the same area for a while before returning to Cardigan where we were provided with a house. This was opposite that large Welsh Baptist Chapel, Bethania, where the noted preacher, the Rev. Esaia Williams served for many years. Our first daughter, Elizabeth Diana was born there on 10 July, 1937. Later on 2 August, 1938, my wife was baptised by Mr. Williams in the chapel, by total immersion this time, so that we were members of the same church. As we became ever more nomadic, however, we worshipped together with many other Protestant persuasions over the next fifty-one years.

Routine police work in a small force without any specialist departments, involved one in a variety of tasks. While one occasionally envied the city police officer who could call on many others to assist in investigating a crime, there was, nevertheless, a lot of satisfaction in pursuing an inquiry to a satisfactory conclusion oneself.

Cases of office breaking were rare in Cardigan and I remember my first one. An office had been forcibly entered, a safe had been removed within the office. The back of the safe had been broken open and contents taken away — some money and a number of postal orders. It looked like an impossible task as we had no likely suspects for an offence of this nature. Almost in desperation I stopped a very young lad whom I had had dealings with when he stole money from a shop till when an assistant's back was turned, and asked what he knew about the office breaking. He said yes he was involved but he was only in the road outside keeping a lookout. I was convinced he was telling the truth when he described some of the money as 'blue paper money' — the missing postal orders. He named the two men who went into the office, one being a relative of his. I saw the men who denied any knowledge of the affair. As I had noted that the fireproofing material had spilled out of the back of the safe, I decided I would take their trousers for further examination and with a sample of the material carried them to be tested at the forensic science laboratory in Cardiff. Analysis of the specimen and of the dust from each pair of trousers showed all contained, in particular, red sandstone sand and the saw dust from five different woods. The sandstone was to be found in the Midlands, where the safe had been manufactured. Unfortunately, the men were found 'Not Guilty' by the jury.

These were the years when King George V died and King Edward VIII had abdicated before his coronation. His brother the Duke of York became King George VI. In Cardigan too we were beginning to read and hear more and more about Hitler and it was not very long before the police, countrywide, were being prepared and trained to cope in the dreadful event that we should find ourselves again at War.

We were all routinely trained in First Aid and many of us helped in training public classes held by the St. John Ambulance Association in our districts. Some of us had also done a lot of First Aid Team Competition work. But in 1938, with some other officers, I was certificated as an instructor in Anti-Gas Measures to carry out local anti-gas training. I remember the sample bottles of the various gases we had to be prepared to encounter — Phosgene, Mustard, Chlorine, etc. One of the classes I particularly remember instructing was made up solely of the clergy in that Anglican diocese. The time had come too for the distribution of gas masks to the public generally.

Then one day I was taken to Headquarters at Aberystwyth, for the day, to do some typing, and then told to stay overnight for a second day's work and on the second day told I was to remain at headquarters. My family would be moved up from Cardigan as soon as this could be arranged. The paper work at headquarters had become massive. So it was a case of a flat for a few weeks for us, then half a house for a few more weeks and then a house in Custom House Street.

The Chief Constable was new to us. After a brief period as a Superintendent in the Metropolitan Police, following a career in the Royal Air Force — he had earned an MC during the Great War — he came to us only months before we were at war again. After so many alarms, it was almost a relief when war on Germany was declared and we thought we knew where we were. It was to be a very long time indeed before real relief really came.

Police Service was declared to be a reserved occupation so that we could not withdraw our services. Release to the Armed Forces would be permitted under control. Certain classifications of men were in due course admitted to the Police for the duration of the War only — they became known as War Reserves. A Women's Auxiliary Police Corps was also created and forces permitted and were indeed required to appoint women to the service, again for the duration. Not all Police Forces had women as members of the force before this. At a meeting of a member of Chief Constables from Welsh Forces at our headquarters, some expressed their disapproval of the proposal and I remember Mr. Wilson the then Chief Constable of Cardiff City Police saying he would not wish to employ anybody else's daughter to do police work he would not wish

60

his own daughter to do. But, of course, as time went on, circumstances required that a number of women were appointed for clerical, driving and general duties in our own Force. The new Chief Constable had earlier secured the services of a woman sergeant on attachment from the Metropolitan Police and this gave us a good start. Before Dublin was blacked out, I accompanied her there, via Holyhead Ferry to bring back a prisoner and, incidentally some rationed foodstuffs and chocolate which my wife and daughter were glad to see. Members of our armed forces going on leave to the Republic were all changing into civilian clothes on their way there. The hotel porter showed me his First World War medal ribbons on the inside of his jacket lapel and wished me luck 'over there'. I have just read a reminder in one of our 1991 national dailies, of the very large number of our very high ranking armed forces' officers who came from Ireland. My luck did hold, for on the day of our return, the ferry was attacked by the Germans.

One of our national daily papers in the first days of the War had a photograph of a placard outside one of London's large cinemas, indicating with an arrow, 'Aberystwyth nearest Cinema Open. 239 miles'. It had been decreed by the Office of Home Security that all places of public entertainment should be kept closed — so as to avoid having unnecessary gatherings of many people in the event of air raids. Our Chief chose to allow our cinemas in Aberystwyth to keep open. Later, the Home Office orders were rescinded.

In April 1940 the Chief Clerk retired and I was promoted Sergeant and Chief Clerk. My father had passed away two years before the outbreak of war and I regretted he was not with us to enjoy this promotion. He was widely known and respected as a stonemason and, as my mother reminded us years later, his monuments were still around us, where he had been the foreman — The 1924 new railway station, Alexandra Hall Students' hostel, the King's Hall, National Library extension, South Marine Promenade extension, all in Aberystwyth. He was working on the latter in 1931 when I had surprised him by saying I was about to join the Police Force. Further afield I remember visiting him when the Lampeter

61

Bridge was being built. He had been the proud possessor of an Austin Seven Saloon EJ 1999 about that time but it was over fifty five years later that I read in my mother's papers that she had bought the car for him with her insurance money. Those were very hard times.

The Chief had also insisted on dismantling the first 2kg German incendiary bomb he saw. He made a gelignite bomb which he thought the Home Guard (but at that time known as LDV — Local Defence Volunteers) would use. We had to see what it would do when with fusc ignited, it was placed under a 4ft x 3ft x half inch steel plate. Later too, he insisted, with me only for company, in tying a rope to a horned mine floating just, on the rocks near Morfa Mawr, Llanon, so that it would not be carried further up the coast, possibly to Aberystwyth, on the next tide. And where, indeed, another mine did explode on the rocks adjacent to the pier some time later. I was ordered to remain in the shelter of a bank on the edge of the beach and I obeyed, without reluctance. When he rejoined me, he showed the strain and the cigarette I lit for him helped him to recover.

During that first hard winter, he took me with him for a shoot in the Tregaron bog area. I slipped and fell on some snow covered ice alongside a hedgerow and so set up a cock pheasant. I turned without getting up and fired my 12 bore with rather a surprising result — no pheasant — but about two and a half inches of that barrel was now flapping. I confess that I never waited to check that the gun barrels were free of snow, for they were otherwise clean, before firing.

The Chief Constable had road safety in mind, when very soon after his appointment in Cardiganshire, he decided that I should go, from Cardigan then, on an advanced driver's course to the Metropolitan Police. But this had quickly to be forgotten with the possibility of war becoming more apparent daily.

Other will have written about the arrival of evacuees in Aberystwyth and the county generally and, later, of the many Dunkirk survivors who arrived in Aberystwyth by special trains. For my part, I had been reorganising the office and the ever-increasing workload and was also available for more duties. A small CID had been created and I introduced the new national standardised crime reporting system. Help was given in the instruction of the war reserve police and there was much liaison work between us and the Civil Defence people.

It was arranged that I should go to Birmingham to collect a very small car that could be used in a playground, with small traffic signs, as an aid in teaching road safety. It was a strange mix at the factory to be collecting this little car for safety purposes while almost alongside they were in the process of tempering armour piercing shells. The car was an ATCO, with one forward gear and a reverse gear, could seat two small persons (or myself alone), was less than three feet wide and less than six feet long and not more than about two feet six inches high. With mini traffic lights (off a battery) and mini Belisha beacons. I was able to set up a mock road system in a school yard and with a showing of lantern slides before hand (pre video and scarce cine film days) tried to teach road safety procedures to classes of school children. A small war reserve constable drove the car and could carry a child in the front (and only) seat with him while the other children played the role of careful and careless pedestrians. We visited a number of schools in the Aberystwyth area, including my own elementary and secondary schools. This, of course, was in the earliest days of the Highway Code.

SWANSEA BLITZ

In June 1941, I accompanied five constables from our Force to Swansea, where, with a dozen other constables from Brecon, Carmarthen and Caernarvon County Forces, we were to relieve, by exchange of duties, an equivalent number of Swansea Borough Police officers who had been under considerable strain and stress during the blitz when acres and acres of the shopping and business centre were destroyed in the bombing. One day one of our constables was on duty at the scene of an unexploded bomb. It was a very hot day. He rested flat on the ground. A senior officer visited and the constable explained that he thought it safer to be lying on the ground than standing if the bomb happened to go off I presume that his superior officer was satisfied about his alertness. For myself, it was a big change to be on patrol for hours instead of being at a desk for most of the day and to be taking a meal break in an old style police box (Dr. Who style in much later days). Night air raids were continuing, though on a much reduced scale and I was teased for reporting one night after the 'All Clear' siren had sounded. What I thought at the time to be the last sound of the Air Raid Warning signal was, in fact, the end of the 'All Clear'. It must have been a comfortable bed I occupied at my lodgings. Before returning to Cardiganshire after our month there, I was given a document certifying my admission to the Worshipful Order of Foot Sloggers, Blisterers and Orange Scroungers, having more or less satisfactorily performed his initial course of instruction of one month's duration amongst the Archaeological Remains of the Fair City of Swansea . . .' and '. . . and also having succeeded in scrounging all the oranges especially sent down to vitaminise the regular permanent police force . . .' It was accompanied by an odd ode of thirteen

Ju Jitsu Team.

Front Row: Sergt. E. J. Evans, Steven Jones, (Chief Constable), Milwyn Jenkins (Instructor, etc.), Supt. Daniel Thomas (D.C.C.), Sergt. J. Richards.

Back Row: P.C. E. W. Jones, P.C. A. I. Williams, P.C. A. H. Jenkins (Hon. Sec.), P.C. K. G. Williams, P.C. T. O. Lloyd, P.C. D. L. Jones.

Aberystwyth 1937.
Opening of National Library Extension.

Sergeant Jenkins with two friends. Aberystwyth 1940

verses, each illustrated by a most delightful cartoon and concluding — 'I expect you are wondering, Sergeant,

> who's the doggerel bard — Take it in good spirit, don't be wild and hard — Recollect your thoughts to a constable on the Beat, who, in the Charge Room, once, stepped upon THOSE FEET'.

It made us all laugh in those stressful days and, fifty years later, thankfully, I can still do so. Perhaps I ought to include the penultimate verse as well. I had cautioned an erring Jewish shopkeeper, and the verse?—

> 'His name is quite notorious for persecuting Jews,
> Books them right and left, if they oppose his views.
> Every Jew he comes across he treats as a traitor —
> Herr Himmler Arthur Jenkins, the Welsh Jew Baiter.'

I remember an invasion scare we had in Cardiganshire, a parachutist had been seen, it was reported but widespread searching for him had been unsuccessful and no trace was found of a parachute. After about three days, when the Home Guard were just about being called off, the matter was resolved when it was found that a worker had carried a discarded zinc sheet on his head before using it to fill a gap in a hedge.

One day, when I was back in my office, an RAF officer from the Air Ministry called on our chief and had talked about investigating a piece of land on the coast between Dyffryn Ardudwy and Llanbedr (both in the adjoining county) as a possible site for an airfield in the event we might have to lose some in East Anglia. On the site, he had seen a very large black barn type building which might have been usable as a temporary shelter by night landing parachutists or whatever, via the adjacent beach, so we would wish to know about the security status of the owner. As I knew the area and the Chief Constable of that county personally, I was able to clear that up in a matter of minutes and later I typed our visitor's preliminary report he had prepared for the Air Ministry. The site soon became RAF Llanbedr and later Royal Aircraft Establishment.

65

Normal policing was continued as much as possible having regard to all the extra demands made on the Force due to war conditions. I would spend some off duty hours with coastguards also on Observer Corps duty on the Castle grounds. I made a number of trips in the lifeboat and was able to assist with some Morse Code signalling on one occasion when we could avoid going in to Aberdovey to ask if the yacht we had been searching for had been traced. The lifeboat was equipped with an Aldis Signalling lamp but no one of the crew present knew any Morse Code when I asked could they not signal the shore rather than go all the way in. They allowed me to try out my little knowledge and no experience and it worked splendidly after I had signalled SLOW.

I remember another occasion I was a passenger and we were searching for one of our aircraft believed to have come down in the sea. We took with us some four RAF nursing orderlies from their Sick Quarters in the town. They were all very sick indeed and could not have helped at all. No aircraft was found.

In September 1942, I tried to get myself released for active war service. At that time release could be obtained if 'specialist qualifications' were involved. I was able to satisfy the Army Intelligence Corps that my own poor linguistic qualifications etc. could be of use to them. Permission to go was refused by the Chief Constable and it was arranged I should also put my case to H.M. Inspector of Constabulary when he was visiting our Force almost immediately afterwards. The Intelligence Corps informed me in due course that although they also had informed those concerned that the Corps was a fully combatant unit, they had been unable to secure my release.

The Projectile Development Establishment at Aberporth was visited by the Prime Minister, Mr. Winston Churchill with Heads of Services and Mr. Winant, the American Ambassador with many other notabilities. They were to be shown something new. It did not go off hitchless but fortunately without injury to anyone. The projectile justified itself after that one hitch though. The visitors had come by special train to Cardigan and some protection was provided for them between the Railway station and the Establishment. I became an armed policeman for the first time. It was thought that I should wear a .45 revolver. It was not needed.

We were all gun conscious in those days and it may have been before or after the above, that one night I was on general duty and a young soldier who had been found sleeping in an air raid shelter, was being taken to a nearby military post. He had admitted being an absentee and that he had missed his transport to his camp and had been advised that the best he could do was to report to the post at once and so reduce the period of his absence to the minimum. He was about to enter the front door of the post with an accompanying constable when, suddenly, he dashed away into the black out. I ran to intercept him but he eluded me and, rightly or wrongly, I called out 'Stop or I will shoot'. Of course I had no weapon so could not have done so. He continued running in to Queen's Road and was soon lost in the dark. I returned to station — no personal radios in those days — reported the situation then continued to Trefechan Bridge where I thought I might yet catch him if he went to leave the town in a southerly direction. I stood in a doorway and listened and, within minutes I heard footsteps approaching. It was the soldier. I dashed towards him and as he again started to run, I repeated the threat to shoot. This time he called out 'Don't shoot. Don't shoot', and stopped with his hands up. I took him to the police station. He admitted stealing the bicycle a constable had brought in earlier from the street near his resting-place-shelter. Later, he was handed over to be dealt with elsewhere for other offences as well.

Chief Constable J. J. Lloyd Williams, MC, tendered his resignation early in 1943. An official inquiry had commenced investigating a number of allegations against him. The inquiry was adjourned for a weekend when his resignation came.

Superintendent W. J. Jones of the Carmarthenshire Force was appointed to the vacant post in January 1944.

I was transferred to New Quay in 1944 and during the pre D-Day days I had to redirect some newly arrived U.S. troops to New Quay, Cornwall when they mistakenly arrived in Cardiganshire. I have not forgotten their amazement and disbelief on learning that the British police was an unarmed service.

Here too I met Wing Commander Ira Jones (author of *An Air Fighter's Diary* — an account of his First World War days.) He tried to show me how to plant shallots one day, on his taking a short cut through our police station grounds on his way home from the Queen's Hotel. He had been awarded so many decorations in his extreme youth so that on one occasion he was arrested in London as a suspected masquerader. He had flown Spitfires in the Second World War before retiring to New Quay. A Dutch pilot who had been forced to land his Spitfire in our area through fuel shortage sought my help to find him. I left them together at the Queen's Hotel.

I had bought an old Austin car to help me cover this mostly rural beat, as well as the town itself, but to my surprise I was refused a travel allowance and therefore a petrol allowance, so I just had to sell it again. I occasionally rode a local hunt's horse to exercise it — out of season — and on one occasion rode it when on duty to cover quite a distance to serve a number of summonses. More horse riding was to come elsewhere later, though I knew it not then.

A bomb of sorts and a threatening letter were found on board the Ministry of Fisheries' patrol vessel 'Alpha' which was based at New Quay. We failed to find the perpetrators. I had obtained specimen hand writings of the crew but found nothing which compared with the letter. About thirty years later I was looking at a house in North Wales as a prospective purchaser, when the owner informed me that he had met me before and that I had at that time taken a specimen of his handwriting. I was thinking about it when he told me of the Alpha at New Quay. He was the engineer and his name was Fish.

I had another unsuccessful case in New Quay. A lady reported she had had some prize specimen Bramley apples stolen from her former lock-up garage on a small lane some distance from her home. With the door open, they would be visible to passers by and yes, someone had been keen to have them and had offered to buy them. She had refused to sell them.

68

There would be about forty to fifty pounds of them. We executed a search warrant at a house a very short distance away but found only other apples but in large quantities. We had noticed a shed in the orchard connected with the house and on inspection found the shed to be locked. The key for it was produced and we found the expected quantity of Bramley apples in a bag behind the door. We were taking him to the Police Station when in passing the old garage, I decided to ask for the shed keys again and immediately found one that unlocked the garage door. The person passed that way several times daily. At his trial, he was found not guilty.

With V bombs now dropping in the London area, one of my sisters, with young twins, decided enough was enough and at last agreed to come to stay with us. Their father now overseas in the Royal Air Force, had not yet seen them. They were a heavy load to push up the steep streets in New Quay and my sister was ever pleased when some or other of the young lads in the London evacuated Nautical School gave her a helping hand with her twin pram. Boys will be boys but I had no trouble with the lads. One of them, unfortunately, was fatally injured in a cliff fall.

Earlier, a young girl who had been evacuated privately to New Quay from the Bristol area met her so sudden death in the safe haven of New Quay. Explosives were being used to excavate an air raid shelter of sorts in the cliff-fall adjacaent to the sandy beach. The beach had been cleared but some children had been allowed to stay in the shelter of a large beached boat. This shelter was adequate in itself but when the children ran out after the explosion, there was a second explosion within moments of the first and one child fell. She had been killed instantly by a small piece of rock which had penetrated the top of her skull.

In New Quay as in Aberystwyth, I was in contact with members of the Observer Corps. One had lived some years in South Wales. He told me of the time he became interested in spiritualism and some of his experiences in this field. After the passage of some forty seven years, much of the detail now escapes me. He had his church in South Wales. On occasion he took services at other churches. He remembered 'seeing' one of his fellow workers helping himself from a collection plate back at his own church but there had been nothing he could do about it. Earlier he had taken part in special services in public halls in many towns in England and Wales and while his fellow workers performed various acts and as mediums, he would attempt to answer questions put to him by members of the audience. He said he knew nothing of what he would be saying and was conscious only that it seemed as if his voice was being used by someone else. Earlier, during the War he had been praying for and laying hands on the head of a young man, and who was still in New Quay but now blind, who had a large growth on his head. There had been no cure but the growth had somehow moved from the back of the head to the side. The youth had been in the merchant navy. He had asked him one day, therefore, if he knew anything of a ship called the *Bismarck*. The answer then was in the negative, but later, of course, had come news of the sinking of HMS *Hood* and the chase when the German warship *Bismarck* was also sunk. I asked my friend what had he seen or heard. He told me that he must have foreseen the sinking of the *Bismarck*. He had seen, as if in a large picture, this warship in flames from shelling and the name *Bismarck* had appeared beneath the 'picture'. There was the time, too, when on visiting another distant church, he had been accommodated at the secretary's home and a shared bed as a separate bed was not available. His companion had fallen asleep and he had followed suit. Later he awoke with a start and felt that the still sleeping man was about to stab him and yet he did not move. Then he said he had sat up and seen a picture at the foot of the bed of a coloured man. The secretary then woke up and asked my friend had he not been asleep yet and so was told what he had seen. The man then started to cry and explained that he had been a warder in Swansea prison. Warders went to Cardiff prison to help look after prisoners awaiting execution and the coloured man was, on his last night in his care. He had sought the prisoner's permission to kneel with him and pray for him.

After this the prisoner had lain down and slept seemingly peacefully until the morning came.

My friend had resisted attempts by some friends in earlier days to attend spiritualists' meetings. He felt that he had been forced to take part. In later years, he had come to realise that a coloured man he remembered meeting as a very young boy on his way home from school, had not in fact been walking home with him but that it was a spirit guide. I can only tell you now, dear reader, that my friend had the clearest blue eyes I had ever seen and to a very suspicious policeman he seemed to be telling me nothing but the truth. These, of course, were only some of the things of which he spoke.

I am reminded of a War Weapons Week at New Quay, to help boost the drive for more savings the better to prosecute the war effort. A most motley crowd of people, in many organisations in the surrounding areas, had come together for a parade in New Quay. They were all to march all the way down the very steep hill and part of the way up the other steep main street again. I had to lead the march. It could only be a slow dawdle.

But the war effort was indeed gathering pace and we were soon all listening to our 'wireless sets' for news of the D-Day landings in early June 1944. Our second daughter, Helen Rowena was born at the Police Station on the 21st June and we little thought then that one day she would be a policewoman in London, standing in line on crowd control, at the funeral of that so great war leader Winston Churchill. It was only the other day that I learnt that a sailor alongside her, also in line had a very runny nose and, at attention, could not help himself she had taken her own handkerchief and wiped his nose for him. The ways in which we serve.

The summer morning, in New Quay, must have seemed a wondrous thing to the young man I found looking at a shop window when I took my first walk of the day around the town. I noticed him because he was a stranger there at that time and there was nothing really to attract his attention in that particular window. I looked more carefully and saw that he could well be a soldier. I spoke to him and I was satisfied he

71

was almost certainly an absentee. He had arrived in New Quay that morning having had a lift from Carmarthen and was on his way home to Aberystwyth. I had to take him to the police station where my wife and I gave him some breakfast. He had deserted in the face of the enemy in Normandy when the fierce fighting and its consequences got too much for him. His unit was continuously in the thick of it as they were relieving others without relief themselves. He had found his way to Cherbourg and overhearing some of the crew of a tanker, gathered they were returning to Swansea that night. He had followed them and smuggled himself aboard and in due course reached Swansea and had lifts by road to New Quay via Carmarthen. I had to pass him on to the police at Aberystwyth. Later, I heard that very shortly after he had deserted his infantry unit, a cable had come from the War Office recalling him as he was under age and should not have been in France. I was exceedingly glad to know that all would be well with him, I would like to think that he survived the war and prospered.

The days of the national government were expected to be limited naturally and before I left New Quay a little later the Labour prospective candidate for the Cardiganshire parliamentary seat, had arranged a public meeting in our hall. To appear in his support Mr. Arthur Jenkins, M.P. had travelled down from London. He was Roy Jenkins' father. I was introduced to them and Mrs. Jenkins remarked on the coincidence that while they had travelled right across England and Wales without seeing a single policeman they had now come across her husband's namesake in New Quay. Today too, I suppose one would miss seeing a policeman, though one might see a real or cardboard cut out police car.

My stay at New Quay was soon to end though I objected to being made to move with our young baby into a house which was condemned at Cardigan. We had to find a place for my sister and children to stay in New Quay as there would be no room for them with us in the little cottage in Cardigan. So I was not surprised some few years later that the Chief Constable was to be reprimanded after a tribunal found some of the charges against him in connection with the administration, morale and efficiency of the Force had been proved. The reprimand had been substituted by the Home Secretary when the Chief appealed against the original decision that he should be required to resign. He then served another year or so before retiring on pension.

I was very happy to be serving for a third time in Cardigan but restless nevertheless. Nepotism and the times, perhaps?

The inspector in charge, like his predecessors, lived in the quarters provided for him at the police station. This meant living on the job but for the duration of my time there, this time, I always worked a late shift until all was quiet enough for me to go home and never had any evening free except when on my official day off. One accepted these things in those days but one was entitled to expect better.

I investigated a report of mysterious lights which were sometimes coloured, showing near St. Dogmael's a little down stream from Cardigan itself, but never succeeded in discovering their source. They were at low level near the river and not high in the sky. These days, I presume, there would have been talk of UFO's?

Some non-belief reminds me of another jury story. This was in Aberystwyth. A lady with a sleeping problem, heard some unusual noise outside and went to peep. She saw men about to force their way in through the fan light above the door of a property nearby used by a wholesale tobacconist. She informed the police who were soon there and managed to catch two of the three men. The third was caught some hours later outside the town. They were members of a Cardiff gang of shopbreakers. Normally their departure from the city into the surrounding areas would be reported to the police forces concerned. This time the gang came further afield. Later I was escorting one of them to Swansea prison on remand. He was in a state because he had broken his promise to his wife on his release from his last sentence, that he would never, never again go out with the gang and here he was caught again on his first outing. At the trial the gang boss was giving evidence for the defence when he was actually warned by the Judge that he might find himself in the dock with the other accused.

73

As one almost expected, the jury did indeed find them all 'Not Guilty' while one was entitled to conclude they would all be convicted and sentenced. I have heard it said and have repeated the story many times that a judge was one day being driven to his lodgings when a fox crossed the road ahead with a pack of hounds closing on it rapidly. The judge said, 'There is just one thing now that can save the fox'. The High Sherif said, 'And what would that be, Sir?' The answer he got was 'a Cardiganshire Jury'. As there are so called good and bad juries, I would advocate a system where only legally trained people should be asked to decide all cases.

The end to the war in Europe seemed to be within reach as the Allied Forces continued their advances but the war in Asia, as yet, looked far from being over.

I had had a hankering for service in Hong Kong in the Colonial Police or Colonial Customs Service. I had started enquiring in April 1945 as I imagined that when we recovered the colony from the Japanese there would be need for replacements for the many officers who would have been interned or kept as prisoners of war. Many would be unable or would not wish to continue in those services.

Was I being selfish in wanting to look for fresh fields? Was I being too uncaring for my family or in the long term, wanting better things for us?

Mothers' cares and worries hardly vary from decade to decade. I shall not forget my wife reminding our seven year old daughter, Diana, to return without delay from a cinema matinee show as if it could be dark before she had to walk a street and a half to reach home. After a few moments, Diana said, 'If someone stops me in the dark and speaks to me, I shall say, "Can't you see I am a policeman?" and then if they'll say, "You are very short for a policeman", I'll tell them, "Can't you see I'm on my knees tying my shoe lace?"' Had we laughed less, would she have said more?

Victory in Europe (VE) Day came and we celebrated and held our Thanksgiving Services.

On 14th June 1945, I was invited to the Colonial Office for a personal interview at the Hong Kong Planning Unit and while waiting for an offer of an appointment and without prejudice to that possibility, I went for an interview on 1st November for possible appointment as a European Police Sub-Inspector. It was 26th November when I accepted an offer of an appointment to the Senior Clerical and Accounting Staff of the Hong Kong Government, made to me by the Colonial Office. I would be seconded for service under the War Office as Hong Kong was under Military Administration.

I rejected the offer of appointment as a Sub-Inspector in Hong Kong as it was insufficiently attractive. I was glad to know though that PC3 Emlyn Thomas who worked with me at Cardigan and who had gone to London with me for interview, had also been offered a sub-inspectorship. He accepted and so we both resigned from the Cardiganshire Force in December 1945 and, separately, we both went to Hong Kong. Resignation was now possible as the police service ceased being a reserved occupation in that month.

TO HONG KONG

The final farewells in Cardigan were brief though I would miss many old friends. There was little time to prepare to go. At least I should be with my family for Christmas and my wife and our two daughters were to stay awhile then in Dolgellau, as no suitable accommodation would be available for families in Hong Kong for some time to come.

Hong Kong was founded as a British Colony in 1841. It consisted of little more than the Island itself with an area of about 30 square miles only. Its cession to Great Britain by China was confirmed the following year by the Treaty of Nanking. The need for more than the island itself and a foothold on the China mainland itself for security reasons, soon became apparent and in 1860, the area that is now known as Kowlon, with some three islands, was ceded to us by the Convention of Peking. As the population increased yet more land was needed to help provide food and water supplies and to this end, in 1898, China leased to Great Britain the area known as the New Territories for 99 years. This would amount to about 360 square miles. In January 1946, 1997 sounded a long time in the future.

Japanese occupation of Hong Kong had only come to an end a few months earlier and the Military Administration would have a lot to do for some time. The Japanese had neglected so much in the way of maintenance and now the Chinese were pouring back into the Colony. Many had been forced to leave to seek some form of sustenance on the mainland. I was given to understand that the population had shrunk to about three quarters of a million before the occupation had come to an end.

I had been told in London that I was earmarked for the

76

post of Secretary for the police department. Originally, I had been expecting to be Secretary to the Director of Public Works but this post had been filled in Hong Kong while I was still awaiting confirmation of my appointment.

I was now to be under War Office instructions so I prepared for the earliest possible departure as they were arranging for my passage by air. First, naturally, were a whole series of innoculations including Yellow Fever. The War Office obtained my passport and a number of visas for stopping points en route. They were even arranging for a supply of clothing coupons so that I could get myself kitted up for work in the tropics. As a civilian, I was issued with a South East Asia Permit to enter the zone of the Allied Forces in South East Asia and instructions to report at the B.O.A.C. Airways Terminal in London at 0730 hours on 9th January 1946.

Though the war in Europe and in Asia was over, it was only after we left the Terminal in a motor coach that I became aware of the fact that we were bound for Poole Harbour down in Dorsetshire. It was a dark, wintry morning and very windy too after we passed Winchester. In Poole Harbour, we found our aircraft was a large four engined flying boat — a Sunderland — with eighteen of us passengers and six crew. Her Reg. No. was 0QZC. There had been a number of these aircraft operating from Pembroke Dock with Coastal Command. This one was converted for civilian use. We managed to get aboard from small boats but the sea was quite rough and it was only after several attempts that we succeeded in taking off.

We were flying into a very strong head wind and our first stop was to be on Lake Biscarrosse some 40 miles south west of Bordeaux. I noted that when we were only about half way, our actual speed over the ground was some 125 mph but our air speed was 166 mph. There was considerable turbulence and one or two of the passengers were very sick indeed. We landed on the lake without trouble just as it was getting dark.

A bus with a Swansea registration number — a Western Welsh — took us to our Hotel du Lac et des Pins. I thought of the thousands and thousands who had crossed over to France in the last five years or so and of the thousands who had not been able to make it back home again. Over some cognac, some of us talked with the locals at the bar but were better able to do so with two who had spent time in Paris, for we were lost really when the others came out with so much that was in their local dialect or patois. Yes, the hotel had been Nazi headquarters for that area. One of the chief Resistance men was pointed out to us. He had worked as a chef in the hotel. He had sabotaged six German aircraft.

And so to bed and under a two foot thick eiderdown and with a hard pillow. We were due for breakfast at 6.45 and then to fly for our next night stop in Cairo with lunch at Augusta in Sicily. I heard that our storm the day before had blown a train off the rails at Bognor Regis.

The flight to Sicily was certainly more comfortable than the flight from Poole but we had a heating problem the first day and again our feet were very cold. I got the young boy steward to bring us a blanket each in our section and then tucked them round our legs.

The Pyrenees in the morning sun were all shades of pink into white with their snows. They were within view for a long time. At about 12.30 we were flying past Marsala on the western point of Sicily and at 9,000 ft. Our airspeed was 168 mph but over the sea we were making 184 mph with a favourable wind. It would then take us about half an hour flying along the south coast of Sicily to reach Augusta and our lunch. I found even the gradual descent very uncomfortable for Sunderlands were not pressurised.

After lunch and refuelling at Augusta we were on our way again for Cairo. Height and speed much like the morning. Names like Sollum and Mersa Matruh sounded familiar. We landed on the Nile in Cairo at about half past nine in the evening local time, or 7.30 GMT. We were accommodated in a houseboat overnight and there was much that was new and strange for me to actually see, smell and hear. I was not looking at pictures but these things and these people were real. Cardigan and Dolgellau were very far away.

Our crew were left in Cairo for a rest while we continued in the same seats with a new crew. We took off about 9.30 a.m.

on the 11th January and headed now, we were told, for Habbaniah, a lake in Iraq a little west of Baghdad. I managed to see Jerusalem through a break in the cloud cover and then looked again for signs of life in the desert areas. We were low enough to see an occasional temporary encampment. I remember little of Habbaniah — just the heat and the flies. We were then soon on our way again for a long flight down the Euphrates and the Persian Gulf to Bahrain. There, we had a late meal and took off, after midnight for Karachi which was then in India.

We were informed there was a severe storm ahead and we would divert a little to avoid the worst of it. I was one who accepted an invitation to go upstairs where a small number of us were able to occupy some low lying cots where we were then comfortably strapped in. I remember thinking as we met some of the turbulent air, that the pilot would be doing his best to get to Karachi safely and there was nothing I could do better than have a sleep. I woke to a gentle shaking of my shoulder and being told, 'We will be landing in Karachi in about ten minutes, sir'. It was very early in the morning when we landed and went ashore.

Again I seemed to be seeing pictures which were suddenly alive. But I was now hoping to meet someone I knew. Douglas Jones was an Inspector of Weights and Measures, like his father, our retired Sergeant Joseph Jones, who told me, before I left, that Douglas was in Karachi. I had advised Douglas, some two or three years earlier, in my office in Aberystwyth, that when he had his expected call-up to the Forces, he should ask to be an RAF Instrument Maker. He had done so and was now a fully trained Instrument Maker with the Royal Air Force in Karachi. He found me first and came to collect me at the B.O.A.C. Carlton Hotel. We spent a few pleasant hours together as he showed me around. He kept his promise to send picture postcards home for me. In 1992 we have just talked on the telephone about that meeting in Karachi forty six years ago and hope to meet soon.

I had slept or tried to sleep under a huge fan at the Carlton and was called at 4.30 a.m. for a very early take off for Calcutta. We breakfasted in flight. We had before us a journey of 1,380

miles to Calcutta and I confess I looked a couple of times to
see if there was anywhere our flying boat could land in an
emergency during this long overland trip! We were flying at
about 3,000 feet only for most of the way so could see quite
a bit of the terrain below.

After about 8 hours flying, we were over Calcutta and landed
on the Hooghli River, between the two large bridges. We were
taken to our hotel and I was able to have a walk about and see
something of Calcutta's street life. The countless beggars, many
exhibiting dreadful physical deformities, gave some idea of the
poverty of the poor. Was there a Mother Teresa then?

We had to leave our Sunderland Flying Boat 0QZC with
her second crew, for they too deserved a rest. I was to see
pictures in my office in Hong Kong, some weeks later, showing
the Sunderland and some of our passengers, taken as we were
leaving Poole Harbour. They were published by the Ministry
of Information to show how transport was now beginning to
resume some degree of normality again after the War.

For the rest of our journey we were to travel in RAF
Transport Command aircaft. An RAF motor coach drove us
in the early hours of 15th January to Dum Dum airport.

Our aircraft was a Dakota (DC3) with bench seats down each
side, lots of noise and none of the Sunderland's luxuries,
comparatively speaking, and what was more we were now
about to fly for hours over the sea without a flying boat. It
could well be that I have been the only one ever even to
think of criticising the Dakota. KN315 brought us safely and
ready for lunch to Rangoon.

It was not long before we were on our way again heading
for Saigon (now of course Ho Chi Minh City). It would take
some five and a half hours.

At Saigon our baggage was handled by uniformed Japanese
and we were taken to the Majestic Hotel on the riverside.
Our evening meal had to be by candle light but only because
there was no electricity. Water was rationed and things
generally were pretty rough. Our washing water was in bottles,
not in a tap. It looked like being a long uninteresting evening
until we discovered that a U.S. Navy ship in the river alongside

Autumn 1942. Road Traffic Instruction at Alexander Road School, Aberystwyth.

Embassy Cinema. Notting Hill Gate, London.

was about to show some films on deck. We repaired to the hotel for a chair apiece and sat ourselves on the river bank and so whiled away an hour or two before bed. The next day was to see us on the last stretch — Saigon to Hong Kong.

Next morning, however, a slight mechanical defect with the pilot's seat, delayed our departure for some time. We were able to start eventually just in time to avoid having to cancel for the day as it was necessary to ensure a daylight arrival in Hong Kong. This flight was estimated at six hours and the weather in Hong Kong was said to be perfect. I remember Hainan Island coming up and then more sea until we were near Hong Kong. Landings at Kai Tak needed to be precise but fine for the Dakota and there we were, later that afternoon, 16th January, having left Poole Harbour on the 9th. Shortly afterwards these flights to Hong Kong were tried out over four days but found to be too trying and so reverted for some time to a week again. In January 1992 the flight from Heathrow to Hong Kong takes about $12\frac{1}{2}$ hours.

The passengers from that Sunderland from Poole in far away England, by this time had become individuals again and each went his own way. I found myself being driven in a Royal Navy Jeep to the Peninsula Hotel in Kowloon to stay overnight. It was quite a few years later that I happened to read that the hotel by then had its own fleet of seven new Rolls Royce cars to convey guests to and from the airport.

The next day I was collected again and taken on the Star ferry to the city of Victoria on the island of Hong Kong and, with my baggage, settled in to Room 510 in the Gloucester Hotel. There I met Scottie Campbell and we shared the room together for several months. The Gloucester Hotel had been requisitioned, of course, and I believed housed many civil servants and military personnel. We were fed in the Hong Kong Hotel which we could reach directly by way of a short walk along a small shopping arcade.

Scottie was a government pharmacist and had been serving in British Guiana. We talked of many things in our off duty hours. I did assist him a little one Sunday morning when he went to work preparing distilled water urgently needed to cope with some cholera cases. Thankfully it never became a serious outbreak. We walked together quite a lot on the upper levels of the Peak area. Occasionally we were able to join others on visits to some of the beautiful beaches. Once we found ourselves at a beach in the Repulse Bay area and as it was dark we decided to divest ourselves of our clothing and plunged in for a cooling dip in the sea. As we walked back to our clothing, we heard shrieks of female sounding laughter. It seems we were pouring phospherescence as we came out of the water and so were seen by a bunch of nurses who were a little further up the beach and we later believed, may well have been doing the same thing themselves.

In January the Hong Kong climate is ideal especially for those straight from a U.K. winter, as it is sub-tropical and after the heat of summer, comparatively cool and dry. The summers are hot and humid. The mean monthly temperature varies from 59°F in February to 82°F in July. The actual temperature rarely rises above 95°F or falls below 40°F. The mean relative humidity exceeds 80% during the summer but in early winter sometimes falls as low as 20% A winter break in Hong Kong was often favoured by some of Singapore's people.

The Japanese had done little if anything to ensure a healthy environment in the city but since our reoccupation of Hong Kong, every effort was being made to clean up the place and this was evidenced in many ways. Every morning, early, aircraft sprayed the entire area in Victoria and Kowloon, at least, primarily, to eradicate the malaria carrying mosquito. All possible was being done too to reduce the rat population. We saw them even at lunch time in the Hong Kong Hotel, and, I found some had even entered a drawer in a small chest of drawers and had almost devoured the bone buttons on a pair of white flannels.

The importation of firewood and charcoal from Borneo which was carried on before the war had ceased during the Japanese occupation and one of the consequences of this was that virtually every unoccupied house on the island had been denuded of every bit of timber by people seeking it for fuel. It was a shame to see big beautiful houses on the Peak area particularly, now standing like empty shells — no doors, no windows, no wooden floors. Such properties, at whichever higher level one could afford, had always been in great demand. Victoria Peak on Hong Kong Island was over 1,800 ft. high and was accessible by roads leading from the several roads which followed the contours, and, of course, there was the Peak rack railway for foot passengers. In the humid summer heat, every 100 ft. of rise out of the city below brought more relief.

The views of the harbour across to Kowloon and the New Territory become more extensive from the higher slopes. The beauty of Hong Kong Harbour is known world wide, for it is in the same league as Rio de Janeiro and Sydney.

With all its sampans, junks and general shipping and with flying boats and all manner of naval vessels lying at anchor, the harbour was an everchanging scene of greatest interest. After dark, the lights added to the picture and the lights on the Peak area being outstanding. As a guest visiting a British submarine one evening, I was invited to see the lights through the periscope. The next guest to look was a member of the Women's Voluntary Services (now W.R.V.S.); her remark I still remember, was, 'Oh, lightning or welding?'

Before I leave the harbour, to come back later, I would like to mention the skyline insofar as it refers to the shape and size of buildings. Its usage would be correct today for don't we all think of the sky scrapers of New York and Chicago say, when we see Hong Kong on our televisions? In 1946, the tallest building, and only a short distance from the waterfront, was the Hong Kong and Shanghai Bank. Its central mass in height was perhaps equal to some fifteen storeys. Some time ago when I was searching a panoramic picture for it, it was an almost inconspicuous little building and noticeable, if at all, only for its being about the smallest. Today, it is a rebuilt bank we see, huge and modern in its own way.

To return to work, I was soon seen by someone in authority over me, welcomed and had it explained to me that the post for which I had been earmarked, in the police department of government, was already filled and I was given the choice of a post in the confidential registry in the Government Secretariat or a post in the Treasury. I chose the former and I was soon settled in. My colleagues were all military personnel in the early days as the Colony continued to be under military administration. Gradually, former staff were able to resume duty and military staff were being released back to other duties. I found my work most interesting, not least because of its extensive coverage of all manner of subjects of interest to any government. I had to acquire a new vocabulary to understand military matters and methods. One day I was handling a file dealing with Report on Airfield Mission to Hong Kong when in came the Royal Air Force officer involved. He was the same man who had prepared that report on the site which became RAF Llanbedr, in Merionethshire and which I had typed for him some five years earlier in the Chief Constable's office in Aberystwyth.

Now that I had arrived and stopped travelling, I realised that I was a free agent every evening and at weekends and that I was relieved of all those responsibilities which had been mine for so long as a police officer. Now, I was just another person. I was shocked, nevertheless, one day when I witnessed something one would hardly see on a police beat in the U.K. There was this young looking Chinese constable, armed with what I took to be a 38 revolver in holster at his hip, standing with each foot on a shoeshine boy's box. The two lads were busy, each polishing one of his boots, while he surveyed the world moving around him.

One evening I was coming back on the ferry from Kowloon, with nearly all the passengers being Chinese, I became aware that a British soldier, some distance away from me, was losing control of himself and obviously under the influence of drink. He became noisy then stood up and looked as if he was about to interfere with some of the glass display cases. My instincts were to behave like a police officer and to approach and speak to him but I refrained until, a few minutes later, he said something which I took to be in Welsh, so I called out, in Welsh, what on earth was the matter with him. His response was immediate — total silence — as he resumed his seat. He acknowledged me on the way off the ferry a few minutes later, by shaking his head.

At other off duty times, I had contact with a Welsh Toc H worker and met other Welsh lads when I tried to get the Hong Kong Welsh Society going again. We met on Sunday evenings then found the need for Welsh hymn books and song sheets. Some of us including Caradog Hughes, a Welsh naval chaplain wrote home to ask that some be sent to us.

As we had done in Aberystwyth, Toc H people organised a canteen of sorts for service people. Some of us also undertook jobs such as painting to prepare for the return of evacuated orphans to one of their orphanages in the New Territories. The provision of wire netting on the windows to keep out the mosquito was a must there too.

One of the Welsh lads I met at the Kowloon Toc H canteen was a young airman who, some five years before, when he was a telegram messenger boy, lived some two or three doors from our home in Custom House Street, Aberystwyth. Elsewhere too I met the Welsh captain of a cargo ship who was the brother of a Cardigan garage proprietor. A few of us had a good Welsh sing song on board one night, before he sailed. We even sang, 'Draw, draw yn China a thiroedd Japan' though none of the nearby dock workers knew it. It was a well known Welsh children's hymn years ago.

One of my earliest surprises in Hong Kong was to note that almost everywhere crowds might gather, there were warning notices to beware of pick-pockets. Every building seemed to have some special security arrangement. All down pipes, for instance, seemed to be swathed in barbed wire and windows barred or otherwise protected. Almost every business place seemed to have its own security guard; usually an armed Sikh with his own charpoy conveniently placed in the recessed shop entrance after close of business. There was an ever increasing number of Chinese returning or entering the Colony every day and new Chinese banks seemed to be opening every other day or so.

Like many other European first-arrivals, I was expecting to see signs of the inscrutability of all Chinese, but, instead, found them to be as capable of exhibiting their emotions as we Caucasians. Their appreciation of humorous situations was always quite evident. I was told by an Englishman who was a member of a conscientious objectors' organisation, and a member of the Society of Friends that he owed his life to an incident which had its share of humour. He was finding his way towards Hong Kong in an area of China which was bandit ridden and was captured by a gang of them. Having nothing that was worth stealing, he was still completely at their mercy and might well have been shot. However, something the Englishman said or did, induced such a response from one of them that his colleagues roared with laughter and it seemed the discomfiture of their colleague was such that they felt they were now on the Englishman's side and they decided to release him immediately and bade him go. He was mightily glad to reach the safety of Hong Kong.

Bandits even held up coach loads of railway passengers in the New Territories. Bandits on passenger boats plying between Hong Kong and Canton had been posing serious problems. Usually they travelled as ordinary passengers, robbed the others and took control of the vessel until they were taken off by their accomplices. This brought counter measures and one such was to en-cage all the passenger accommodation so that the crew would be protected. Then there came an incident when the ferry, still virtually stern on and tied up to the jetty in Hong Kong, but ready to leave with its full complement of passengers, caught fire. Trapped as they were in the steel cage, very few escaped with their lives.

While we were still under military administration, a number of us who had come to Hong Kong as civilians under War Office control, were treated in our off duty hours as if we were service personnel. For example, transport was arranged for some of our leisure activities, picnic trips to some of the beaches and visits to Royal Navy ships. One visit was to the battleship HMS *Duke of York*, then at anchor in the harbour, which is one of the finest natural harbours in the world. She proudly showed us one of her battle scars — a hole made by a piece of shrapnel from one of the *Scharnhorst's* shells when that formidable German battleship was trapped and sunk on Boxing Day 1943. Several British destroyers and the cruiser HMS *Jamaica* were endeavouring to protect a very important convoy bound with aid to the Russians to Murmansk and when off the north coast of Norway, the *Duke of York* arrived in time to help save the convoy and play a major part in the sinking of the *Scharnhorst*.

Scottie Campbell returned to U.K. to continue his leave from British Guiana and I acquired a new room mate. The warmer days were returning and we were soon back to tropical heat. The day came too when other accommodation became available, and I, with others, moved in to the requisitioned Jesuit Mission building which stood behind the Hong Kong and Shanghai Bank and nearer to the Secretariat. Here too I acquired a new room mate. He was an assistant superintendent of police who had been interned for the duration of the occupation but had elected to resume duty before taking up his leave. He still showed signs of malnutrition and was quite lame.

I was now finding the heat and humidity very trying. And I was not alone in this. I had become used to seeing the local populace, carrying small packages, by a convenient loop of string. I now understood that had they carried the entire package in hand, the contents would have become saturated with moisture from the perspiring hand. One bought one's fish live — they were fresher this way. There was something new to be seen every day. The variety of new experiences helped a little to ease the ache of missed family and home.

I had already decided that until I knew for certain whether I would be staying in Hong Kong permanently, I would not attempt to learn to speak Chinese. The Chinese dialects are of course, numerous. The standard spoken Chinese though is Mandarin. In Hong Kong, as in southern China, the more common language is Cantonese. Was I not told too that words had to be spoken in the right tone or pitch — there being five tones? It could be inconvenient, perhaps utterly futile to use the wrong tones. I am no sinologist so I say no more. I did hear though that some Europeans learning the language by

87

living in China, would have recourse to a sleeping dictionary!!
The same will apply in other countries too.

Early in June, I was transferred to the Department of Supply,
Trade and Industry and to take charge of both its Procurement
and Requisitioning Sections. The Department was then located
in the Mercantile Bank Building. This was at the changeover
from Military to Civil Administration.

Soon after the Japanese occupied Hong Kong after its
surrender to them in 1941, we commenced planning for our
re-occupation of the Colony. Apart from the physical efforts
that would be needed for its recovery, arrangements had to be
made for the earliest possible resumption of all normal services
provided by government. It would also be necessary to restore
to manufacturers and dealers, their abilities to function, in
progressively improving conditions until normality was achieved.

It had to be presumed that in the recovery of Hong Kong
much of what was still available during the occupation would
either be destroyed during any actual fighting or by the Japanese
themselves in pursuit of a burnt earth policy, where property
that could not be kept must be destroyed rather than left.

Elaborate programmes of procurement were prepared and
the action to implement them in various stages planned.
Equipment for example, would need to be ordered and its
shipment, reception and storage arranged.

A power to requisition goods could provide additional sources
for the procurement of supplies. My two sections, Procurement
and Requisitioning, related to goods, although the Department
for some time was also responsible for the requisitioning of
Animals and Transport. A planned distribution of goods was
also necessary, not only to secure an equitable distribution, but
a distribution controlled for the benefit of the community. This
involved a system of priority and price control and was
consequently a natural function of the Department of Supplies,
Trade and Industry. We thus had other sections of the
department which dealt with Storage, Marketing and Price
Control operating as well as other sections relating to the
rehabilitation of industry.

On the re-occupation of the Colony it was found that much

of the stores placed in the godowns (as warehouses are called) in 1941, surprise, surprise, still remained in the godowns. These goods formed an important source of supply upon which we had been able to draw, by means of requisitioning, to provide Government departments, public utility companies and essential industries with much needed stores and equipment.

Foodstuffs were requisitioned for controlled distribution at fair prices. Raw materials were requisitioned to enable manufacturers to resume production of essential goods and provide employment.

I found, within a week of my transfer, that I was having to make representations for better staffing of the sections, for I found work in arrears — I had had no time for proper instructions and the two senior staff sergeants were returning to the U.K. that weekend. I had to report that what one of them had told me was true — information which should have been recorded in proper form had only been committed to memory due to shortage of staff. But these are only examples of difficulties we encountered and that had to be overcome in all departments of government and, I have no doubt, in private businesses in those difficult times.

At this time and distance, I can still remember a number of cases which may be of interest.

The routine handling of all indents to the Crown Agents in the U.K. for supplies by individual departments of government showed up all manner of interesting information. Why such a demand for such heavy calibre ammunition by the police department? Because 38 or 303 ammunition was not guaranteed capable of penetrating the skulls of buffalo! Also railway engines were needed as replacements on the Hong Kong Canton Railway.

Orders had been prepared in the U.K. before the recovery of Hong Kong for such things as torches and batteries, as it was anticipated that all electric power plant might have been destroyed. I think the order still stood for some million batteries to half a million torches — it was certainly not less than this. We had reached a stage where the Industry Section was busily trying to rehabilitate the Hong Kong torch manufacturing capability. My section's help was being sought to secure supplies of the raw materials — tin plate particularly. There was naturally a world shortage and I had addressed a cable to the U.K. ambassador in the United States pleading for pressure on the U.S. government to release supplies to Hong Kong. I had discovered that the long standing order for all those torches and batteries was still awaiting execution, so I had promptly cabled U.K. (War Office and Colonial Office) cancelling it. The copy of cancellation cable was seen by my department head and at once queried of course. Copy of my tinplate cable served to confirm my explanation. They were very busy times and action had to be immediate when possible. (By chance I see that 15 years later Hong Kong exported 2,908,370 dozen torches in 1961).

It was essential that food supplies were maintained at an adequate level and a full resumption of fishery capabilities would have been required as early as possible. To this end it had been foreseen that the fishing fleet would need to be brought back to pre-war levels at least. It had been calculated that a unit of fishing boats would comprise of a set number of vessels needing to be built. Then what each unit would require in its various parts. The quantities of nails that would be needed were so calculated. Somewhere along the line the order for certain nails had been executed by the hundred weight instead of pounds and I could only imagine the situation when these had arrived in one of the godowns, for I was assured that this had actually occurred — before my arrival in the department, naturally.

Our Marketing Section was able to secure a sale of surplus supplies of sanitary buckets and hurricane lamps to the Philippines. Maybe some of the nails went there too.

Hong Kong paint manufacturers sought government assistance to find linseed oil. This was in world short supply and by international agreement the Hong Kong allocation was 500 tons for the year and this was to be available to us in India. India, however, would only release this to us provided we found for them an equivalent amount of mustard oil. Two of our representatives in India found their mustard oil for the Indians in their own country.

Someone else came to me needing supplies of pyrethrum for their mosquito destroying products. They were found in east Africa.

A very large firm of building material importers contacted us to say that they had been trying to obtain glass from the U.K. but had been advised it could only be supplied on government orders. They wanted some half million square feet — some in 18oz and some in 24oz. How was I to know — unless I spoke to the people who ought to know — the government department of Public Works? I was informed that government used nothing less than 24oz as anything lighter (thinner) could be lost in greater quantity in typhoon winds. It was deemed prudent, therefore, to suggest that only 24oz should be ordered so that less replacement would be necessary. To conserve Hong Kong supplies it was also deemed prudent to prohibit the export of glass and this was at once arranged through the department of Imports and Exports. We placed the order through the Crown Agents with Pilkingtons and the importers would take over the shipment on arrival in Hong Kong with all paid by them to that point. As a matter of interest I have just checked with a local glass company and they tell me that they recommend nothing less than 32oz glass for windows and they talk too, now of course, of glass in millimetres.

From time to time we had our typhoon warnings and in that first season one or two more severe blows. One saw how very large windows often had the added protection of strong beams slotted across them so as to lessen the danger of them being blown in. To many, a visual signal to indicate the need for a higher degree of alertness, was the submerging of the large naval floating dock. Sampans and other small vessels would be herded close together for better protection in the harbour in what was called a typhoon shelter.

An example of the need for requisitioning goods in order to ensure a fair distribution at fair prices, was with knitting wools. If a shipment of wool from the U.K. was less than adequate, the entire shipment would be requisitioned and held until another shipment arrived when the total would then be released under controlled prices. Knitted cardigans, pullovers and the like were in demand in the cool season.

There was the case I remember particularly where large numbers of parcels of cotton goods were ariving at the GPO from Australia. By chance, a partly opened parcel was seen to contain wool and not the declared cotton goods. A decision was taken to inspect a number of such parcels and the contents were found to be wool. Names and addresses of intended recipients were found to be very similar and left us in no doubt that all the parcels were part of a big scheme to save on import duty and or avoid the requisitioning. We decided to requisition all the parcels found to contain wool and there were hundreds of them — some of the GPO parcel bays overflowing — and we paid for them at the declared valuation plus ten percent. We received no complaints.

More expatriate staff had joined us during the year and Hong Kong's population was still increasing rapidly and had reached about one and a half million towards the end of the year. It had increased about three quarters of a million in some twelve months. In 1992 the population is over 5 million. I had long since become accustomed to working with Chinese staff and can only speak well of them.

As there was little prospect of family quarters becoming available for expatriates in the immediate future, I had to decide whether I should return to the U.K. to join my family or continue the separation for an indefinite period. I chose the former.

The time soon came then to see about my return passage to the U.K. I found I could have passage in the aircraft carrier HMS *Illustrious* or, alternatively, on a Blue Funnel cargo ship which would be carrying some twenty four passengers. Much as I would have liked to travel on an aircaft carrier, I imagined that I would see far more if I travelled on the S.S. *Menelaus* and this is what was arranged.

In the meantime, I prepared to take my leave of many friends I had made in Hong Kong. Changes of police station in my police days had taught me to enjoy new surroundings and the finding and making of new friends. There was always a wrench though when leaving friends and familiar faces.

In Aberystwyth, in the early days of the War, I had become a member of Toc H and in Hong Kong I had continued contact and now that I was on the move again, I would be leaving some very good friends. Toc H, the signaller's way of saying T H, was formed during the First World War, and the initials stood for Talbot House, a club, if you will, where servicemen meet and talk and be refreshed. Talbot was an Army chaplain. It was an interdenominational club or organisation. I would like to remind myself now of our main resolution — 'Remembering with gratitude how God used the Old House to bring home to multitudes of men that behind the ebb and flow of things temporal, stand the eternal realities and to send them forth strengthened, to fight at all costs, for the setting up of His kingdom upon earth, we pledge ourselves to strive — To listen now and always for the voice of God; to know His will revealed in Christ and to do it fearlessly, reckoning nothing of the world's opinion, or its successes, for ourselves or this our family; and towards this end to think fairly, to love widely, to witness humbly, to build bravely.'

And the Toc H prayer — 'Oh God, Who has so wonderfully made Toc H and set men in it to see their duty as Thy will, teach us to live together in Love and Joy and Peace; to check all bitterness; to disown discouragement; to practise Thanksgiving and to leap with joy to any task for others; strengthen the good things thus begun, that with gallant and high heartedness happiness, we may work for Thy kingdom in the wills of men. Through Jesus Christ our Lord. Amen.'

Of Hong Kong I now remember so many little things but they will have to remain memories. The great respect of Chinese for family, the use of chopsticks, my first view of a Chinese funeral when 72 people shared, at the same time, in the carrying of the coffin and the mourners in white, walking together within an enveloping open-topped tent like affair carried around them. Then my first visit into the New Territories, with my Cardigan colleague who was by now a

Sub-Inspector of the Hong Kong Police. I remembered a story showing how little, some who ought to have known more, knew about Chinese in the now distant past. In England, some big people in cotton business were at a dinner with some Chinese guests. One, feeling he had to make an attempt at conversation with his guest, 'You likee soupee?' was his first approach and received a nod of approval. His next effort was, 'You likee fishee?' and so it went, till speech time. One of the speakers was the Chinese. He addressed his hosts in faultless English. He sat down to approving applause and turned to his neighbour, with a well concealed smile and said, 'You likee speechee?'

After the strict food rationing in the U.K. I had found Hong Kong's food supplies, in quantity and variety, almost unlimited. The special dishes of Shanghai, Peking and elsewhere were all available, as well as all sorts of European dishes. I found the service marvellous too. Having the hottest of wet hot napkins handed to one by a waiter with his serving chopsticks was something new for me and entirely pleasant. There was a lot to be said too for the small cup of hot tea, constantly being topped up.

I can still hear the sound of mahjong tiles being played by the gamblers, the sound of the abacus in the banks and counting houses and the clatter of clogs of early risers walking to work before the day's big traffic rush.

I do not forget the shock though of seeing so much poverty and the attempts being made by so many to exist on so little. I saw a small shed which was being lived in, had been built of empty cigarette tins. Cylindrical tins had been flattened so that they could be used as shingles on some sort of wooden frame. More durable and more permanent than a London cardboard box shelter.

At my own little party, on the eve of my departure, I think I must have said that I had had many a rickshaw ride but had never been carried in a sedan chair. Some of these were still in use more usually perhaps to carry people up and down steps from one street level to another and where rickshaws couldn't go. So another memory is of my being carried in a sedan chair that night but not by its Chinese team but by Royal Navy chaplains.

The next day, 19th February 1947 and at 10 a.m. Mr. Lai and Mr. Pun, senior members of my staff, with other friends saw me off at Murray Pier to board a launch which took me across the harbour to Holt's Wharf, Kowloon, where I boarded the Blue Funnel's *Menelaus*.

I find I am sharing a cabin with Mr. P. B. H. Kent. We leave Hong Kong at about 1 o'clock. The view is lovely — the sampans, junks and other ships and then the islands. It is bitterly cold though and perhaps more so after the summer heat. The China Sea is rough so only a few of us take tea. Several are seasick and the ship creaks and groans.

The night too was rough for I spent a rolling sort of night and was very glad of the tea the steward brought us at about 6.45. On deck later, I see there is still a roughish sea but the air already seems a little warmer. We put the clocks back 20 minutes. I get to know a missionary and his wife who are going home for the first time since before the War. There is another elderly couple. Then three men who share a cabin — one is an American/Pole from Shanghai who sells films and is on transfer to Singapore. Then an 18 stone Scot who tells of his 200 acre estate near Bangalore in India, and the third, a very small Latvian/Russian returning to India. I have already noted their excellent appetites. There is a young Irish ship's doctor returning to the U.K. for final course. Two other youngish men; Two W.V.S. women homeward bound but only as far as Singapore with us. Then a woman with an invalid boy and two other women bound for the U.K. with the wife of a Butterfield and Swire man taking a boy and a girl to school in U.K. She also has a 14 month old little Janet and their northern Chinese amah. With a Cable and Wireless man and Kent and myself, quite a mixed bag. We have seen no land since Hong Kong and the islands and only one ship in the distance yesterday. Only needed one blanket last night.

21st February. Clocks back another 20 minutes — we are making to the west as well as south. Really hot on deck despite the breeze. Still plenty of white horses and a steady roll. Feel

I have now found my sea legs. We lessen our speed a little so as to reach Singapore Monday morning instead of Sunday night. I have found the real ship's doctor to be an Irishman named Murphy who had a practice in Rhyl for 25 years but has only been to sea for one year.

Our ship, a ten thousand tonner, is now 25 years old but can do about 14½ knots on good coal. Crew of 57 Europeans and some Chinese firemen. I am told she hardly saw a thing of the War except on one occasion when she was able to keep clear of a submarine said to have been following her. The officers share tables with the passengers. Ship still rolling — a funny little fish flew on board from a big wave — it contained some inky substance. I played with little Janet for a short while today. Our Rowena is now 2½ ! !

Saturday 22 February. Hearty breakfast of pomelo, porridge, egg and bacon. Saw some flying fish today. Slept on deck after tiffin. Winds blowing from astern giving us huge following waves.

Sunday 23 February. Much like yesterday but more rain. Sing song in Smoke Room in the evening as several of our passengers are leaving us in Singapore tomorrow.

Monday 24 February. Found we had anchored at about 7.30 a.m. till weather clears, to navigate carefully the remaining miles into Singapore. Very wet and hot. We arrived about 5.30 p.m. and about twenty minutes later. I received a letter from my wife. Grand to feel in touch again. In Hong Kong, mail any day might have brought me news of them all, but at sea, for days, no mail could reach me. So till now even though I am homeward bound, I had felt more cut off. Many ships in the roads and it sounds as if we shall be here for some time. Had a long chat with the chief steward who hails from Anglesey.

25 February. We have moved to another anchorage, closer in, this morning. Have had passport cleared to land. Very busy all round us. Very wet. We unload cabbages galore which had come to us from China. Another sing song.

26 February. Went ashore in ship's lifeboat — over a mile. Saw a little of Singapore, including the famous Raffles Hotel.

August 1949. Police Station/house, Port Stanley, Falkland Islands.
A Welsh family far from home. Diana was 12, Rowena 5 years old and our new baby,
Sarah, 3 months.

William Ellis from near Castell Brychan, a former school chum from Aberystwyth — visiting the family in St. Vincent. He was then a captain of a Canadian Bauxite carrying ship.

Saw a French aircraft carrier also a big French liner, the *Marechal Joffre* packed with troops. Plenty of other big ships around us also at anchor.

27 February. Still at anchor. Holds being cleaned and ship being painted. We load rubber and sacks of sago flour.

28 February. Morning tea in bed, as usual. Went ashore again in the lifeboat but extremely hot walking around. Posted letters home. Had my haircut but by a Chinese girl — a new experience, especially as she also massaged the back of my neck. First time I had seen or had this done. Back to ship for lunch. After tea, had cold salt water bath with washdown after in fresh water. Mr. Kent came back aboard about 4 o'clock. He had got very dirty under some tarpaulin when it rained, so then washed his suit himself. It rains every day in Singapore at about 4 in the afternoon. So they know the time to hang out their washing here for I noted that almost every house or flat window had a very long pole of sorts, protruding out above the street with its washing hanging out to dry. (I remember this today as I write this again as I see TV views of the so very high rise flats in Singapore with all the very long poles full of washing sticking out, just as in 1947, but now from upwards of a score and more storeys not just two or three floors).

St. David's Day. Wrote letters. Lazed in the heat. Due to go alongside at last tomorrow morning.

2 March. Went ashore with Jones, the chief steward, to the Union Jack Club for a Welsh service at 7 p.m. but we found only our ship's carpenter there. No one else turned up so we left to go for a meal and returned to the ship at 10.30. Very hot and the mosquitoes a real nuisance at night.

3 March. Still alongside and very hot all day. They say the hottest day for four months. Very busy loading rubber in 195 lbs bales.

4 March. Went ashore this morning and bought white shirts. Back for lunch under boiling sun. Lazed and perspired the rest of the day. In this climate, as in Hong Kong's high humidity and heat, there is a need for a Dutch wife — an inanimate one of course. My cabin mate, Kent, and I, more by unspoken

mutual agreement, I think, have kept apart when away from our cabin so as to enjoy our separate meetings with others. Then back in our cabin, we have always had something new to say to one another. Our discussions daily, for the trip so far and for the weeks that remained, covered a wide range of subjects and our long hours spent together, passed most happily. P. H. B. Kent, O.B.E., M.C., was a barrister-at-law; formerly Legal Adviser at Peking to the Ministries of Finance and Communication also of the Chinese Government's Salt Administration; author of *Railway Enterprise in China* and *The Passing of the Manchus.* I have his book *The Twentieth Century in the Far East* in front of me as I write in 1992. He kindly sent me a complimentary copy after our long voyage. Kent had been very many years in China and had been and had been interned there by the Japanese, but in the earlier part of the War, as he was over sixty five years of age, he had been one of many who had been exchanged and handed over in Laurenco Marquess, in Portuguese East Africa. (Now Maputo in Mozambique). Later in London, he became involved in the planning arrangements for a sort of War Crimes Tribunal with special reference to South East Asia. He had returned briefly to China, after the Japanese surrender and now, in Singapore, he was in touch again with a Brigadier Davies who was now concerned with the War Crimes Trials in South East Asia.

I now quote again from some diary notes I made on 5th March, 1947 — 'Brigadier Davies called for Kent and myself at 9.30 a.m. and drove us out to Changi Prison. We sat in at one of the courts trying two Japanese civilians for shooting an Indian and then inspected the prison, now full of Japanese. Much impressed. Saw twelve Japs including a general, in the condemned yard. They had a priest with them. Saw the Execution Shed and examined the gallows. There were three of these, so three could be executed simultaneously or separately. Later, after lunching us at the Pavilion restaurant, Brigadier Davies sent us in his car so we could shop a little before we returned to ship about 5.30 p.m.'

At Changi Prison that day we saw several courts sitting in

the prison compound. I still have the copies given to me of the charges and some abstracts of evidence in a number of the cases, which involved cruelty and illtreatment in P.O.W. camps in Saigon and other places in South East Asia as well.

Much of the internal discipline of the Japanese prisoners was the responsibility of a Japanese sergeant major who was pointed out to me as a former Olympic champion. I was impressed by the disciplined appearance of the prisoners seated in a very large dining room, with their mess tins lined up in precise straight lines at each long table.

I have recently bought a book, *Priest in Prison* by Canon John Hayter, now in its second edition. It tells of Changi and much else in Singapore during the war years, and for £6.00 can be obtained from Boldre Enterprises, Talbots, Rope Hill, Boldre, Lymington, Hants.

I am still complaining of the heat and mosquitoes and that I shall be glad to leave Malaya altogether. I quote again:

'7th March. Blisteringly hot today again. See in today's paper about a woman found dead in a car in a snowdrift in the Aberystwyth area. (The very cold weather persisted in the U.K. to the second week in May!!) Mr. Kent went to see Lord Killearn in the afternoon and the Governor (Malcolm MacDonald, son of Ramsay MacDonald).

8th March. Went up town with Kent in the morning and bought myself rattan lounge chair for the deck. (This survived quite a number of years in Wales too!) I also bought two large, pinkish fleshed pomelos which the Chief Steward undertook to keep for me in cold storage till we reached home. (They were deliciously edible when we did get there and something we had not tasted there before.) Terrific rainstorm with thunder and lightning in the afternoon. A bit cooler afterwards.

12th March. Left Singapore late afternoon on 9th March for Port Swettenham in Selangor, Malaya. We arirved next day. Went up river for a few miles and had to anchor out in the stream — no loading, just waiting for a berth along side the jetty some 2-3 miles away. Still at anchor on 11th and today when it was very hot all day with a bit of a storm in the late evening.

Had my hair cut by a Welsh sailor from Amlwch in the afternoon.

13th March. Still at anchor. Went off in a launch at 7 p.m. and then on to Klang some 6-8 miles inland to a club where planters (rubber plantations) meet and attended a dance. Back to ship very late and captain took us to his cabin for a drink before bed.

14th March. Still at anchor. Saw porpoises swimming by. Went below, late at night — some 40ft. down into the engine room. Very hot in the higher places but not too bad under the air vents lower down. The Chinese duty stoker was from Hong Kong.

15th March. When I awoke I found we were approaching the jetty and well within the port limits. We tied up just after breakfast. Only two ships can go alongside at once. Malayan railway comes on to the wharf. Loading started at once. Bales of rubber 224 lbs each and pumped on 1,000 tons of palm oil. (This I found had to be kept warm in our specially heated tanks for the rest of the voyage.) Went ashore with Kent and explored small place. Birthday cable to my wife and bought a penknife and some Parker Ink. Mr. Snelling a new passenger came aboard today.

16th March. Stretched legs on jetty but found it too difficult to get to the creek on foot in search of crocodiles. At 4 p.m. went with a party by launch but still saw no crocs.

17th March. Very hot all day so just lazed on the ship and read a lot. Heavy shower tea time.

18th March. Went to Kuala Lumpur, 11 of us, in a truck then on to the Golf Club where we had wonderful swimming in a lovely pool. Lunch, then more swimming. Captain talked me into diving from second highest board — higher than I had ever dived before. Anxiety made me flatten out sooner than I should have done but it could have been worse. Return to ship via an experimental agriculture station and saw rubber plantations, tin mines and tea drying. Rain caught us and terrible ride back till truck broke down before reaching Klang — so a bus ride to Klang, a big dinner there and taxis to ship.

19th March. Busy finishing loading and left gladly at 4 p.m.

Lovely night at sea and passed a Blue Funnel ship — *The Samiti* at 11 p.m.

20th March. Saw Penang Island before breakfast. Tied up at wharf about 12.30 p.m. Mail from home. Walked round part of the town in afternoon and then dined on board. The capital is Georgetown and the place reminds me of Hong Kong.

21st March. Moved out to anchor and made room for a big liner, the *Alcantara*. Very hot aboard but did not go ashore.

22nd March. Went ashore 10.15 by launch, then with Mr. and Mrs. Allen and Alec by taxi to Botanical Gardens which with monkeys about as well we found interesting. Went then to a swimming pool at the edge of the sea, bathed, lunched and had tea there. Saw plenty of coconut trees, bananas and lovely flowers. Shared a huge ripe pineapple. By sampan to ship by 6.15 p.m.

23rd March. One of the hottest days yet. Too hot to sleep. Big lighter coming alongside with the interminable rubber, caught its huge mast in some ropes when swept back by the tide and had it broken. Hear we leave at midnight tomorrow. Good news!

24th March. Still busy loading rubber. Another passenger came aboard today. Big awning put up on deck. Started heaving the anchor about 11.15 p.m. Marvellous display of lightning almost round us. Could see the Pole Star and Southern Cross in the sky. We are 6° north of the Equator. Singapore was only 1°20 north. We are about 100° east of Greenwich so have a long way to go yet. Lovely breeze blowing and so goodbye Penang. Everyone very glad. We put clocks back 55 minutes after we start sailing again.

25th March. Breakfast seemed an hour late this morning. We are heading westwards for Ceylon (Sri Lanka). Lovely gold and red Kingfisher flew on board before breakfast. Sumatra just visible for most of the afternoon.

26th March. Large tanker met us in the morning about two miles off. Two four-engined aircraft flew over high up. Watched a wonderful sunset. We all start keeping a lookout for the green flash at the moment of sunset.

27th March. Good sleep again last night. Played deck quoits. Washed some more shirts. Flying fish galore now.

28th March. Started ironing a shirt in the morning but the Chinese amah insisted on finishing it for me. Spent an hour on the bridge talking to the 3rd Officer, from 10.45 p.m. Kept lookout for Ceylon's lights. (Some 1250 miles from Penang?) Storm coming on when I turn in.

29th March. Land in sight when I get up — south coast of Ceylon and followed it round till we reached Colombo about 2.30 p.m. Made fast to buoys in harbour and went ashore. Caught by the rain and almost went in to a Hindu temple. Bought picture postcards. Meal in a Chinese cafe. Saw lots of Buddhist priests, shaven heads, saffron robes and black umbrellas.

30th March. Went ashore with three others this morning then by car to Mount Lavinia, Grand Hotel — sandy beach, waving palms, crows everywhere, surf riding before lunch — catamarans. Met some other passengers there too. Back to ship after tea in time for dinner. Very busy loading tea and coaling. Hope to leave tomorrow.

31st March. More letters from home (posted 24th March!) so glad to feel in touch again. Went ashore and had haircut and joined Snelling again. Made some purchases including a doll. People wearing most colourful clothing. Back to ship for lunch. Talked to a Ceylon policeman on the ship. Left Colombo 9.30 p.m. in fresh breeze. Made myself a cup of tea then a drink and chat with Scott on the port side then bed. (The word 'posh' — smart or tip top — is, I think, originally a word used to describe people who could afford to travel, in east and west bound ships in eastern waters, on that side of the ship away from the direct sun. Port Outwards (eastwards) and Starboard Homewards).

1st April. Very nice to be at sea again. Ship a bit cleaner again after the coaling. It will be at least seven days before we sight land and Aden. Saw porpoises and later went up to the bows to see a school of them — 14 or 15 — swimming ahead of the ship's bow — almost touching, turning over and at times leaping right out of the water like salmon. Tails like mackerel. They were some 5 - 10 ft. long.

2nd April. It is six weeks today since I left Hong Kong! Saw two ships, one, the *Lycaon,* a Blue Funnel ship, which our captain had told me we should see in about an hour — they had been in wireless touch. From above, the flying fish look much like aircraft. Ran into terrible rain and thunder late evening and had to slacken speed. Played bridge.

3rd April. Saw another two ships today.

4th April. Good Friday. Archdeacon Shann (whom I'd met in Hong Kong) took a special service in the Smokeroom at 7.15 a.m. There were about fourteen of us present. Grand day. Sun and breeze all day. Sun sets about 6 p.m. and dark almost immediately. Saw a ship flashing us at 10 p.m. — a new ship to Hong Kong for Butterfield and Swire.

5th April. Another wonderful day of sun and breeze. Saw a ship's funnel above the horizon. Slept after tiffin. After bath and changing went with Forsgate and Snelling to captain's cabin for drinks before dinner. In the morning, I examined typewriters! Mr. Kent's (borrowed from the Chief Steward), the Purser's from the Fort Langley and then coached Forsgate in shorthand typing for an hour!

6th April. Easter Sunday. There was a Communion Service at 7.15 a.m. which I did not attend. I took the collection though at 10.30 a.m. service — £7.3.3 for Seamen's Mission. Land on our starboard side all morning — islands of Socotra, The Brothers. Convinced I saw whales blowing in the distance. Saw two ships. In the afternoon saw Africa — Cape Guarefui — Italian Somaliland (now Somali Republic). Forbidding look about the high cliffs. Could see the lighthouse and later saw it blinking every five seconds. Lovely sunset but still no green flash.

7th April. Saw scores of dolphins or porpoises at the bows before breakfast. Ironing and polishing shoes afterwards. I've lost one of my sandals — it fell overboard in Colombo when I put my foot on ship's rail. Dr. Lynch did the same thing in Singapore.

8th April. We were outside Aden when I got up early this morning. Just rocks and barren, jagged peaks. Went down the

103

ropeladder with Snelling and Maxlow about 9.30 a.m. Ashore saw camels, women with hidden faces. Most shops were closed. Taxi to the town then to NAAFI club at Steamer Point for lunch and bathed most of the afternoon in swimming pool. Watched two servicemen, I think, who happened to be diving in turn and found themselves competing really, for both were most expert divers and really entertained the rest of the people using the pool. Saw destroyer *Finisterre* which came into Colombo just before we left. Very hot and dry. Scores of coolies loaded 1,000 tons of coal in 10 hours. (This sounds impossible today but the coal was carried aboard by a seemingly endless chain of coolies, like a conveyer belt non-stop for ten hours!)

9th April. Ashore with the Fort Langley engineer early and breakfasted ashore with some others. The ship filthy with coal dust! Swam in the pool again and in the adjacent sea area enclosed with anti-shark wire netting. Left Aden 1.45 p.m. Many ships and tankers about. Turned into Red Sea about 9.45 p.m.

10th April. Seven weeks yesterday I left Hong Kong. See a number of rocky islands — some called 'Twelve Apostles' also a volcano. Lot of shipping sighted. A northerly wind blows into our cabin and as a result it is passably cool on deck and not too hot in the cabin.

11th April. Visited the bridge and examined charts. We all wonder when we shall arrive in the U.K. It seems we are making extra calls to renew the company's pre-war connections. Drinks with captain.

12th April. Up very early as we now retard the clocks every night we are on the move. We see several ships, land, an island? porpoise, hundreds of jellyfish. Sand on the sea. It was agreed at the table we would not speak at breakfast and neither a "No" or "Yes" at lunch. I won the latter. We all managed to keep mum at breakfast.

13th April. Had new lock fitted on my big box in the hold today to replace one they broke when moving it the other week. Came into the Gulf of Suez today. Met many ships. Overtook three sections of a big dock on its way to Malta from India, so got to the Canal before them and we thought, saving a few days delay. Arrived Suez about 8 p.m. — dark, plenty of lights and some ships. Welcome mail from home. We are to be at anchor till 5.30 a.m. It has blown almost a gale all day with big waves — all feeling the cold!!

14th April. Woke to find we had entered the Canal about 5.30. We see a train, camels, donkeys, army camps, airfields, sand, scrub and trees. A road runs alongside the Canal for some miles. People wave and whistle, especially soldiers. We see a German P.O.W. camp. We meet a dredger and two ships. See a York, three Mosquito aircraft and three Spitfires. Arrive Port Said about 5 o'clock. Go ashore with Snelling. No mail here. Dinner ashore — departure delayed till morning.

15th April. Awoke to a rough sensation and found we were in the Mediterranean. Strong wind blowing cold and very rough sea which made our 10,000 ton ship pitch up and down considerably. I find it bearable on deck but many are seasick I sleep in a deck chair on deck in the afternoon, fully clothed with overcoat as well later in the day. Saw two ships in the morning, one pitching very badly. Nice to hear English news on BBC but sad news about the price of cigarettes, Bruce Woodcock beaten and Tommy Davies knocked out too. Nice then to go to bed under double blanket again.

16th April. The sea has moderated and most of the sick reappear. Plenty of sun but wind still cold. Sit on deck most of the day but well clothed. Visited the bridge after 4 p.m. Herron on duty — he used to be in Aberdovey! One of the North Walians — from Pwllheli — is at the wheel and I take over for about ten minutes — Course was N 63 W. We should see the lights of Crete this evening. Wind increasing again but the ship much steadier so far. At about 10.30 p.m. saw the lighthouse on island south of Crete — supposed to be highest in the world. Then to bed.

17th April. Lovely day today, wind chilly but not too strong — sunbathed, quoits, hair cut on deck: an Italian with us catches a small bird like a yellow hammer but we release it later — there are two or three resting on the ship and fly with

105

us, also a couple of doves. I see one ship during the day. Next landfall will be Straits of Messina tomorrow mid-day.

18th April. A very interesting day today. Awake early and soon saw high land showing over a cloud bank on the starboard side — it was the toe of Italy, then, presently, I was the first to spot the top of Mt. Etna in Sicily. The top was all I could see but it looked like a little island high in the sky peeping through some cloud. It is 10,870 ft. high and had a lot of snow on it. Then the Straits narrowed right into Messina — 1½ miles wide so we could see all sorts of things on each side — houses, railways, vineyards, etc. Wide waterways now dry — a big sunken ship, ferry boat. That was at lunch time. Before tea we saw Stromboli with its live volcano. It is about 3,000 ft. high, some 20 miles from the coast with a population of 1,853. We were close enough to see houses and gardens and a cemetery. We also saw smoke coming from the crater which is on the N.W. side of the island. We had boat drill today too.

19th April. Bitterly cold day with mist and a little rain. Hoped to see the island of Monte Cristo but out of luck. We notice the cold as we are travelling further and further north.

20th April. Lovely sunny day chilly first thing. Heard we passed a floating mine in the early hours. Saw Genoa before breakfast and then into the harbour. Very impressive looking city on the hills. Saw many wrecks and wreckage in the harbour. Many big ships here. Went ashore with Mr. Wilson and walked and walked. Lunch in a 'British Restaurant' sort of cafe — Visited a church — Much bomb damage. Returned for tea. A pound sterling brought one anything from 900 to 2,000 lira — about 200 to go ashore in a boat. Everything very expensive and shops seemed full of almost everything in consequence. At the restaurant I had hardly touched my bread roll and I could see a lady at a nearby table, well dressed and clean and tidy, looking at it almost hungrily I thought. I was right too for as we showed signs of leaving, she approached and signalled if she could take it and this she did, wrapping it carefully in her napkin, when I indicated approval. Had long chat with a French/Italian watchman who had been a P.O.W. in Germany so we spoke in German, doubtless haltingly. Saw ruins of a house where it was claimed Christopher Columbus lived as a boy.

21st April. Went ashore again this morning — shops nearly all closed yesterday. I got my watch repaired for five cigarettes. Managed to buy papers 2 London 1 Paris of two days ago. Sailed for Marseilles about 1.30 p.m.

22nd April. Arrived Marseilles about breakfast time. Many damaged ships and wrecks visible. Ashore after early lunch with Mr. Wilson. Quite a lot in the shops but points or 'tickets' for almost everything. Even for some of the cakes in a tea shop. Climbed to Notre Dame a la Garde. Saw model ships, aircraft, etc., hanging inside. Went back down in "lift". The cathedral fabric was pitted by shells and nearby saw a tank memorial to three men killed. Saw Count Monte Cristo's prison.

23rd April. Left about 11 a.m. for Gibraltar. Very windy and cold — a bit of a sea splashing over our starboard side. Listened to a St. George's programme from Windsor.

24th April. Awake very early then 6.45 Snowy brought us our morning tea. Bit warmer today. I see Minorca on our port side about 10 a.m. and later we see Majorca and the mainland. See several ships and a number of fishing motor boats. Quite hot in the sun now that we are so far south again. A Spanish aircraft flies over us and see a lighthouse in the evening.

25th April. See snow capped mountains to starboard. Meet many ships and pass one. About 4.30 p.m. we sight the Rock — Gibraltar. It is rather long and high — very steep on one side. We are in to the anchorage by 5 p.m. We cannot go ashore till tomorrow. Spanish boatmen from La Linea try to sell us things. I buy a watch! A good sing song after dinner. Only Mr. Kent had a letter — so far!

26th April. Went ashore in a launch — down the long rope ladder — about 10 a.m. and examined Gibraltar. Saw Trafalgar Cemetery, the 1529 Casemates, Moorish castle, etc. Too late to get a pass to see the Rock itself. Heard bits of Cup Final. Lunched with Scot and Wilson. Saw the water carts, horse taxis, (Spanish) and spoke to some German prisoners. Returned to ship at 6 p.m. Postmen and policemen English style. Still coaling.

107

27th April. 20 years ago today I joined the RAF. Still in Gibraltar but no one goes ashore. Just before breakfast we see a big American cruiser enter and just before we sail at 11 a.m. our own troopship HMS *Devonshire*. We then pass through the Straits and see both Africa and Spain for some miles. We see Cape Trafalgar too. Wind getting stronger and seas rising. After dinner, too cold and rough to stay on deck.

28th April. Sea very rough. Several passengers sea sick but I am not. See several big ships including one very big four-masted sailing ship, Spanish, believed to be a training ship but had little sail up because of the strong wind.

29th April. Sea still very rough and it is bitterly cold. Several sea sick again. We enter the Bay of Biscay!

30th April. This is the third day of bitter cold wind and almsot mountainous seas and now that we turn a little north eastwards to cross Biscay, the seas and wind are on our beam and the old ship rolls badly as well as pitches! The sick are still sick and the rest of us hope for better weather soon. I hear there is more snow in North Wales. Roll on Liverpool. I managed to do a little washing in the morning.

1st May. I wake up to find seas not quite so rough and there is only a little creaking. I start a little packing and hope to reach Le Havre tonight. We see Cherbourg and a number of French minesweepers at work. We do reach Le Havre but have to anchor outside as no pilot comes out.

2nd May. Into Le Havre harbour in the morning and we are buoyed almost alongside the *Europa*, a very big ex-German liner and the wreck of the *City of Paris* which has been on her side since 1938. There are many wrecks visible and terrible destruction of the port works. I go ashore with Mr. Kent in an L.C.T. (Landing Craft Tank). Wet and very cold. Welcome mail received. The bombing has resulted in a terrific amount of damage. Very interesting place. I try out some more of my French. Understand we shall be here for several days.

3rd May. Ashore again soon after breakfast and go with some ship's officers (Brown, Jumper Collins, Bradshaw and Nairn) to fix up soccer match. We do this at a Merchant Navy club and meet Kempton, an old Southampton pro and trainer of Coventry team, who referees us in the afternoon. I lunch at the club and at 2 p.m. the rest of the two teams arrive. Then by tram and a walk to a huge ground with stadium. I play outside left for Supernumerarics against crew of our good ship *Menelaus*. We lose 7 nil! I enjoyed the game but acquired a big toe blister. Meet Munkley who was a soldier here in the last War (1st World War). He is from Cardiff.

4th May. Recovering on board mainly because of my toe! Remarkably unstiff.

5th May. Still in Le Havre. Ashore with Mr. Kent and Mick — our midshipman. We find a tram and go to see the fortifications — part of the German West Wall on top of the cliffs. Two girls picking wild carrot warn us about explosions then a soldier tells us they are blowing up mines on the beach and by another fort they are blowing up something else but we see as much as we want of the ruins of forts and smashed guns. Most shops closed again today. (They have to close for two days a week in France). We had tea in the Merchant Navy club but back to ship for dinner. (I forget the detail now but I remember I was given a lot of francs for a tin of cigarettes).

6th May. We are at long last leaving today for our final trip to Liverpool. I send a telegram through the Purser to say I shall be in Liverpool the day after tomorrow. Roll on Thursday morning. We leave about 1 p.m. Outside I see the French submarine *La Creole* at exercise. She lay alongside us in the dock. I watch her submerge for practice. It is cold in the Channel and we start a gentle roll.

7th May. When I go on deck before breakfast I see Land's End coming into view and the lighthouses — Wolf Rock. A very welcome sight. I do some packing and I have a drink with Captain Savery in his cabin before tiffin. I play a while with Janet (her mother asks for my address too and we exchange addresses). Before dinner the Chief Steward and a couple of others join Kent and I in our cabin for a gin. Then, after dinner I have a drink with Robson and Collins, engineers, and later help Kent do some packing. I had spotted two or three of the islands off Pembrokeshire, far away in the haze. — So I am passing through Cardigan Bay now at 10.15 p.m.'

That was the last entry in that diary, for the next day our slow, slow ship from China — or rather our slow, slow trip from China — brought us at long last to Liverpool. It had taken eleven weeks and two days!! My wife with our two daughters were there. There have been so many other partings and reunions especially these last few years, so ours was only different in that it was our own long awaited reunion. Rowena now very nearly three and Diana soon to be ten, spotted me, and the others, waiting on the dock, as we made to tie up, heard Rowena say, 'There is my Daddy. Where is Diana's?' And seeing the funny side, they all laughed and relieved their own tensions. Today, the 2nd of March, 1992, I reminded Rowena, now a grandmother again of this.

I kept in touch for some time with Kent. He found London with rationing and no domestic help in their flat and no help with shopping quite tiring. I had so enjoyed his company.

We overnighted in Liverpool and the next day, 9th May, Falmai and I, with our two daughters, travelled down to Wales.

HOME AGAIN

When I came home again to Wales, it seemed as if I had brought some tropical weather with me. After the long cold winter and snows, my wife and children had to travel in winter wear to Liverpool but the day I arrived, the weather changed so that it was necessary for her to buy some summer dresses for the girls before we left there for Dolgellau.

We were all now to stay with Falmai's parents on the outskirts of Dolgellau on the small farm 'Trefeilia' overlooking the town and with most marvellous views of Cader Idris, the Mawddach Valley and the surrounding hills. I still remember the joy of hearing Rowena chattering away and only in Welsh of course. Diana was already in primary school. I remember the green of the country. Despite the beauty of all those other places I had seen, there had been nothing to match the colour of our own land.

My baggage duly arrived and there was the unpacking of gifts such as one could bring from Hong Kong and such as one could afford. The nest of camphor wood chests, ivory carvings, doll dresses and dolls, embroidered table cloths and such like. The so large pomelos I had bought in Singapore were soon eaten.

I had not expected to wear my tropical kit in Wales but in no time at all, I found them most useful in the warm weather of that sudden summer. I was there to help with hay making and harrowing too for that matter. The 'tractor' for the harrow was an old Austin car chassis with engine and with the body of a two-wheeled cart (the type normally drawn by a horse) affixed to complete conversion to a small lorry. While using it to draw the harrow one day, I had placed a tin which had contained 50 cigarettets but now with 20 very small cigars I had bought in Malaya in the body of the open back lorry. They had bounced out and I was able to retrieve only two of them. Not a great financial loss but still remembered after all these years.

Much of the rationing in the U.K. which I had forgotten about in Hong Kong, was still in operation.

I kept in touch with the Colonial Office and was offered an appointment as Chief Constable of the Falkland Islands and Dependencies. I would also be the Colony's Gaoler and Superintendent of the fire brigade in Port Stanley. I did know something about the Falklands but it surprised me to learn how many there were who could only think they were up Scotland way. Many then, of course, had no idea where they were. I was soon gleaning all the information I could, and I was anxious to be on our way for this time we would be going out there as a family. I was asked later if I would attend a course of instruction in fire fighting and this was duly arranged for me at the National Fire Service training school at Manchester. It was a general course for fire station officers and all of my class fellow trainees were ex-Royal Marines already employed as firemen in Naval establishments. I was to take over the Port Stanley Fire Brigade from the untrained local volunteer.

During the War, all local authority fire brigades and the auxiliary fire service had been merged into the National Fire Service and training standardised. I was soon to hear of the advantages of this and the disadvantages of the old system when fire fighting knowledge could often only be acquired from what could be gleaned through experience alongside other firemen. I found the course most interesting and over many years since, I have endeavoured to pass on to others titbits of useful information I had gathered at Manchester. The rungs of ladders should be used both by feet and hands. Each rung is tested by hand before body weight through foot is applied — they are far more easily held on to if a rung breaks under one's foot than attempting to hold on to the invariably too thick and wide sides. And do I remember my first climb up the 120 foot turntable extension ladder! All my uniformed firemen

1954. Sarah starts school, St. Vincent.

Grenada, 1951.
Ceremonial Uniform — including Spurs!

In the Office, Georgetown, British Guiana.

1958. Signed copy by Countess Mountbatten visiting Kaieteur Falls, British Guiana. The falls at 741 feet has the world's longest uninterrupted drop.

fellow trainees climbed the whole length of the ladder in turn before me and there was I the odd man out in civvies (private clothing) saying 'Can I go now please?' with lots of lookers-on having a good look to see how I fared, I set forth. In the event, fortunately, I climbed succesfully to the topmost extension piece which I found to be exceedingly narrower, of course, than the lower sections which had to accommodate the lower sections when retracted. Are you there with me? With the top well clear of the nearest building, it swayed through some four or five feet. I found the smallest of steps or flap attached to one side which could be brought into use with one's foot to allow a more comfortable stance for working at the top (it measured perhaps twelve inches by three inches or so). There was a telephone there for us to communicate with the ground crew. Quite exciting for the novice. The instructor told me that during the War when they handled so many recruits, they often had cases when the trained 'froze' when perhaps only some ten to fifteen feet up a ladder and they literally had to be fetched back down.

Back home there were all the other preparations and packing. We should be going through the tropics to mid winter in the Falklands. I was given extra clothing coupons. There were goodbyes to be made. We would be leaving in the knowledge that we would be away for three years before coming home on leave.

TO THE FALKLAND ISLANDS

The Colony of the Falkland Islands and Dependencies in 1947 included not only South Georgia and the South Sandwich Group but also the South Orkney Islands, the South Shetland Islands and Graham Land and that part of the Antarctic Continent which lies between the 20°W and 80°W longitudes. Since 1962 only South Georgia and the South Sandwich Group remain as part of the Colony with the Falkland Islands. The others became a separate Colony named the British Antarctic Territory in that year, and bounded by the 20°W and 80°W longitudes and by the 60°S latitude for the territory's northern boundary and thereby the southern boundary to the Colony of the Falkland Islands and Dependencies. Had the South Pole been a measureable pole, it could then have been said that I was also Chief Constable of one sixth of the South Pole! So my daughter told me!

Now back to our geography. The Falkland Islands include with the two main islands, East and West Falkland, separated by the Falkland Sound, a number of smaller inhabited islands such as Sea Lion, Speedwell, New, Weddel, Carcass, Keppel and Pebble, and numerous other inhabitated islands including the Jason Group. In all then the Falkland Islands cover some 4,700 square miles. (Wales has 7,400 sq. miles). They lie in the South Atlantic with Cape Horn some 480 miles to the South West. South Georgia though is some 800 miles east south east and the South Sandwich Group are a further 460 miles south east of South Georgia.

The coastline of the Falklands is deeply indented and affords many good anchorages. Most of the land is hilly with Mount Usborne on that East Falkland rising to 2,312 ft. Port Stanley is the only town and lies in the inner harbour entered through

114

the narrow Narrows from Port William with Cape Pembroke and its lighthouse at its entrance some seven miles to the east. The next largest settlement is probably Goose Green, also on East Falkland with Darwin nearby. (Darwin went there in the *Beagle*). These were the very large farms of a number owned by the Falkland Islands Company.

Darwin, for instance, sheared some 90,000 sheep each year.

The population of the Colony which has rarely exceeded 3,000 in total permanent residents is almost equally divided between Stanley and the Camp. All land outside Stanley is known as the Camp, derived from the Spanish word 'campo' meaning countryside.

The Islands are in the same latitude south as South Wales is north but there are very marked climatic differences. The Dependencies, of course, have a most rigorous climate of Antarctic character. The main feature of the Falkland's weather is the very strong wind which blows throughout the year. It was said you could tell a Falkland Islander by the angle of his body when walking and navy sailors claimed they were issued with two-anchored buttons.

So after reading up as much as we could about our future home, we duly left Dolgellau's winter on the long journey to autumn in the Falklands. We entrained for Tilbury to catch the R.M.S. *Highland Brigade* which would take us to Montevideo. I remember we were a 102 first class passengers as we sailed out of the Thames.

The weather was wild and stormy and we were soon in rough seas. We could not drop the pilot but had to take him all the way down Channel to get off for Southampton. We soon lost sight of fellow passengers. In the Bay of Biscay conditions were even worse. I was one of the very few who turned up for meals. I confess I rather enjoyed myself. Chairs were tied to tables. The tables' fiddles did keep some things on the table but all was usually awash. All the soup was lost one night. How the cooks managed to produce anything at all was a mystery.

I did what I could for my usually prostrate family but Diana did venture on to the deck with me one day. We managed to

115

get on to a couple of deck chairs but had them tied so we would not slide away to the ship's rails. We were carefully watched by one of the deck stewards for the first ten minutes or so otherwise we had the deck to ourselves for well over an hour before we moved back in.

In the lounge one evening I was sitting on a settee resting on the wet cloths laid down to prevent slipping. However, the cloths did not work well enough for the settee started sliding across the wide open floor space — almost the ship's width — and gained speed until I thought we would have to crash into the partition between us and the open deck, when it came to a full stop, momentarily only though, no time to get off, as the ship was now ready to roll fully back again on to its port side, and so backward we went till we regained the precise spot we had so suddenly and unexpectedly, recently departed from and again came to rest. I was later told that our ship had kept going when most other ships in the area had been hoved to and we had suffered quite appreciable damage to some of the rails at our upper levels as well. We reached Vigo in northern Spain on the fourth day and most of the passengers came for their first real meal.

Our stay in Vigo was brief and we found it difficult to get our own sort of cup of tea ashore and our first bits of Spanish had to be learnt — tea with hot water and cold milk had become a must.

It was then onwards to Lisbon where we took on several hundred steerage passengers, emigrating to Brazil, and then on to Madeira.

By this time we had met several passengers who were bound for the Falkland Islands. Two ladies were first timers like ourselves, one to become a teacher in Stanley and the other the wife of an engineer. One of the islanders was Eva Betts who later became the police sergeant's wife there. She is now widowed and living in England.

All now seemed to be enjoying the voyage with its variety of entertainments, rationless meals and warm looking comfortable seas. Some of us were treated perhaps a little less gently at the Crossing the Line ceremonies when we reached the Equator. The crossing of the Atlantic was completed when we arrived at Recife, or was it Salvador, before the run down to Rio de Janeiro. Our family trip ashore was a pleasant interlude though a short one. We did a little shopping, a little sightseeing and visited Copocabana Beach. Rio is dramatically sited with the Sugar Loaf Mountain and a giant statue of Christ, with arms outstretched, on the peak of Corcavado Mountain, looming over the city and its magnificent bay. Perhaps even more striking than Hong Kong. Copocabana and Ipanema are sleek beachfront suburbs where royal palms and Bougainvillaea line the streets. But the immediate backstreets are on the edge of the most dreadfully soul destroying shanty towns which climb up so much of the surrounding hillsides.

A German taxi driver told us as we drove along, having just been passed by a motor car followed by a police car that we should see what would happen then — the car would be stopped, the police would be handed monies and the driver then allowed to drive away. He was right — it looked like that and he explained that the police pay was a mere pittance and in consequence the police existed on the bribes they were able to collect. They even had to buy their own uniforms.

On another brief visit ashore, I wondered why it was that so many people seemed to be admiring (?) my knees. Realisation came fairly quickly though for it looked as if I was the only one in sight wearing shorts! I was improperly dressed for Latin America and I soon found my way back on board.

We were soon on our way again and about 1,000 miles further on the *Highland Brigade* brought us to Montevideo in Uruguay. As we sailed into the River Plate, we saw the upper parts of the German pocket battleship *The Graf Spee* still showing above the water where after the 1939 'Battle of the River Plate', she was scuttled after she had been made to leave Montevideo, a neutral port, under international rules of war. Had she ventured further out, she would have met elements of our Royal Navy waiting to deal with her.

We had taken over three weeks to arrive at Montevideo and reluctantly I think, disembarked into a strange world, though anxious to reach the Falkland Islands. Some of us were taken

117

to the Hotel Florida to await onward passage. We had to wait twenty more days before the S.S. *Lafonia* came for us.

The hotel was very Spanish. I think we had to make do with the best we could muster Spanish and some German. Everyone though were most helpful. Excellent accommodation and food and did we enjoy the bowlful of peaches always available on the table!

The main streets of Montevideo were very wide tree-lined avenues with wonderful displays in the shops. We were there for a very large carnival which was all very impressive indeed. It took ages for it to pass us — mounted police very impressive too though the horses were generally much smaller than we expected but very active and efficient. In line abreast, the various elements were spread right across the very wide avenue, numbering perhaps fifteen to twenty persons or horses in each row.

The days passed comfortably, still very warm by day. Shopping expeditions or rather window shopping expeditions, gave us exercise and there were afternoons we spent on nearby holiday beaches. I was surprised at the extent of German influence I saw in ordinary day to day things. Perhaps where we had long since become accustomed to Italian shopkeepers in some of our Welsh towns, Montevideo had its Germans from pre-war days.

I was now learning that while there was close co-operation between Uruguay and the Falklands, at least insofar as normal commercial matters were concerned, there was virtually none between the Argentine and the Falklands. I was told that the Falklands did import most of its butter from Buenos Aires though, but that may have come through Uruguay. I also heard that Falkland Islands passports were impounded by the Argentinians as being valueless because the Islanders were deemed to be citizens of the Argentine. So there was no question of our using Buenos Aires.

During our later days in Montevideo, we became aware of the latest problems down in the Antarctic when Argentinian naval/military units were found on bases in the Falkland Islands Dependencies zone. HMS *Nigeria* was leaving Simonstown, the British naval base in South Africa in great haste to get to the Falklands before proceeding south to the Antarctic. A news reporter of a London national newspaper — the *Daily Express* — had flown out to Montevideo and just managed to join us on the *Lafonia* for our voyage down to Port Stanley.

The *Lafonia* was a small cargo/passenger vessel bought by the Falkland Islands Company in 1946, to replace another of the same name sunk in the North Sea in 1942 after being requisitioned for the war effort in 1941. Our *Lafonia* was before that the S.S. *Perth* and had operated as a rescue ship in the North Atlantic during the war.

We were very glad to be on our way again and now met some more Falkland Islanders returning. We were joined too by the Bishop of South America, south of the Amazon. He was the Rt. Rev. D. Ivor Evans paying a routine visit to the Falklands from his base in Beunos Aires. The Bishop was a Welshman from Lampeter in Cardiganshire so we had much in common. I had not expected him to teach my daughter Diana to play cards.

We had heard a lot about the sea trip between the Falklands and Montevideo. It could take anything between four and a half and seven days depending on the weather. The weather through the 'roaring forties' could be bad and we were to find that the *Lafonia* was not the *Highland Brigade*. We met some very rough seas indeed but made quite a good passage. It had been a good chance to hear at first hand, and in Welsh of course, from the Bishop, a good description of life on the Islands and at the settlements. I still remember his description of life in a typical 'cookhouse'. On the larger settlement, the single men would be accommodated and fed communally at their own 'cookhouse' — or bunkhouse in western cowboy parlance. These single men would be Islanders with occasionally labourers/shepherds brought out on contract from the U.K. Some islanders would look for futures beyond the Falklands and from time to time, along the years, some would leave for the U.K., (or Home as it was called by most islanders) New Zealand or Australia. The shortage of labour would then be met by the Falkland Islands Company, usually by importing young

119

men on contract from U.K. and indeed in recent years, on occasions, even single women as shepherds.

After the weeks at sea and in Montevideo, I was really anxious to sight land as we approached the Falklands on the 29th February 1948. It was a Sunday too and I caught my first glimpse of its north east coast. There was some general excitement as we entered Port William and then we were through the narrow Narrows into the inner harbour Port Stanley. It was 4 p.m. With customs and immigration formalities quickly over, it was not long before we were installed in our new home. Home this time was a combined private quarters of the Chief Constable and Gaoler, the police office and chargeroom and then the prison. A room attached to the police office, with its own separate entrance, was the Islands' small telephone exchange. I found the entire building, that is our private quarters, police quarters, prison and exchange was centrally heated by a peat burning boiler. The same boiler also provided central heating for the Catholic Church in the adjacent compound. All this on Ross Road, the front road running alongside the harbour.

Sgt. Jim Norris who had acted as Chief Constable pending my arrival was a Berkshire man who had come from England to work at Goose Green some twenty five years before but joined the police force at the end of his contract period instead of returning to the U.K. He was now a widower. We met his mother-in-law some time later — she was one of many McLeods on the Islands — and had arrived from Lewis in the Hebrides (now our Western Isles) as a young girl to marry her man who had gone before her in the days of sail. She told us the voyage had taken months, and that the conditions were so dreadful she had never been able to think of going back for a holiday in Scotland. Another of her daughters, Marion as a young girl during the Great War of 1914-18, was rewarded by the Lords of the Admiralty, for her part in helping to get information from the south coast of East Falkland, near Fitzroy, to H.M. ships at Port Stanley that German warships were travelling eastwards in the direction of Stanley. On October 30th 1914, a naval battle between German and British ships at Coronel off the coast of Chile, occurred in stormy weather. In the action which lasted about an hour, H.M. ships *The Good Hope, Monmouth* and *Glasgow,* cruisers, engaged the *Scharnhorst, Gneisenau, Leipzing* and *Dresden. The Good Hope* and the *Monmouth* caught fire and sank; *Glasgow* was not greatly damaged. This defeat was soon avenged though for elements of the British Fleet had come to search for the Germans and were at Port Stanley refuelling on 1st December when they were alerted to the approach of the Germans and the Battle of the Falkland Islands resulted. Four German warships, the raiding cruisers *Scharnhorst, Gneisenau, Nurnberg* and *Leipzig* were sunk by the British ships commanded by Admiral Sir F. Sturdee. The Battle Memorial overlooks the Port Stanley inner harbour. Marion McLeod showed me the beautifully inscribed silver teapot. One of the *Good Hope's* small boats, she had left behind, was still being used in Stanley harbour in 1948 and probably much later too. I wonder if it is still there. One year in the late 1980's, Marion McLeod as a senior Falkland Islander laid a wreath on the Cenotaph in Whitehall.

So here I was, once again a police officer. I was now Chief Constable over a vast area, with few people and few policemen to help me. There was one Sergeant, Norris, and constables O'Sulivan, whose father was once the Chief Constable, Shakell, a London born man who doubled as a barber — I hoped he would be listening more than talking, as barbers are wont to do — Williams, a Kelper (all born Falkland Islanders are called Kelpers — kelp being seaweed which grows in great abundance around the Falkland coasts and is often an aid to navigation as it indicates presence of rocks. It is often tree-like with thick trunk attached to the seabed and with long trailing branches some of which have been known to grow to several hundred feet in length); Fleuret of some French ancestry — and who after returning from his first visit to England was so impressed by the roads compared with those few miles in and around Stanley that he declared, 'The roads in England were smooth as billiard tables' : Bill Jones who was a Captain of the Boys Brigade and keen P.T. instructor; Goss (his brother was our constable in South Georgia and whom I never saw

121

until twenty years later when we met at a Falkland Islands Reunion in London!). Constable O'Sullivan was also a captain in the Falkland Islands Defence Force while Constable Bill Jones was a lieutenant in that military unit which was a volunteer organisation.

I was also the official Gaoler or Prison Keeper (with my wife as Gaol Matron); the new Superintendent of the Stanley Fire Brigade (with about 60 volunteers) and Sanitary Inspector. Police also undertook registration licensing of motor vehicles (but only some 250 then in all!) and I also later became Driving Examiner. We were also responsible for issuing dog licences for example. There was rarely more than one prisoner at a time and often none at all.

The prison accommodation included, I was shocked to find, a 'padded cell' — the only one on the islands, as there was no mental institution. I was also shocked to find that the female accommodation of the prison was only accessible by ladder and trapdoor from the male section of the prison or from the landing on the first floor in the Chief Constable's quarters!! Later we did have a female prisoner — for one month's imprisonment — but then I realised there was no need to use the upper floor accommodation if there was no male prisoner on the ground floor area. It had been twenty years since they had a female prisoner in before. Our prisoner was also the first woman to be put on our 'black list'.

Serious crime was not very prevalent and crimes of violence rare. There was considerable drinking and the majority of offences were attributed in lesser or greater degree to drink. The licensing laws gave a court power to have certain persons placed on a black list. Where it would appear that a person's estate or health or behaviour was being adversely affected by liquor, application could be made to the court by his dependants or the police for a prohibition order to be issued. It would then be an offence for anyone to supply such person with drink, in any place. An offence too for the black-listed person to consume or possess liquor. I had cases where an 'alcoholic' approached me himself to ask to be placed on the black list. I should explain too that there was no availability of beer on the islands but a varied supply of other liquors. Rum was probably the favourite drink and occasionally it would be consumed with the addition of other liquors. One man I knew always drank milk with his rum.

A shepherd on his long rounds on horseback would rarely be without a bottle of rum in his saddle bags.

The last judicial execution of a man convicted of murder had been some forty years earlier. He was a coloured man named Jenkins, from the West Indies and he was hanged, although many of the islanders had petitioned for a reprieve. So, with a memory of that execution shed at Changi still fresh in my mind, all I could do now was hope that there would be no need for an execution in Port Stanley for another forty years!

The prison, on 29th February 1948, held two men. Both were from a visiting British warship. One was serving 21 days imprisonment and the other was remanded in custody charged with larceny from a dwelling house. He was from H.M.S. *Nigeria* on her visit to the Antarctic Bases.

The Police building was one of but a few buildings of stone construction. It had a corrugated zinc or galvanised roof. Kitchen and bathroom were of wood construction though and there had been additions to the end of the main building. The central heating was augmented by an open peat fire in the living room and the cooking stove in the kitchen too of course was peat fired. All dwellings in Stanley were connected through a Tannoy (loudspeaker) system with the broadcasting station. This was therefore always available for distribution to all households of information and notices which would be of interest to most. For instance, after the mail had been collected from the *Lafonia*, the post office would announce the time the post would be open for the collection of letters. This would be followed by a notice of availability of the parcel post, perhaps an hour or so later.

We were shocked to see the colour of our water supply in Stanley but we did get used to it. It was coloured from its peat sources and the bottom of the bath, if well filled, for instance could hardly be seen. For tea making it was alright but as cold drinking water it hardly appealed. We rather envied but did not complain that fresh water was fetched to Government House for the Governor's domestic needs daily in a motor cycle combination (that is with sidecar) with containers from a spring well out of town, as it was clear spring water.

Our peat shed at the back of the premises was a large barn type building with better than well ventilated wooden walls to allow a free flow of air into and through the year's supply of peat blocks. One's entitlement was spoken of in cartloads for those provided with it. Private householders were allocated their own sections of the peat beds where they cut and dug their own supplies to be dried by weathering in heaps or ricks, before being carried home each summer. Rowena, our three year old, was heard to say, in Welsh, that first day I think it was, 'Look, clean coal'. The deeper the peat — some beds were ten to twelve feet deep — the blacker was the dried out block and it was some of this type when broken up into smaller lumps, we called 'pastry peat' for it burned almost like coal. Our open fires were never normally allowed to go out and we would bank up the fires overnight by adding the lighter, top sod, peat blocks as these would be very slow burning. No coal was imported.

Peat was the main fuel at all the settlements. It is a very expendable commodity and Stanley's peat beds were retreating further and further from the town. In some places the peat beds left clay and rocks exposed. Peat beds can become very waterlogged and on occasion have been known to slip where the bed is sloping. There were two very bad peat slips in Stanley years ago when peat was still present on the brow of the hill on slopes of which Stanley was built. The town is built from harbour level along parallel streets running east and west on the north facing slopes. One night in 1878, a mass of water-logged peat, several feet deep slipped at a good walking pace across the town so that one part was completely cut off from the rest of the town, except by boats. There were worse results in 1886 when two lives were lost and a lot of property was damaged, when another slip occurred in an adjacent area.

The *Lafonia* which brought us from Montevideo, after discharging Port Stanley passengers and cargo, would then visit some of the larger settlements. The Falkland Islands Company was under contract to carry twelve mails a year to and from Montevideo and this was our only regular link with the outside world. But as I write this in 1992, how things have changed!!

The Governor and Commander-in-Chief was Miles Clifford (he was knighted later) but he was away on H.M.S. *Nigeria* in the Antarctic dealing with an international political problem. Constable O'Sullivan, who had spent some time in the Argentine before he returned to the Falklands and joined the police, had also travelled on *Nigeria* as a Spanish interpreter if needed. I thus saw the Colonial Secretary on Monday, 1st March, the day after I arrived. There was a lot to be done.

One of the musts on arrival for duty in a Colony is the signing of the book at Government House. One pays one's respects to His Excellency, the Governor, thus on arrivals and departures and special occasions and, for example, after receptions and other visits to Government House at the invitations of the Governor. This I did.

We were still in early days of the settling in process and shopping too was a must. The largest shop — store — in Stanley was the Falkland Islands Company owned West Store. It could provide a very wide range of goods, but even so there was never such a wide range of choice as there was milk. There were other smaller privately owned stores. Virtually everything had to be imported from the U.K. and had, therefore, to be ordered by our stores in good time to catch the infrequent sea transport available from Montevideo — the monthly steamer from the Falklands. Very occasionally stores could be brought direct to the Islands by a vessel coming to collect the seasonal wool clip. Wool was the principal export and at that time it would total about four million lbs.

Fresh meat was available in Stanley and beef could be bought occasionally for 4½d (almost 2p!) a lb but mutton was for years sold at 3d or two thirds the price of beef. These were exceedingly low prices even in those days. Mutton was delivered, usually by the quarter, and kept, as a rule, in a wire mesh meat safe hanging on an outside wall — refrigerators in an ordinary housheold were then an unheard of luxury. Most people in Stanley and in Camp, kept their own poultry. Pork was available sometimes. In Camp, shepherds living away from the main settlements — usually several hours riding away — would have a cow for milk and butter for their own use only, a pig and some poultry. I was surprised the first time I saw a shepherd throw Upland geese, just shot by him, into his pig for feed. The Upland goose is found all over the islands but in dwindling numbers near Stanley and within too easy reach of guns in the settlements. It is very good eating. I saw the research vessel *John Biscoe* leave Stanley on one of her routine visits to the bases in the Antarctic, with scores of geese hanging from every available place on her deck. A treat for the men down south.

There was no official rationing on the islands but sometimes unexpected shortages would occur, so it behove one and all to ensure they had good stocks always in hand. Mutton was never in short supply. It was always available and due to the frequency of its appearance on the table, was sometimes referred to by other names. I remember in my RAF days, corned beef being listed on the menu as 'Viennese Steak'!

It was Wednesday 3rd March when I was sworn in as Chief Constable and Gaoler by a Justice of the Peace who was also the Registrar General and the Stanley Magistrate, but he was without any legal qualification. There were no qualified legal practitioners in the Colony!

The Law of the Colony was based on English Statute Law and Common Law together with the Colony's own Ordinances relating to its own particular requirements such as control of sealing, peat and penguins. An 1851 Ordinance applied the British Laws to the Falklands and this was continued until 1900. Since then only those subsequent laws of the U.K. declared by the Colony's Ordinances to apply are available. I had to do lots of re-thinking — stealing had to be dealt with under an 1861 Act instead of the more familiar Larceny Act of 1916. I had no Children and Young Persons Act of 1833 for instance nor a Road Traffic Act of 1930 with all its amendments.

While provision was made for the appointment of a Judge for the Supreme Court, it was the practice at that time for the Governor to act as Judge.

So the law was quite a problem for the Colony. Then on the 8th March I went to discuss the general legal situation with a recently arrived Legal Adviser from England. He was there to advise Government and assist in a revision of the local laws. It was the first of many meetings we were to have as we worked closely together to introduce some more urgently needed changes. The increasing traffic demanded our early attention as did the control of firearms for instance.

At a later date, the Legal Adviser was also undertaking other duties and for some time acted as the Colonial Secretary so that it is probable that some of the legal aspects of his duties could not be proceeded with to the extent originally intended.

On the 8th March too, I attended Court when our sailor was further remanded in custody. I am reminded too that I had to send on the sum of £500 for Captain Biggs in South Georgia. We attended our first cocktail party at the invitation of the Colonial Secretary.

On the 9th the Governor returned to Stanley on HMS *Nigeria* and on that day too we had to report the petty officer and two ratings of the naval shore patrol for drunkenness to be dealt with by the naval authorities. The next day, our time-served prisoner was handed over to them. That evening it was cocktails on HMS *Nigeria*. The public dance in Stanley that night went on till 1 a.m. at the gymnasium nearby. For the next year or two, this was in use instead of the burned down town hall. It was also used as a cinema. At that time one took one's own cushion to film shows.

On the 11th I prosecuted in Rex v. Campbell. He was sentenced to six months with hard labour for larceny from a dwelling house. I see from my papers that he was released on 21st August and 'put aboard *Lafonia* for the U.K., via Montevideo'. He had hoped he would have been dismissed from the Navy but I do not know what befell him after leaving us. His hard labour had mainly been the carrying in of the peat for the police and prison, and general cleaning up in and around our building and at Government House.

After Court that morning I was called to see the Governor and our meeting lasted an hour. Sgt. Norris went to investigate a report of theft of some poultry. Then another dance until 1 a.m. which I see I visited at 11.45 p.m. Some worthy citizen wrote to me on the last day of that first month in appreciation of our efforts '. . . to ensure better behaviour in the gymnasium. For the past ten years or so the behaviour at dances has left a lot to be desired. In fact it has often been so disgraceful that decent folk could not possibly find any enjoyment . . .' If one allows for a little exaggeration, it will be seen that excessive drinking was indeed one of our major problems.

I have to admit that it has been quite interesting to look again at old papers of yesteryear about matters otherwise long since forgotten. Why didn't I keep more? I would commend the practice but be as selective as you would wish.

The settling in process is taking some time. I find I have quickly accepted my role as Gaoler. Sergeant Norris and the constables are most supportive. I am arranging for the police to be relieved of a long standing obligation to ring the work bell and close the yard gates of the Public Works Department compound on all working days. I am conscious that in the Falkland winds, the risk of fire spread is greater and as I was soon to find out, a chimney fire in a peat burning chimney is particularly fierce. I prefer the police to patrol rather than be gatekeepers.

We have the Bishop to tea on the 15th March so I presume now that he went on his round of the Camp and has just returned to Stanley. We shall miss the Welsh but there is so much that is still new to us. Diana is not yet twelve and goes to the John Street School. Rowena not yet four will soon be starting at the infants' school under Greta Pitaluga. Miss Whiddon our fellow traveller, is to stay teaching in Stanley and visits us regularly.

There were only itinerant teachers in Camp. Some shepherds would live in houses usually referred to as 'outside houses', which were quite a distance from their settlements and meant

128

Author and wife Falmai attend a ceremonial occasion.

Sarah with her parents at Gobowen Orthopaedic Hospital.

hours of horse riding in some instances. Where there were children, the teacher would visit regularly to stay with them briefly and set more work until the next visit. Later the radio was to become an additional aid. Children at the settlements were taught likewise.

'At least once a year, the Islands are visited by one or more of H.M. ships, and the sailors', I wrote in 1952, 'will testify to the loyalty of the Islanders and the warmth of their welcome. The Islanders were almost invariably able to prove their superiority at rowing, shooting and football. With a population of British stock and that not going back more than a few generations, the traditional ties of the Islanders are purely British and Britain is still 'home' to the many folk who have never ventured out of the Islands.' It was now that I was seeing this for the first time.

Our rifle range had targets at all the usual ranges including the 900 and 1000 yards which in Falkland breezes could be particularly difficult. But the Navy brought us problems too. I have already referred to some of them.

The return of H.M.S. *Nigeria* on 9th March brought back Constable O'Sullivan and I had his verbal account of the voyage and some of the proceedings. Formal written protests were made to the Argentinians at our bases but then *Nigeria* played them at football. Major Wilson of the Royal Marines on H.M.S. *Nigeria* had handed the protest to the senior Argentine officer. I believe it was not very long after this that it was agreed internationally that no armed vessels — warships — would sail further south than the 60° latitude. Much has happened since then of course.

Here are some extracts from a few of the following days:

Visited several licensed houses with Sgt. Norris. At 9.45 p.m. he arrested one James Hanrahan, a greaser on R.R.S. *John Biscoe*, for assaulting William Tucker. Prosecuted Hanrahan in the Magistrate's Court. He was fined £5 and bound over in the sum of £5 for 12 months.

Discussed police matters with Hon. Colonial Secretary.

Requested by Mr. F. to find his wife and child and other

129

children after family quarrel. Mrs. F. called at Police Station where I spoke to both.

23rd March. Sgt. Norris brought into custody Leslie F. Summers at 9.45 p.m. on a charge of being drunk while a prohibited person. He was fined £10. Mrs. F. called to complain about her husband. I went with the Sgt. and we found F. alone at home — apparently sober and calm.

25th March. Attended Magistrate's Court at 2.30 p.m. An application by Mrs. F. that her husband be blacklisted was adjourned *sine die*. Visited Sappers' Hill, Mullet Creek. Visited S.S. *Fitzroy* on her arrival from Montevideo. Examined two horses at Hallet's.

26th March. Instructed Sgt. Norris and P.C. O'Sullivan to investigate alleged theft of potatoes from Captain Roberts' paddock in John Street. I spoke to Mr. Hallet re condition of the two horses I saw yesterday.

27th March. Visited scene of fire in peat shed at 70 Davies Street — Accidental — ignited by improvised boiler in adjoining boiler shed.

28th March. Discussed fire, etc. with Chairman Town Council.

29th March. (I had to arrest two pesrons at public gymnasium for being drunk and disorderly). Sgt. Norris arrested James Hanrahan for being drunk in Villiers Street also Louis Lee for D. & D.

All pleaded guilty and were fined. I had an interview with Hon. Colonial Secretary re Fire matters and later spoke to Mr. Hardy the Chairman of Stanley Town Council and superintendent of the fire brigade. I shall now be taking over.

More cases involving drink were dealt with in the next two days and perhaps it was all this that induced the worthy citizen to write his letter.

April 2nd was our first Easter in the Falklands and on the Sunday my family and I were invited to lunch at Government House. I do not remember much about the lunch but Mrs. Clifford and His Excellency the Governor, were greatly entertained when on taking our leave of them, young Rowena kissed his hand. She could only just about reach that.

I was still trying to get used to the idea that there would be no postman with mail from home. Only twelve mails an year could be expected and in Stanley the mail would have to be fetched from the post office. No daily national newspaper every morning neither. I had prepared myself for this to some extent though by ordering an airmail edition weekly copy of, I think, it was the *Daily Mail* which was available in those days. So I should get four copies perhaps by each steamer bringing back the mail from Montevideo. All airmail being sent to the Falklands would just have to sit in Montevideo until our ship went to collect it. We were going to be relying a great deal on the BBC overseas broadcasts on the short waves for news of home and even for this our aerials needed to be correct.

The U.K. was a very long way away to the north. From Stanley we could see Twelve O'Clock Mountain in the north and now, of course, as we looked towards it, the sun travelled from our right to our left instead of left to right as we had always seen it travel in the U.K. It took a little while to get used to this. From the house, too, we could see the sailing ship *Fennia* — now a hulk used as a storehouse — at anchor in mid-harbour and for ever swinging to face the wind and tide.

The *Fennia* was a steel masted barque of over 3,000 tons of French origin. She was beaten by Cape Horn weather and made it to Port Stanley in 1927 and was still there twenty years or so later.

Someone, some years ago, had written that from the number of hulks in Port Stanley, the place might well be named the Cape Horn Mausoleum. In the days of sail, countless ships had managed to get to Stanley after storm damage and many had to be abandoned there. There were so many other ships which had failed to reach safety and there was a history of ship wrecks on the many miles of the island's coastline.

One hulk in Stanley, pointed out to me, had been used to carry slaves and was said to still have some of the iron shackles in place. It may well have been the American schooner *Farie* which was a former slaver. She was said to have had immense spars for she was built for speed, not only to shorten the time

131

at sea with her load of slaves but to be able to avoid warships hunting for such slave runners.

I was also told about an American ship the *Philadelphia* which had apparently reached the entrance to Port William the outer harbour — and had been there for some time before attempting to come in without a pilot. She had struck the notorious Billy Rock and had sunk with all hands. That was around the turn of the century. But it was always talked about.

But the most famous hulk of all was that of the S.S. *Great Britain* — Brunel's historic steamship. She was built at Bristol and launched in July 1843, as the largest ship in the world and considered to be a marvel of engineering. Although she had been designed originally as a paddle steamer, she had been redesigned during construction for screw propulsion. She was the first iron-built screw-driven ship to cross the Atlantic. There were very few ships in those days of over even a 1,000 tons, but *Great Britain* was over 3,500 tons. She had been inspected by the young Queen Victoria who was said to have been very impressed with her sixty four state rooms, boudoirs, music room and twelve hundred yards of scarlet and purple carpet.

In 1846, the ship ran ashore one night on the north-east coast of Ireland but without loss of life or cargo as she grounded safely between two protecting ridges of rock. Brunel crossed to Ireland and made her safe and well protected in that position until early 1847 when she was successfully towed off. After some delays she was refitted for the Australian emigrant trade and in 1852 began the first of many voyages over a period of twenty five years only interrupted by trooping service during the Crimean War and Indian Mutiny. On that first voyage about six hundred and thirty passengers were taken to Australia. On those runs she called at Stanley many times to refuel with coal specially sent out for her from Wales in chartered sailing ships.

Originally *Great Britain* carried six masts but these were reduced to five in 1847 and a few years later to four. The ship had then been laid up in 1875 for sale. She was bought eventually in 1881 and in the following year, she made another appearance in the Mersey but this time as a sailing ship with her masts reduced to three and her iron hull completely sheathed in wood. She made two voyages to San Francisco then on 6th February 1886 she sailed for the last time. She was bound for Panama with coal from South Wales when she ran into a gale off the Horn. She was damaged badly and partially dismasted, she ran for the Falklands and managed to reach Stanley. There, however, in due course she had to be condemned and was sold as a hulk.

She was some hulk though because for another forty-seven years, until 1933, she was used by the Falkland Islands Company for the storage of wool and coal. She then lay unused at anchor for several years. Attempts were made to obtain funds to restore and preserve this historic vessel. Despite appeals in the U.K. and in Bristol in particular the attempt had to be abandoned because of the high costs anticipated. And so it was that this lovely old ship was then condemned to be towed out to sea and sunk. But this was not to be, either. Instead, she was moved from the inner harbour to Sparrow Cove on the north shore of Port William, Stanley's outer harbour and there, in fairly shallow water she was beached. In 1937 holes were made in the stern and bow to let in the sea so that she sat comfortably on the bottom.

Constable Williams told me he was one of those who helped to take her there, as he was then working for the Falkland Islands Company. Like so many of her visitors, I too climbed aboard, though warily, and took pictures of her. In 1952 I almost sent a picture to the Science Museum in Kensington as the one I saw on display there was not such a good one. I did not imagine what more was in store for that very old, very frail, great lady with her beautiful lines still showing as she lay in Sparrow Cove.

In her centenary year 1943, someone on the Falkands had written of her resting in the land-locked peace of Sparrow Cove and saying — 'On a fine day, when the sea and sky are blue, her old timbers gratefully absorb the warmth, and glow grey and amber in the sun, against the honey-coloured grass, and she rouses herself from sleep to tell tales of the Antipodes and the windy Horn, to respectful deputations from the penguin rookery on the hill above the Cove. Perhaps these little gentlemen remind her of the Mayor, the Aldermen, the Dean and the sixty resident clergy of Bristol, who accompanied Royalty in procession to her christening one hundred years ago.'

That was how I last saw her. There was, however, continuing interest in this wonderful ship. A naval architect, Dr. Ewan Corlett, had taken particular interest in her for some years before advocating her salvage. There was such an excellent response to a letter he wrote to *The Times* in 1968 that he went to the Falklands to verify that she could, in fact, be moved. He reassured himself that it was possible. The Americans had for some time been showing interest in researching the history of a number of hulks of vessels of U.S. origin in the Falklands and in 1966, a Maritime Museum in San Francisco had even shown an interest in restoring the *Great Britain*. When the Brunel Society issued its appeal in 1969, for monies with which to recover the ship to Bristol, the Museum offered considerable help with the organisation. Funds were soon available and the committee in London went to work rapidly. The old ship was prepared and by early 1970 she was ready to be lifted out of the water, by means of a submersible pontoon, and be carried to the U.K. on the pontoon.

As the *Great Britain* was 320 feet long and 51 feet in the beam, the salvage operation was going to be some task. A British-German consortium accepted the contract to do just this. In March, a very special pontoon and a very special tug arrived in Port Stanley. The pontoon, of over 2,500 tons, was 265 feet by 80 feet. The hulk had to be patched and strengthened, particularly in one section, and the masts had to be removed. Two of the three were over 20 tons each and were taken with the ship on the pontoon. But the third, the mizzen mast, was left in Stanley where it still commemorates the long years she had stayed in the Colony.

The next major stage was to have the ship actually floating again. Powerful pumps, working for hours, enabled her repaired hulk to rise slowly off the bottom. But all was not easy for it was then found that the depth of water under her was not enough to allow the pontoon to be brought underneath. So the huge pontoon had to be moved again into deeper water and preparations made to move the ship to a position above the resubmerged pontoon. All this was accomplished and the pontoon surfaced so as to bring the ship right out of the water and she was then some ten feet above sea level. In all it took about three weeks to complete the recovery to this stage for weather conditions too created constant problems and it was with wind and swell giving them a very rough passage, the flotilla of tug with laden pontoon and the local smaller tugs assisting, moved out of Sparrow Cove to a bell-pealing welcome of the inner harbour of Stanley, some four miles distant. Later at a simple ceremony held beneath the massive bows of *Great Britain*, the Governor officially transferred her to the Project Committee.

The tow to Bristol was a record and a story in itself. *Great Britain* now lies in Bristol again and as I write this only a few days ago I watched a television programme showing how in 1970 she was prepared for and made the journey from Sparrow Cove to Bristol.

A Board of Survey at the Colonial Secretary's Office occupied me some hours on three consecutive days. I attended a Board of Health Meeting and submitted the monthly report.

I inspected drains near Dairy Paddock Road.

Dr. Sladen reported that a mental patient from Fitzroy settlement needed to be brought in to Stanley. I detailed Constable O'Sullivan to go the next day to collect him in the Government launch *Porvenir*. That was on Saturday, 10th April. He arrived on the 11th and reported hoping to be able to leave for Stanley on the 12th. He only got as far as Bluff Cove where they were delayed by the weather and it was the afternoon of the 14th when they arrived in Stanley. By this time the patient seemed normal again and was allowed to go home with his wife. Mr. Winter, the Legal Adviser, came and visited the prison on the 15th and that evening I broadcast a special appeal from U.N.O. for Children.

On the 16th the Governor laid the Foundation Stone of the new Town Hall and we attended that ceremony at 5 p.m.

On 19th April we received information that Fred Davies had not been seen since he went out in his boat on the 16th with his young boy. P.C. Fleuret reported that Mrs. Davies was not expecting him back until the next day.

On the 20th we enquired again about Davies. He was then said to have left Stanley at 10 a.m. on the 16th after purchasing 'more' liquor and to have gone to Johnson's Harbour settlement (some 18 crow miles north of Stanley) for geese and tussac grass from Kidney Island. (Tussac grass was growing at this time only on small islands where there were no sheep which could destroy it. Tussac was a most nutritious feed for animals and would be brought by boat to Stanley and sold to feed cattle and horses). We searched Port William's north and south shores including Sparrow Cove but found no sign of Davies.

21st April. Enquiries by radio and telephone. People at Johnson's Harbour were requested to make a detailed search of the coast of Berkeley Sound and Volunteer Lagoon. The weather was very bad.

Over the next two weeks the search was continued over a colony-wide area after radio and telephone calls to most of the settlements. Visits were repeated by us in Stanley to most beaches and coves in the Port William and Berkeley Sound area. For example, at 7 a.m. on 24th April, the Research Vessel *John Biscoe* ferried 97 volunteers to Sparrow Cove to repeat searches and 40 others landed by 9 a.m. in Mengeary Point area round to Kidney Island. We made radio broadcasts to shipping generally and to all on the Islands without success. They were lost to us and yet some hope lasted a long time because, some years earlier, Davies' grandfather had also disappeared with a young boy and their boat had survived 62 days at sea until they were rescued off the coast of the Argentine some 900 miles north of Stanley. They had existed on their load of vegetables and swedes.

Meanwhile, routine matters occupied my time, together with much work on new legislation.

Up to now all cases brought to court had been straight forward and without problems. As there was no legal assistance available to those prosecuted, I spared no effort to ensure that the police evidence was in all ways without prejudice and that what could be said on behalf of defendants was never unsaid.

I also wanted all to realise that any police action was without regard to personalities or position. A careless driving charge following a road traffic accident was perhaps the first case since my arrival, where this, hopefully, would have been apparent. The defendant was a justice of the peace and he was convicted and fined.

On the 12th May I attended at Government House for a meeting of the Legislative Council. The Government at that time was administered by the Governor aided by an Executive Council and a Legislative Council. On 1st January, 1949, the composition of these was varied slightly so that from that date, the Executive Council consisted of three ex-officio members (most senior government officers) and five nominated unofficial members while the Legislative Council was composed of three ex-officio, four elected, two nominated unofficial and two nominated official members. The Chief Constable was not a member of either of these Councils.

One needed to be a Jack of all trades in a small community that of necessity had to be self sufficient. I must have been dragooned into giving a talk about the Salvation Army to members of the Tabernacle Church on Friday, 14th May, as I had no qualification to talk about that world wide Christian Army. I had already seen that a Falkland Islander could turn his hand to a variety of jobs that elsewhere might properly have been left to specialists or artisans. Some of the islanders were capable of erecting their own houses and did so. Carpentry, brickwork, plumbing and electrical work was often done by the same person.

The Tabernacle was the church of nonconformists and in those days was called the United Free Church for it was available to members of all Christian denominations. The Anglicans and Roman Catholics had their own churches in Stanley. It was probably named the Tabernacle after the Metropolitan Tabernacle in London for it was the famous preacher, the Rev. C. Spurgeon, of that church who sent a Baptist minister to Stanley in 1888. In less than four years, the members had erected the Tabernacle in Barrack Street and with another Baptist minister to serve them. The building, in sections, had been imported from England and is still in use. The minister I met there was the Rev. Forrest McWhan. He had gone to the Falklands originally as a member of the Church Army when a young man and served there for many years. He too had to be a man of many parts and for some time produced the Colony's small weekly newspaper. He was the only one I knew at that time who took a daily swim in the so cold Falkland waters. Too cold for any of the rest of us to attempt it even once a year. The church had a thriving Sunday School and its picnics too are well remembered. Sankey and Moody hymns were most popular. People in Camp were able to share in worship through the Government radio broadcasts of services from the Tabernacle on Sundays alternating with the Anglican Christ Church Cathedral services and Roman Catholic services from St. Mary's Church.

Another Moody, this time Governor Moody, had much to do with Anglican church services in the Falklands before the Colony had a church or chaplain, for he led services himself in a government building. His brother, later appointed as the Colony's chaplain, arrived in 1845 and it was not very long before a church building had been erected and brought into use. This building though was for some time used for other purposes as well as was its successor, in a new Exchange Building. It was then the Holy Trinity Church in the early 1860s.

For half a century earlier and more, there had been much missionary activity in southern South America, in Patagonia and Tierra del Fuego. One of the missionaries, the Rev. Stirling, had been recalled to England to be made Bishop of the Falkland Islands in 1869 but it was two years later that he was installed as Bishop of the Falkland Islands in that Church of the Holy Trinity. Twenty years later, on 21st February, 1892, Bishop Stirling consecrated the new Christ Church Cathedral. Its centenary was celebrated recently and we have all seen it on our television screens regularly since 1982. Incidentally the huge Whalebone Arch we see adjacent to the Cathedral was given to the Colony by the Falkland Islands Company in 1933 in the Colony's centenary year.

We were still having far too many cases of petty theft and the detection rate was not as good as I would have wished. This was partly due to the fact that there were strong ties between so many people in a small community. It was said there, as of so many places in the U.K. that whereas before the War, house doors were often left unlocked, people now found that they dared not do so. It was my estimation later that 95% of all police cases were attributable to excessive use of intoxicating liquor.

On 1st June at 8.55 p.m. a fire was reported in the extensive gorse bushes at Government House gardens. I attended with the fire brigade and returned there again before midnight to ensure there was no more immediate danger. The Governor was away in Camp. Gorse thrives in the Falklands. For its colourful bloom and properties as a windbreak, it is encouraged but in the immediate vicinity of buildings, it is a fire risk. This was very much the case at Government House. There was a telephoned false alarm of fire the following evening so the possibility remained that the gorse had been fired maliciously.

The Stanley Fire Brigade's fire fighting equipment was very limited when considering there was no further fire fighting force available to come to its assistance but the availability of its members and in such numbers added to their keenness, ensured that the best possible use would be made of what it did have. At the first chimney fire I saw the brigade in action, I realised that a peat-smoked chimney fire could be something more than a coal-smoked chimney fire but I had not expected to see a fireman get on the roof to direct his hose into the chimney pot. I did appreciate though the way in which rapid care was taken in the house to minimise water damage. Thereafter they extinguished chimney fires in the approved way.

There was no fire mains with hydrants and water supplies had to be drawn from the harbour. I was told that with the Coventry Climax trailer pumps they could supply adequate water to all but the top street. There was no large 'first aid water carrying engine', so there was a delay while water was brought directly from the harbour — side pump or to a portable canvas dam by another pump operating in relay up the hill and the third pump in that case, drawing its supply to the fire from the dam. Being fresh from the training school in Manchester and hydraulics a brand new subject still fresh in my mind, I needed to solve the problem. It was a 3,000 gallon dam and I was able to calculate that the actual filling would take four minutes from the time water was arriving at the dam until it was full. On the day we attempted to do this at practice, we succeeded. This was to the relief of us all. I was able to give practical and verbal instruction in due course and for them I produced detailed written notes for study in their own time.

On 10 June I attended the King's Birthday Parade and afterwards at Government House. Later in the day I went to Cape Pembroke Lighthouse where there had been a theft of meat. There was no proper road to the Cape but jeeps could be driven there. The ubiquitous Jeep and a lot of surplus equipment had been left on the islands by the British Forces who served here during the War which had only been concluded about three years earlier. I remember, particularly, berets which were most useful in the Falkland winds and the camouflage netting which was now in general use in most Stanley gardens as a frost protector. Potatoes and cabbage grew well and there is nothing more frustrating for the gardener than to have his potato crop ruined when already perhaps in flower. Sudden squalls of hail could still do a lot of damage but out of season frost could be ignored under netting stretched two or three feet above the potato patch. We were always amazed how lupins thrived so well and withstood the high winds and gales.

Road building outside Stanley had always proved impracticable if only from the financial point of view, owing to the smallness and wide distribution of its population. Apart from a very few miles of dirt tracks on some of the bigger farms, roads beyond a radius of three or four miles from Stanley did not exist.

Settlements had only been built where there were ample peat-beds near sheltered waters where ships could safely enter for stores to be brought in and wool taken out. In some instances the ships might be able to anchor very close to the shore or if not drawing too much water, alongside a jetty.

While virtually all goods had to be transported by sea between Stanley and the farms, people travelled on the islands on horseback between the settlements, outside houses and Stanley. The terrain though was very rugged or in some areas, especially, it could be boggy and in the southern part of East Falkland was flat or only gently undulating over long distances and that brought its own problems. Even experienced campers have been known to lose their way. I remember on some of my earlier trips in the camp, travelling over an expanse of flat ground, with its cover of the common white grass, being shown the glint of a bottle here and there as we rode along and being reassured by 'Look, another bottle — we are on the right track!' Riding in company is better too for even the best of horses can stumble on very rough ground or be troubled in boggy ground. The shepherd has to cope on his own.

My duties continued to provide variety. I see that on 19th July, for instance, I acted as Chairman of a Surprise Survey of Cash and Postal Stocks in the Treasury. Then the next day yet again a report of missing people. Two men were missing and after making enquiries we decided to drag the waters round the East Jetty. Both bodies were recovered over the next two days. Both were found to have died from drowning and we could only presume that both had fallen into the water after dark.

On 1st August one of the constables failed to report for duty through drink. He was officially reprimanded.

On 4th August I received a report of storebreaking at Port Stephens and after discussing the matter with the Colonial Secretary and the Legal Adviser, I decided to go there myself. Port Stephens is on the south west of West Falkland some 160 sea miles or 120 crow miles from Stanley. The *Lafonia* was due to sail on a southabout (clockwise from Stanley) trip round the Islands, so I boarded her at 11 p.m. and we sailed at midnight, in a gale. It was quite a wild night and by 10 o'clock in the morning we were back in Stanley with the ship listing quite seriously. Her cargo had shifted during the gale. It was an unusual cargo for there were quite a number of ex-Army Bren Gun carriers — heavy tracked motor vehicles — to be delivered from Stanley to a number of settlements where it was hoped they could be put to good use.

It took all that day and most of the next re-stowing the cargo before we could resume our voyage. Turning back in the storm with the ship listing had taken most of the night so we had not reached our first port of call. We sailed again at midnight. We arrived at North Arm in the Bay of Harbours, on the south of East Falkland by 9 a.m. and by so doing had added about 30 miles to our sea miles. I went ashore and met Mr. and Mrs. Vinson but we left again, late afternoon, to arrive off George Island after dark. We left there in the very early morning and arrived in Fox Bay by 9 a.m. Fox Bay is about 30 miles north of George Island and on the south eastern side of West Falkland. I went ashore to both Fox Bay East and Fox Bay West but then had to stay ashore as a gale had blown up. In the meantime, I was arranging for a Justice of the Peace to travel with me from Fox Bay to join another J.P. who was also travelling on the *Lafonia,* so that a Court could be held at Port Stephens. I had also been hoping to arrange my transport back to Stanley. Actually the Government MV *Philomel* would not be available to collect me and if possible I was to continue on the *Lafonia.* The *Philomel* was an ex-Admiralty fishing vessel. She could carry about 40 tons of cargo with a small handful of passengers depending on conditions. She was used too, to carry patients into Stanley and generally was very much in demand. So, in the afternoon, I left Fox Bay on the *Lafonia* and arrived at Port Stephens at 8 p.m. Running up to Fox Bay had added another 50 miles to our trip.

Having slept ashore I was able to complete my enquiries into the store-break-in. The Court was convened and three men appeared before the two Justices. The prisoners had been drinking excessively and after the farm store at Port Stephens had been closed to them, they had broken in and stolen more liquor, tobacco, sweets and other articles. They pleaded guilty and were fined. By charging them with theft, we were able to dispose of the charges before this lower court. So then at

142

9 p.m. it was onward again, northward now, to arrive at Roy Cove early next morning after negotiating our way between a number of smaller islands on the west coast of West Falkland. I stayed ashore overnight here too and would record the unfailing hospitality shown at all the farms to their often unexpected guests travelling around as I was doing — and for that matter to all horse riders who come passing by at any house or farm in Camp.

From Roy Cove we left for Chartres Settlement, roughly 15 miles in a south eastward direction this time on now the 13th August, arriving about 2.30 p.m. Here too I spent the night, this time with the Luxtons.

It was nearly 40 sea miles back past Roy Cove to West Point about a three hour trip arriving at 6 p.m., then in another hour to Carcass Island before arriving off Hill Cove Settlement about 10.30 p.m. There, it being Sunday, 15th August, I went ashore about 11 a.m. but we were ready to leave about 3 p.m., to arrive, after negotiating a maze of interesting looking islands, at Pebble Island on the north coast of West Falkland at 6 p.m. There I had dinner with Mr. Betts and so the voyage proceeded — 16th August on to Port Howard on the Falkland Sound where I was glad to go ashore again. There was a gale that day too — 17th August across the Sound to San Carlos about 20 miles.

18th August to Teal Inlet about 50 - 60 sea miles away on the north coast where I spent the evening ashore and at last, on the 19th August, late in the evening, we sailed from Teal Inlet for Port Stanley to complete our circumnavigation at 1.15 a.m. but did not disembark until 7 a.m. on the 20th.

I had naturally found it all most interesting — and all so unlike Hong Kong — BUT from 4th August to 20th August — to deal with a simple case of stealing liquor, we travelled all those sea miles — maybe 650 to 700? I was realising also how remote the settlements were from one another and from Stanley. It had been an excellent opportunity for me to meet more of the people too.

The first telephone to be put into use on the Islands was installed about 1895 which connected the lighthouse at Cape

143

Pembroke with Stanley. All shipping entering or attempting to enter Port William could be seen from the lighthouse and a telephone message from or to the lighthouse was going to be so much better than having someone to ride his horse seven miles in each direction. Gradually more lines were installed between Stanley and some of the main settlements as well, and eventually there was a network on the East Falkland and a separate one, as in my time, on the West Falkland. Later came radio/telephone links and an extension too of the rediffusion system existing in Stanley to the residents in the settlements. With the loudspeakers left switched on, maximum use could be made of the system. The Falkland Islands Government Broadcasting Service was already operational as well before my time.

Strange as it may sound today, the Police Department had no transport of its own. Occasionally, for some special purpose we could be provided with motor transport from the Public Works Department but only in the Stanley area. On some occasions I was driven into Camp in a privately owned Jeep. For other travels on land, a horse or horses would be provided by the Department of Agriculture. All the farmers were most helpful for they would also provide guides and relief horses as and when necessary, and on occasion, if available, motor transport as well. Government's Harbour Department helped with water transport or, as I have already said above, passage could be taken on the Falkland Islands Company steamers, the *Lafonia* or *Fitzroy*.

Later, when Government Air Service became operational, we could take passage by aircraft.

FIGAS, as the Service became known, was created in late 1948 with two light aircraft and the one pilot. They were Austers and equipped so that a patient and stretcher could be carried. Suitable landing strips were not available everywhere so their use was rather limited. Now there was an aircraft available for emergencies and a beginning was made with the dropping from the air of often long awaited letters when the mails had arrived at Stanley. It was not long though before even better arrangements were available. For a second year,

144

June 1985. A happy family reunion at Annedd, Gwalchmai, Anglesey.
Left to Right: Diana, Arthur, Sarah, Rowena, Falmai.

Arthur Hughes Jenkins — Gwalchmai 1989.

Falmai Wyn Jenkins — Gwalchmai 1988.

severe conditions in the Antarctic at the crucial times had prevented the relief by sea of a number of scientists at one of our special bases on the Dependency.

It was now imperative that this should be accomplished at the end of what had now been a two-year unrelieved stay at that Base. To ensure that this could be done even if the ice would not perimt the approach of the relief vessel, it was decided to take aircraft on the Research Vessel. Another Auster was taken to Beaumaris in Anglesey and there fitted with floats. This would be a back up for a Norseman float plane which was a type being used so extensively in Canada. The Norseman could carry nine people. When the big day came, the ship was able to sail into Stonington Island and the need to use the aircraft did not arise. When they all arrived back safely in Stanley, the Government Air Service took over the two aircraft for they were in perfect shape. Flight Lieutenant St. Louis of the Canadian Air Force and Sergeants K. D. Hunt and Bodys of the Royal Air Force, with our two pilots, Vic Spencer and Maurice Smith were with the aircraft when I photographed them in Stanley. Robin Pitaluga, a Kelper, is also in the picture. The Air Service was now really established for they could land at any of the places visited by ships and schooners.

There was more crime than one should really expect in a community of about one and a half thousand. Far too many drinking offences were still adding new names to our 'black list' and a number already on the black list were committing further offences.

I was out riding with the Agriculture Officer and together we impounded sheep we found grazing on the Common. It was a novel experience for me to be trying to round up sheep while on horse back and riding cowboy fashion. As we drove them back with us to town, my companion threw well aimed stones at road junctions to help keep the sheep going in the right direction. My riding seemed to be improving rapidly. Horses were neck-reined. I understood that if you wished to go right you merely held the left rein closer to the horse's left neck and the horse moved as if away from it, to its right and vice-versa. Basically that was it — to hurry the reins were moved forward and to stop or slow, you drew the reins towards you. And of course use of knees and body weight. There were very few English or Australian type saddles. One rode Falklands style. A special wooden frame, securely in place and well covered with sheep skins was the saddle. Stirrups varied a lot but an open box type was favoured too, so as to lessen the risk of a foot being trapped if the horse fell suddenly on boggy ground. One needed good knees as well when travelling across country. I did have such a fall but maybe it was because I only had the one, I was never able to claim to be a good rider. I think I must have managed to learn to sit well though, for I remember being so pleased when told by one of the shepherds, at an outside house, that he thought it was Constable O'Sullivan who was approaching. O'Sullivan had ridden a lot in the Argentine and for years in the Falklands. He sat well.

There is a long and most interesting history to the introduction of horses, cattle and sheep to the Islands. Since earlier days, all items of horse gear have borne Spanish names as used by the South American gauchos who came to deal with the wild cattle. The colour description of horses is usually Spanish too. Many place names in Spanish live on as well.

One day we rode to Ordnance Point to investigate the finding of some unexploded shell. It proved to be a Falkland Islands Defence Force smoke shell unaccounted for at one of their exercises in that area. We had taken one of their Bren guns with us and I was permitted (!) to use it to explode the old shell. Though I was well accustomed to shooting with .22 and .303 rifles, this was the first time I had handled the Bren. I was told it could fire off single shots although set on automatic, if this was attempted gently. I found that to be correct. Today, unfortunately, ten years after the surrender of the Argentine's forces in 1982, there are acres and acres of beach and land which have had to remain fenced off as dangerous minefields. We have already managed to find and destroy thousands of their mines.

We were alerted one morning with a report that an armed vessel had entered Port William. We knew then what might be

146

threatening. While I was driven to a point above Yorke Bay where with binoculars I could have a good view, all concerned in Stanley were being alerted. What I saw though was a 'whale catcher' for I could clearly see the harpoon gun up in the ship's bows with the elevated gangway, to reach it quickly, from the deck housing amidships. Arriving back in Stanley, I found His Excellency the Governor with senior Government Officers already gathered together. The Governor directed that the MV *Philomel* would take him to Port William at once accompanied by some Defence Force members, myself and one or two senior government officers, to investigate further. The catcher was one of Onassis Olympic whalers, *Olympic Cruiser* and had come in to shelter temporarily after a storm and later with one or two others left on their way south about their lawful business.

We were only too well aware of the claims being repeated regularly by the Argentinians that the Falkland Islands were their Islas Malvinas. The Jefe V Brigada of The Argentine Air Force at Base Aerea Militar 'Coronel Pringles' at Villa Reynolds, the Argentine sent me on several occasions, a descriptive list of conscripts who had deserted! One envelope was addressed 'El Sr Jefe de Policia, Arturo Jenkins, Port Stanley, Las Islas Malvinas, Argentinas Interior via Montevideo'.

We searched for the *Indiana,* a small sailing cutter with a crew of two. We were told she had been out of Stanley for nine days instead of the usual two or three and we had had several gales in that time. I requisitioned the *Philomel* and went to search an area where she may have been fetching tussac. We were about to search Kidney Island and Cochon Island at the southern end of the entrance to Berkeley Sound when we saw her at Kidney just hoisting sail. She refused our offer to tow her back with us.

We had another scare when she was again reported overdue but this time with children aboard, on a picnic. As we were about to leave the jetty in the dark to look for her, she returned to harbour.

Another day, the lighthouse keeper phoned to say that the *Indiana's* owner had just rowed ashore from one of the nearby islets and reported that his companion whom he had left on board, while he himself was ashore cutting tussac, was missing when he returned to the *Indiana*. A launch was available in Stanley to take us at once to the scene and almost within the hour, we recovered the body of his companion, with grappling irons, in some four fathoms of water. He had been subject to epilepsy and had undoubtedly fallen overboard.

Not long afterwards, the *Indiana* was reported long overdue yet again. This time she had been taken to the Falkland Sound — some 100 miles from Stanley — to fetch seabirds' eggs. It used to be the custom to collect them in large quantities and bring them to Stanley to sell and of course a lot of people were able to collect their own penguin eggs and pickle them for use in winter, when eggs would be scarce. The collection of penguin eggs is now under strict control with licence fees on a sliding scale. Jimmy, the owner and his *Indiana* had last been seen some three weeks earlier when she was sheltering in Bull Cove on the southern tip of East Falkland. Our telephone and radio calls brought us no news. The weather was too bad for the Auster to take off from the temporary airstrip on Stanley's racecourse. I sent a constable off with the crew of a government auxiliary ketch to search for her as I thought it possible she might have got into trouble out of sight on Sea Lion Island some ten miles off the coast from Bull Cove. This proved to be the case. Jimmy and his mate had been forced to run back from a head on gale when they had tried again to make it to the Falkland Sound, and made for the shelter of Sea Lion Island.

With both *Indiana's* anchors out, the two men had gone ashore in their dinghy during a temporary lull only to see her drag her anchors and wreck herself within the hour as the wind had backed and strengthened.

The men were most fortunate in finding both shelter and food which kept them for the three weeks in the only house on the island. The house was unoccupied for the greater part of each year as the island was only being sheep farmed each summer and it was the practice to leave all foodstuffs that would keep until the following season. Nowadays there is a thriving tourist lodge on Sea Island catering for those who wish to study and enjoy its fascinating and varied wild life.

When Jimmy came to see me, he had a tale to tell of a partly exposed human skeleton at the top of the cliffs near Bull Cove. But more of the skeleton later. Jimmy had always been a bit of a dare devil but after all the dangers he had run into, he was to succumb to the calm waters in a sheltered harbour. Only a few short weeks after the *Indiana* was lost, Jimmy with two companions was boarding a dinghy at the jetty in Stanley harbour in the dark when it capsized. Their cries brought help as a man in another dinghy nearby rowed quickly to the spot. He grabbed two people as his boat brushed past them in the dark. He saw no one else. It was only after my arrival some ten minutes later that it was realised that Jimmy must have been with them. The two men were rushed to hospital and survived. We recovered Jimmy's body the following morning. That made seven such drowning cases in this small community in less than twelve months.

I decided to investigate the Bull Cove skeleton matter myself. I hired a Jeep which took me in three hours out of Stanley to Rollons Cove where I transferred to a motor boat. This took me to Fitzroy Settlement — a good hour away — where I stayed the night. Early the next day I started riding the next part of my journey. The Manager himself was my guide and he was proudly extolling the virtues of his Welsh cob as we began the next stage to reach a shepherd's house (quite some miles from the nearest habitation) and had some lunch and were met there by Mr. Gilruth, the Darwin manager with a Land Rover, the first of that new breed of four-wheeled drive vehicles to reach the Falklands. I then sat in and grimly held on to the Land Rover for about three hours until we reached Darwin where I was so well looked after. But we were on our way again in the Land Rover at 5 a.m. to arrive at North Arm farm at 8.30 a.m. for breakfast. I do not need to describe the capabilities of these vehicles but to me, at that time, they were awesome and for some of the ground we had to cover, they had to be.

Here Mr. Gilruth left and returned to Darwin while I was

provided with another horse and guide. This part of the Island was only gently undulating without landmarks for miles and miles. After some hours we were met by the shepherd who lived in the outside house nearest to Bull Cove so he then became my guide, the other returning alone to North Arm. My new guide was Peter Duncan, a bachelor aged 69 years, who had lived alone at Fanny Cove for nineteen years, with his nearest neighbour two hours (horse riding) away. He was a tough old shepherd and I noticed he was wearing gloves. He explained that a fortnight or so earlier, he had lost himself for two nights and a day, when his horses left him in the dark during a snow storm at one of the very few fences. His fingers were still painful from frostbite and he told me that had he not kept on walking the whole time, he would have perished.

We arrivced, to my relief, at Fanny Cove where he made us some quick tea then we rode on again to the coast, with fresh horses. I described the place I wanted, as detailed to me by Jimmy, and he brought me to the cliff top within fifty yards of the skeleton. I photgraphed it and completed its entire exposure as only the skull and leg bones were visible at first. The earth on the sea side of the cliff top had been weathered back some twenty feet from the actual cliff top, aided by sheep sheltering there too from time to time, it seemed to me. So it looked like a genuine burial some three feet deep in the soil at that time. I concluded it had been buried many years ago and that it had probably been the body of a young shipwrecked sailor. The teeth looked so good. The whole of this coast is a graveyard of ships smashed up rounding Cape Horn. I decided to rebury the bones some fifty yards further inland. Peter had brought a shovel with him so this is what we did.

We then rode back to Fanny Cove about 7 p.m. as darkness fell. Fried penguin eggs and some more of Peter's bread — such a huge round loaf which had been baked in peat ash — which tasted better than any other bread I had tasted, made an excellent supper. For those who want to know, it is usual to dispose of about a third of the 'white' of the egg which is equivalent to about $2\frac{1}{2}$ to 3 chicken eggs. When fried the 'white' is not white but almost transparent. I have seen them swallowed raw too.

Peter had a good radio and his knowledge of politics and affairs in Britain really surprised me. Had we been less tired, we could have talked all night.

It was 4 a.m. before I had a chance to start appreciating my bunk bed with its depth of sheepskins under me. I must have fallen asleep very quickly. After breakfast we were off again before 5 a.m. The stiffness of the first two days was soon jolted out of me. You ride limply entirely, for your horse does not normally trot or canter but moves quite rapidly nevertheless when not walking. It is the only way to ride for long distances or hours.

We were making a detour westwards to Blind Island as I wanted to see the round up of the horses which had been wintering on the island in the tussac grass (in 'bogs' which grow 8-10 feet high thus providing wonderful shelter and food). In the spring/summer season, each shepherd needs a troop of seven to ten horses — a change each day as feed is of poor quality and work hard.

After the round up of nearly two hundred horses, they were driven in batches of about 50 from the corral into the sea and with a boat each side of them in the channel, induced to swim back on to our main island perhaps some quarter of a mile distant, and watched by inquisitive seals which came up all around snorting and grunting. Only one horse was lost in the process. Then came a long ride behind a bunch of these horses which had again been resorted in some corrals to be gradually detached in several directions as they progressed. Peter and I rode back to be met in due course by the Land Rover for the tiring trip back to Darwin, for a welcoming hot bath, drinks before the cheery peat fire, good food, a pleasant conversation and a most comfortable bed — I remember a most marvellous fur bed cover — at the Gilruths.

The next day another long ride in the Land Rover until this time I was met by the Jeep from Stanley, while Mr. Gilruth drove back to Darwin. The dusty rugged dirt track — surface top soil was removed to expose harder surface a few inches beneath it — now gave way to open land which gave us a very rough ride. We hoped to reach Stanley that night but it was not to be. When attempting to cross a creek to save driving some mile or two round the end of it, the Jeep's nose went down and the water was up to the footboards. We scrambled ashore and surveyed the scene. We had either missed the spot where a safe crossing could be effected or had a much higher tide to contend with. We could not drive out. With luck we were not so far from a farm where it was known they had a big ex-army QL lorry. After retrieving the Jeep and ready for the tow back to the farm, came a roaring gale with driving rain and we were drenched and frozen by the time we reached the farm. The Jeep had to wait till next morning to be dried out when it was soon fixed and this time we reached Stanley without undue incident. The driver had come out from Stanley with a bundle of stakes to mark his path through a particularly boggy area. The surface had recovered and was not showing clearly where he had driven the previous day but the stakes marked our track and so he retrieved them as we went along. I gave him full marks despite the creek bath. Shortly after this, he sold up his property and set out to Australia.

Back in Stanley all seemed very busy after the long almost lonely hours in Camp. My family was well settled in to our new life. My wife joined a thriving Spinners and Weavers Guild. They produced special jersey/pullovers and stockings for sale to the men who were working in the Bases down south. Diana was keen on riding whenever possible in and around Stanley. I see in front of me a licence which allowed her to cut grass on Victory Green for a full year for the sum of 2/6d (12½p). We were able to visit some of the nearer penguin rookeries and occasionally some of the beaches. It is always interesting to observe penguins both at the rookery and moving to or from the sea. They seem to stop to have a conversation with the other penguins they meet. At the nests the noise is quite something. The penguins are constantly helping themselves to nesting materials from neighbouring nests and it was interesting to watch the movement of a piece of stick identified by an added bit of string or coloured ribbon as it was stolen by bird after bird in turn. It was when handling some of the very young penguins that Diana told us she now knew where cotton wool came from.

I played a lot of badminton and football and used the indoor .22 rifle range in winter and the Open range with .303 in summer. They were all first class shots and the Falklands have always been represented at Bisley and at various postal shoots with teams overseas.

I have to admit that I made the most of every opportunity to go to Camp. My wife though had no such opportunity. Here was another trip. Theft of money at Salvador Settlement. Salvador lies at the entrance to a very extensive inlet of the sea on the north coast of East Falkland. I left Stanley with Constable O'Sullivan at 6 a.m., 29 October. We rode some fifteen miles to reach Estancia, then on to Malo, another ten perhaps, and continued to Teal Inlet Settlement, probably another twelve to fifteen miles. What I remember particularly about that ride is the rough going, the detours to follow the most suitable track, having to ride our horses across a creek where they had to break the surface ice still lying on the eighteen inches or so deep water so as to enable us to save another detour of a mile or two round the head of the creek. I also saw Drunken Rock, so called, I was told, because it was a favourite stopping place as it provided a shelter from wind in any direction and where the many empty bottles had accumulated over the years and still lay around.

We interviewed two men at Teal Inlet that evening and the next day we left at 7 a.m. by motor boat to cross the Inlet to Salvador some ten miles to the north. There we made further enquiries but bad weather and damage to our motorboat delayed us there until the next morning when we were able to return to Teal Inlet for yet more enquiries. That was a Sunday, so the following morning, 1st November, we rode our horses from Teal Inlet at 10 a.m. and arrived back in Stanley at 7.05 p.m.

The following Sunday was Armistice Day when the Special Memorial Service and Parade was held at the Cross of Sacrifice.

One entry in my diary for the Sunday after that — the

153

14th November, reads: 'Son born to Princess Elizabeth and Duke of Edinburgh' and on the 15th — 'Public Holiday — 21 Gun Royal Salute'. So I recorded the birth of Prince Charles.

H.M.S. *Sparrow* arrived 27th November. There was always a big welcome for H.M. ships from all sections of the community. I acquired a dog, some of the crew had kept aboard as a mascot from the West Indies. I see from my dog licence, issued on my behalf, by Sgt. Norris, for 6/- (30p) under Ordnance No. 6 of 1853, that it was a female, black and white pointer. It later produced a litter of pure black puppies.

We were making good progress with the revision of the legislation and naturally I was finding it all very fascinating to be so close to actual law making as well as its enforcement. I had a slightly different role in the matter of civil cases, as we did 'wait upon the Court', as it were, when these were being heard. There was one particular case brought before the Supreme Court (a legal requirement) where the Governor sat as the Judge and with a jury. The jury was being prepared to go to their retirement room, on the Judge's instructions, as he was retiring as well, when I felt I had to intervene. I drew the Registrar's attention to a procedural flaw. I had indicated to the sergeant to hold the jury in the Court while I whispered hurriedly to the Registrar. After a few moments, it could hardly have been minutes, the Registrar indicated that the jury should retire and that the matter should continue. They found perversely against the plaintiff. It was a matter which merited an appeal and the Judge, it seemed to me, was intimidating to the plaintiff that he could do so.

I now found myself again in a situation which was entirely new to me. The Legal Adviser was at this time acting for the Colonial Secretary and had nothing to do with the court but I advised him of the position. An appeal could be made only to Privy Council and I undertook to prepare 'grounds of appeal' for the plaintiff, with the unspoken approval of the Colonial Secretary and the Governor. So I borrowed the appropriate volume of Halsbury's Laws of England so as to know the precise form of such an appeal. The written appeal was duly submitted and some three years later the plaintiff (appellant) was fully satisfied.

The sergeant had introduced me to fishing for mullet on cold beaches with rod and line. The only bait we used was — yes, mutton. My wife did not always approve of my habit of cutting into the finest part of a leg for bait but she did appreciate the fish it produced. An angling club was formed in Stanley and on occasion, we would hire a lorry to take us to some of the nearer beaches or hire a motor launch, even the *Philomel* sometimes, to take us to creeks where we would spend part of the time fishing with our rods and lines. Before returning, we would use a long net from beach and back to beach to catch more than our personal needs which we would sell in Stanley to meet our hiring expenses. This sale would be made at two or three road junctions in Stanley after notifying all households over their loudspeaker system.

Several species of indigenous trout existed in the small rivers but I saw none myself, neither did I attempt to fish for them. Other trout were being introduced to some of the rivers on both West and East Falkland during my first two years there and have thrived. Excellent fishing is now available to tourists and the Falklands record, which had stood for about five years was beaten, in 1992, with a monster fish weighing 22 lbs. 12½ ozs. and this beats even the British record by 4½ ozs.

Readers who are stamp collectors, will know more than I do about Falkland Island stamps, so I will not attempt to write about the various issues for the Islands or the Dependencies. They are, however, always in great demand and have consequently been a valuable source of income for the Colony. As commemorative issues are made twice a year, in keeping with other countries, surplus stocks need to be destroyed to ensure good sales of the new issues. I had to supervise and assist in this process. A sixty stamp sheet of one pound stamps had its value of £60 increased to £300 the day after that issue was withdrawn. This was one example I remember and can now picture myself with two others sitting by the open fire door of the large peat burning central heating boiler, crumpling sheets galore, at £300 a time, into the furnace. That is how it was and somebody has to do it still I presume.

And something different yet again. H.M.S. *Bigbury Bay* was in need of gun firing practice. The very old tug *Royder* was due to be taken out of harbour to be sunk. *Bigbury Bay's* captain kindly allowed some of us, including Dr. Vivian Fuchs (now Sir Vivian) who was the leader of the scientists who had been 'marooned' at Marguerite Bay earlier, to be aboard to go out to sea some ten miles south east of Port William where the old tug now sat to become our target. We fired various weapons at diminishing distances until *Royder* sank after a second depth charge had been thrown. The navigating officer was from Tenby. Old photographs tell tales too. I must remember to write what, when and where on more of them.

With rationing still in force in Britain, we felt we were lucky to be doing so well in the Falklands. Occasionally, others, like ourselves would send fat, in some form, home. We had posted a large tin full of dripping which we knew would be so welcome. Shortly afterwards we had news of the sinking of the *Magdalena,* a large, brand new passenger ship on her maiden voayge. She had just left Rio de Janeiro, in daylight, on her homeward bound trip when she struck a rock and sank. She had been carrying Falkland Islands mail to the U.K. We were compensated by the Post Office for our loss.

Live sheep and frozen mutton had been exported from the Islands from time to time since before the turn of the century but never with much success. Shortly before World War II, the possibility of succeeding with a freezer plant in the Falklands was being considered but nothing was done until 1947 when the Colonial Development Corporation offered to provide finance. Work on the freezer began in 1949 but not completed until four years later. In the meantime, of course, while all meat was so much needed in Britain, in the Falklands, we were, shall I say, wasting so much mutton. Thousands of sheep were being killed off regularly, as the quality of their wool deteriorated. Only the wool and hides were recovered. Seabirds cleaned the carcasses. The bones often burned in heaps.

There had been a lot of opposition to the scheme and probably a lot of it justifiable, for after three years the whole impressive establishment had to be closed down. Problems of transport, communications, distances, costs of change of style of farming to intensive meat production, had all been too much. Some of what was still standing, after major dismantling earlier, was in 1982 used by our Army Hospital units as a place to treat those injured in the fighting on land and sea in the conflict to recover the Islands. Do you remember seeing the pictures on the television screens and the time the medics worked on with an unexploded bomb, dropped by the Argentines, within feet of them? Wonders were performed at Ajax Bay then. Ajax Bay lies on the western shore of San Carlos Water and opposite the settlement of San Carlos.

When the Norseman float plane became available, I was able to make a different sort of trip to Camp. I needed to go to West Falkland to deal with a case of larceny at Hill Cove, a hundred air miles away. We took off from the harbour at Stanley, landed for a brief stop at Ajax Bay and arrived at Hill Cove within some 75 minutes. This was unbelievable and I enjoyed every moment. I can savour it all again as I look at my maps. With my enquiries soon completed that day, I was able to make arrangements to go on horse back to Fox Bay West the next day, taking my prisoner with me. I also arranged for the Justice of the Peace at Port Howard to travel to Fox Bay West as well, so that a court of summary jurisdiction could sit there. A second justice was already at Fox Bay. I stayed with the manager and was well looked after.

The next day and it being almost mid winter, we started riding before daylight on our 50 mile or so journey. The three of us, that is the prisoner, our guide and myself, were soon climbing on to a nasty ridge called Hell's Kitchen. After a while we descended on to lower ground with the going at times uncomfortable. About mid-day we were met with change of horses for the prisoner and myself by a guide from Fox Bay while the morning guide returned to Hill Cove. The journey was quickly resumed but even so darkness had fallen again long before we reached Fox Bay West. I had no idea what the going was like but it was not easy. I could hardly see the guide ahead of me and found it difficult to keep up with him. He told me to give the horse its head entirely and that the horse would pick its own path. I held tightly with my knees as the horse swerved left and right. I was glad to arrive. We completed the trip in about nine hours. The justice from Port Howard must have had as long a day in the saddle too. I appreciated why a shepherd needed a troop of horses. I needed a bed but had travelled quite well.

At Fox Bay I stayed with Chris Perry and the following day was soon able to charge the three men there, as they did not deny their guilt. To avoid expense and considerable trouble to all concerned, I brought the lesser charge of larceny instead of storebreaking in each case so that they could be disposed of there and then instead of at Supreme Court proceedings at Stanley. Fines were inflicted in all cases but I have just seen again that the only one who asked for and had been given time to pay failed to do so and later served a short period of imprisonment for his sins.

Weather and transport problems kept me at Fox Bay West ten days before the Norseman called to take me back to Stanley. We stopped at Ajax Bay briefly on our return journey too.

Our third daughter was born on 27 May, 1949 at the King Edward VII Memorial Hospital at Stanley. Forty three years later, and certainly thirty three years later, to a Kelper, Malvina might not sound such an attractive name but Sarah Malvina, we thought, was just right. Between British discovery and earlier occupation of the Islands, the French too had had a settlement there. They called the archipelago Isles Malouines for it was from St. Malo that many French expeditions had set sail to these southern seas. There was a sale of sort to Spain at Port Louis and the Governor of that French settlement was succeeded by a Spaniard Ruiz Puente. So Iles Malouines for them became Islas Malvinas. The name Falkland though had already been established a long time before that.

Routine police work continued at Stanley. The jail was occupied briefly from time to time. One new prisoner, a Shetland Islander working under contract on Falklands was found crying in his cell. The sergeant came to tell me that he had eventually succeeded in getting him to understand that executing the warrant, which had been mentioned, did not mean the other execution. His contract expired shortly afterwards and he returned to the Shetlands.

One of the farm managers reported that some six hundred sheep had been stolen and that quite a number of older sheep had been substituted for his younger ones. This was rather startling and an unheard of thing from what I could gather. But the matter would have to be investigated and I decided we would do this together with the Government Agricultural Officer. It was a long and tiring ride there and we waited the next day while a round up of all his sheep was being completed. There was no reason to suspect anyone of the crime if there was a crime. The sheep were duly counted and drafted. Previous gradings of wool were checked and various figures checked and rechecked. Later we sought advice from some other more distant and experienced managers and had to conclude that the complainant was mistaken and his losses and poor gradings were really the result of his own inexperience and mismanagement. The size of the farm and size of his flocks demanded a lot of management experience.

Secondary school education was not available in the Falkland Islands in those days. Government did, however, provide a small number of scholarships to enable a few children to continue to secondary education in Montevideo. Diana was one of these in 1950 but just at that time my wife lost her mother in a tragic road accident and it was decided that she should travel home with our three daughters while I would follow when my home leave became due. As Diana would be able to start her secondary school education in Wales, her scholarship could now go to another in Stanley. It was agreed that I would accompany my family as far as Montevideo on the *Fitzroy* on her next trip.

We were fortunate to find that *Fitzroy* on this trip was going via Punta Arenas, the most southern city in the world, in Chile, on the Magellan's Straits. With a population of over 30,000 it was much bigger than Ushuaia, the southernmost town in the world which with a population just about like Stanley, is a little further south in Argentina's Tierra del Fuego.

We were in the Straits when an earthquake occurred and one or two lives were lost when a resulting landslide carried some cottages into the water some miles ahead of us but we saw nothing of it. In Punta Arenas itself a little later, we had a substantial shake, though negligible damage I think, and were told when we got back aboard that the ship had rocked a little against the jetty. The town bore some resemblance to what I thought a wild west town would look like. We did not see much of it though. Then it was back into the Straits again and then northward for some four or five days to Montevideo. The *Fitzroy* sailed back with me to the Falklands before my family sailed for home on the *Andes*.

It would be weeks before I could receive letters from home and weeks before my letters could leave Stanley with three weeks or more to reach Britain after that. It was possible to exchange cablegrams but they were too costly except for special occasions. Today I can press a few numbers on the telephone beside me in Anglesey and in a matter of seconds I can speak to an old friend in Port Stanley and hear him so clearly. Diana now a newly qualified radio 'ham' talked to someone in Stanley from her home in Buckinghamshire. I renewed acquaintance with Harold Bennett in Stanley after I recognised him on my television screen when Mrs. Thatcher visited the Falkland Islands and he was seen to give her a rose. Shortly afterwards he visited England with his wife, Grace, and was able to stay with us, so briefly though, before returning to the Falklands. He had been the Senior Magistrate and Registrar and a Member of Legislative Council before he retired after many years service.

There was but one doctor in Government Service for both general work and hospital duties. Occasionally, for very short periods, he might be assisted by a doctor attached to the special teams of scientists of the Falkland Islands Dependencies Survey. It was one of these, in fact, who stayed on in Stanley later and looked after all of us and continued to do so for many years. Dr. Slessor. Dr. Arthur of the survey accompanied me to Darwin when I was myself going to deal with an alleged offence against a young girl. We had the most atrocious weather for hours. We were breasting one ridge and the wind virtually stopped us in our tracks. We returned to Stanley several days later and for the latter part of the journey we sailed from Fitzroy, on the *Philomel* in some seven hours of lovely sunshine. I am looking at a picture of Dr. Arthur asleep on the deck of the *Philomel* as I write this.

The Falkland Islands Company at times had their own doctor and everybody benefitted from that too. Having flown out together to Camp once, I remember acting as his 'dental assistant', in that I was ready to hold the patient, if necessary, when he extracted some teeth for two patients at Goose Green. There was no dentist there in those days so the doctor did whatever he could to help.

I do not remember any grave emergencies for doctors to deal with but it would have taken weeks before a patient could be taken to Montevideo if this had become necessary. In 1992, patients are flown to Britain in a couple of days and our forces' helicopters fly out to fishing vessels to bring emergency cases to Stanley where the hospital now is more appropriately staffed and equipped.

One season, the Dependencies' Survey vessel found herself trapped in an extensive icefield. It became necessary for relief work at the other bases down south to be continued in the short summer, on the Falkland Islands Company's *Fitzroy*, so her routine visit to Montevideo had to be delayed. I suppose we would have found the ten week wait for that next mail from Britain even worse had we known it was going to be such a long wait.

My first round the Islands trip on the *Lafonia* had taken a fortnight. The convenience and speed of air transport proved a great blessing to those in Camp and especially so for all on West Falkland and island settlements like New Island, Beaver, Carcass, Saunders and Pebble. Morning radio calls to any or all settlements provided up to date weather reports, and flights by the Norseman could be arranged for the day.

The Deanery in Stanley was next door to me, so with the

Catholic Church on the other side of me, I was well looked after, I hoped. The new man who came to take charge of the Anglican Cathedral, was the Rev. Maldwyn Lloyd Jones who hailed from Mallwyd then in Merioneth. He brought me a flavour of that county where my family was awaiting me in Dolgellau. We were soon exercising our Welsh and with the Bishop as well when he visited us. We thought the occasion of Welsh clergy and police called for photographs under the Whalebone Arch at the Cathedral's front doors. Some thirty years later Maldwyn Lloyd Jones came to see me in Barmouth. After meeting the Navy at Stanley, he had later become a chaplain in the Royal Navy and so served for many years.

Tragically, the Bishop lost his life in a freak accident when travelling a mountain road in the Andes on one of his long circuits of his diocese.

With the end of my three year tour approaching, I tried to arrange to visit South Georgia and the bases in Antarctica when the season's reliefs and replenishments of the Dependencies Survey was again under way. I was really looking forward to this as I was now offered another police appointment and this would be my last chance to see these so interesting areas of my long beat. There was so much I had not seen including many of the island settlements and historical sites. The history of the Falklands makes most fascinating reading.

My departure on leave to the U.K. was scheduled for the end of March when the *Fitzroy* would sail for Montevideo. Before I could go south, however, the Governor of the Windward Islands had now asked if I would defer my leave and proceed direct to Grenada, as serious disorders had broken out in that West Indian Colony. I agreed to do so. It was imperative therefore, that I was available to catch the *Fitzroy* so my Antarctic trip had to be cancelled as time between my scheduled return from down south and departure for Montevideo would be too short to risk any delays by ice conditions.

There was urgent contact with my family but excitement about my new posting and all that might lie ahead of us, would help ease the pain of delayed reunions. I tried to gather as much information as I could about the West Indies and

Grenada in particular and prepared for my departure with my main baggage to go to Wales and only air freight to accompany me to Grenada. Some dozen lovely lamb skins helped to protect our camphor wood chest on its journey home.

So the time came quickly to say goodbye for I knew it would be most unlikely that I should see the Falklands again. Gladly though, I have been able to maintain some contacts and renew others. I attended that reunion in London about twenty years later and met many besides PC Goss. I see the weekly Falklands paper fairly regularly and, shall I say, devour all I can see on the TV set since 1982. All in all, I feel very much a Kelper and easily share the Exile's Lament —

'It is a long road and a weary road
That leads across the sea,
To an isle amidst the storm winds
Where I ever wish to be;
To hear the sea birds crying
And to watch the storm clouds frown —
But I'll see no more Malvina
For the years have chained me down.

I love the misty curtain
That hangs above each hill
I love the calm, sweet scented days
With harbours mirror-still;
I love your mighty tempests,
Your torrents peaty brown;
But I'll see no more Malvina,
For the years have chained me down.

GRENADA

The three years of so much that was so different to the preceding three years, had now come to a close and it was all change again with a long way to go to Grenada in the West Indies. There was joy at the thought of seeing my family again, sadness at leaving friends and a hope that all would be well for us in the Caribbean.

As the *Fitzroy* pulled away from the jetty at Stanley, there were so many there to wave their farewells to relatives and friends. It was ever thus whenever and wherever long distance ships and trains depart. It was March 25, 1951, and we were soon through the Narrows and in to Port William. Stanley was out of sight as we headed for Cape Pembroke before turning northward for Montevideo. We had a good passage which took us four or five days. Accommodation was already booked for me in Montevideo and air passage was reserved for the flight to Trinidad and thence to Grenada.

I boarded a Clipper airliner of the Pan American World Airways and our first scheduled stop was Porto Alegre in Brazil, then to San Paulo, both brief stops and after dark we were over Rio de Janeiro and circling for some time before landing. The view at our height of all the city lights was quite breathtaking. There was an electric storm in progress too for we then had a display of lightning both above us and below us. As we descended gradually, we could see the city lights in greater detail and then we were flying at a lower level than the lights on the hills and on the statue of Christ on Corcavado Mountain. It almost seemed a pity to be landing.

I was glad to be on our way again though and we had a long run this time to Belem just south of the Equator and the Amazon delta proper — some 1800 miles from Rio. Having left Belem we were soon across the Equator and we were given special cards and certificates signed by the Clipper's Captain indicating we had crossed the Equator on April 2nd, 1951. No rough stuff airborne as when we were seaborne. Hours of flying over seemingly endless rain forests were not so boring for I looked for and very occasionally spotted clearings where there were some signs of human activity.

This flight to Trinidad and beyond too, I presumed, was called the Milk Run for the number of stops we were making and now in French Guiana, Dutch Guiana (the name Surinam was then coming into use) and British Guiana (now Guyana) with its airport, Atkinson Field, some twenty miles up the Demerara River from Georgetown. This was one of a number of bases handed over to the U.S.A. in return for the fifty old destroyers we had so badly needed to help us in the Battle of the Atlantic convoys. From this base U.S. aircraft then had been flown across the Atlantic to Africa to continue their fight against our common enemy in Word War II so recently concluded.

From Atkinson Field it was but a short flight of some 350 miles to Trinidad's Piarco airfield on 2nd April. We had a good view of the limit of the muddy Orinoco and Amazon waters carried so far offshore into the Atlantic and I was all eyes, of course, to have my first view of a West Indian island. Here I was to leave the DC6 Clipper and fly to Grenada. After the 4,000 plus miles from Montevideo, the 90 miles from Piarco to Grenada would be but a short flight indeed. I wondered what the situation was in Grenada now. I had had no real detail of the troubles since I was asked to postpone my leave and that was some time ago so all sorts of things may have happened since then.

In 1951, Grenada was a colony administered by an Administrator, assisted by an Executive Council consisting of the Administrator, the Attorney General, the Colonial Treasurer as 'ex-officio' members and such other persons as may be appointed with the approval of the Secretary of State for the Colonies. It was one of four colonies in the Windward Islands (the others being St. Vincent, St. Lucia and Dominica) at that

165

time. The Governor of the Windward Islands presided at meetings of the Executive Council when present in the colony (he had his seat at Government House in Grenada). Then there was the Legislative Council consisting of the Governor who was President (with a casting vote only) the Administrator (with an original and a casting vote when the Governor was not present). The Attorney General, the Colonial Treasurer, four nominated members and seven elected members.

The Windward Islands are the southern half of the group known as the Lesser Antilles and lie north of Trinidad and Tobago (as that territory is known today). In sequence northward, they are Grenada, St. Vincent, St. Lucia and Dominica. (Martinique, a French territory lies between St. Lucia and Dominica).

Grenada is 90 miles north of Trinidad and 70 miles south of St. Vincent. The chain of smaller islands between Grenada and St. Vincent are the Grenadines. The colony of Grenada included the islands of Carriacou and Petit Martinique and several other smaller ones. North of Petit Martinique, the other islands and islets of the Grenadines were part of the colony of St. Vincent.

The island of Grenada is 21 miles long and its greatest width is 12 miles. Irregular oblong shaped north to south and wider in the southern half, it has an area of about 120 square miles and Carriacou is about 13 square miles. It has been described, structurally, as an eroded volcanic pile. With its somewhat disordered mix of mountains and steep sided valleys, the island is remarkably beautiful whether viewed from the sea, the air or the land. Mount St. Catherine at nearly 2,800 ft. and Mount Sinai at 2,300 ft. are the highest points. Generally, the mountains slope eastward and gradually towards the sea but on the whole of the west coast, the mountains run right down to the sea. Every valley is well watered except in the extreme south of the island where the rainfall is much lower than elsewhere. The rainfall does vary considerably according to locality and from about 30 inches a year in the extreme southwest to 200 inches in the mountainous interior. On Carriacou the average is about 50 inches.

166

The climate is good and when the north east trade winds prevail during December to April it is delightful. There is a wet season and a dry season. The dry season lasts from January to May. The temperature in December and January is most pleasant and dropping to 65°F even in the lower lands at night. In the wet season, it is hotter and rather oppressive because of the humidity but never unbearably so. Despite being in the low latitudes of the Tropics, Grenada almost invariably escapes the hurricanes which usually start up even a little further south and east in the Atlantic, for by the time they are as westerly as Grenada, they have already passed well to the north of the island. (An exception in recent years was Huricane 'Janet' in 1955 which wreaked considerable havoc and caused heavy loss of life along its path. In Grenada in particular the losses in plantations of cocoa and nutmeg were very serious — nutmeg trees for instance grow to over 'fifty feet in height but not quickly like sugar cane or bananas. Grenada produced about one third of the world's annual crop of nutmeg and, of course, its mace).

Evidence of the volcanic activities in the distant past is to be seen everywhere. St. George's, the capital, is built around the inner sides of an old crater which is now the harbour. A branch of the harbour called the Lagoon was said to have shown some signs of volcanic activity in 1902 when the Mount Pelee volcano erupted on Martinique and again in 1929.

While my concern was going to be the people, and very much so, I needed to learn all I could, quickly, about Grenada past and present. It is probably true to say that Christopher Columbus was the first European to 'find' Grenada. It was certainly known to people of other races who inhabited the place at various times many centuries before 1498 when Columbus came there. There are still some traces of very primitive people but more is known of the more recent Arawaks and the people who ousted them and who were called Caribs by the Europeans who came to the New World. The Caribs also occupied the other islands in this area which was then called the Caribees. Nowadays it is called the Caribbean.

About the middle of the 17th Century, Grenada's Caribs

167

were eliminated entirely but a few survived on other islands in the group. The last of Grenada's Caribs, rather than give in to the French settlers by whom they were being attacked on the island at that time, committed suicide by leaping into the rocky sea from a cliff top on the north coast of the island. The spot known as 'Le Morne des Sauteurs' is also known now as Leapers' Hill and the small town at that place today is named Sauteurs.

The island was 'owned' privately by a number of French people after a much earlier attempt by some British merchantmen to settle there had failed. It became French crown property in 1674 but was conquered by the British in 1762. It was lost to the French though in 1779 but restored to the British in 1783 when it was ceded to us by the Treaty of Versailles. The French influence remained though and after the French Revolution in 1789, there was more trouble in the islands and Grenada had to deal with a very serious rebellion.

Wilberforce's efforts to abolish the slave trade in the British Empire succeeded with the passing of the Act in 1807, but slavery was eventually abolished in British Colonies by the Act of 1833, the year William Wilberforce died. This brought an end to many problems but brought others in its wake. In Grenada, many former slaves chose not to continue working on the estates, so other labour had to be imported. Labourers were brought from Malta, then came Portugese from Madeira and, soon after, even other liberated slaves from Africa. In the late 1850s, East Indian imigration commenced. So the population was changing and I was to find a most interesting mix of peoples. Some of this detail was not available to me during the time I was awaiting the day I would actually arrive in Grenada but I was very aware indeed that I was soon to see and experience much that was going to be very strange to me.

The colony of Barbados had been British without interruption after the arrival of the first batch of some 80 English settlers about 1627. I only mention Barbados to explain the arrival of a number of the descendants of those settlers in Grenada. The economies of most of the territories in the West Indies had been considerably affected when slavery was abolished in the early 19th century and, unusually, there was this English labour force in Barbados who had become to some extent redundant. Many of these were thus brought to a number of other Caribbean islands to better fend for themselves and Grenada had its quota. They came to be called 'the poor whites' but keeping themselves much to themselves, in Grenada, they all settled within a small area and were noted for their industry. They were very hard-working and self supporting small farmers and planters. (It is only in this last quarter of the 20th century that they have 'emerged' when a number of the younger folk emigrated and the others have now become absorbed into the general Grenadian community.)

The Colony's exports were limited entirely to agricultural products; its few industries manufactured nothing for export. While much food for local consumption was produced, it often fell short of the minimum requirements. Estate agriculture was responsible for the major portion of exportable crops but peasant agriculture was of considerable importance. Hand cultivation was practised almost exclusively, for all crops, as the topography of the island made any extensive use of machinery impracticable and especially in the case of tree crops.

The principal export crops were cocoa, nutmeg and mace, raw cotton, copra and lime oil. Some banana production was exported before the War but lack of transport facilities stopped it completely during the War. My first purchase of bananas in Grenada was one whole stem which naturally filled the boot of my car. I had seen none in the Falkland Islands! I paid 2/6d (12½p) for the stem.

All manner of spices are obtainable in Grenada, including allspice, saffron and cloves and cinnamon. The island is known for this reason as 'The Isle of Spice'. (The reintroduction of banana production on a large scale after Hurricane 'Janet' aided the economy considerably). Sugar production and rum was not enough to meet local requirements.

There must have been a surplus of labour available for many years and this probably contributed to a long period of trouble

169

free labour relations in the colony. Grenadians had been going almost everywhere in the West Indies in search of work. Some came back home and found conditions unsatisfactory and suddenly, strikes, which had been an almost unheard of thing in Grenada were being encouraged and in February 1951 serious disorders broke out as a result of widespread strikes on the sugar estates. There was intimidation and incitement to violence, burning of buildings and destruction of crops. The stupidity of burning the people's own schools and sick dispensaries, for instance, never seemed to occur to those committing such crimes.

Police reinforcements had to be obtained from St. Lucia, Barbados and Trinidad. In one instance two of the Trinidad police officers were members of a party of sixteen police sent to deal with a riotous mob of about four hundred people. There was much violent behaviour and tear gas used in an attempt to disperse the mob. A number of police were hit and injured and, at least, in self defence, some of the police opened fire, killing three people and wounding others. These police reinforcements had returned to their own forces by the time I flew in to Grenada.

The total population in 1951 was probably in the region of 82,000 (nearly 90,000 by 1960 census).

The island was divided into six parishes with the island of Carriacou as an equivalent seventh. There was a familiar ring to parish names for they were St. George's, which included the capital St. George's, St. John's, St. Mark's, St. Patrick's, St. Andrews and St. David's, and in that order clockwise with St. George's at the southwest. The population of St. George's would have been about 7,000. The as yet unfamiliar to me place names were very often French.

When making his 'Observations on the Office of Constable', in 1754, Saunders Welch wrote — 'It is a glorious opportunity of doing all possible good : to secure and protect the innocent from the hands of violence : to preserve the public peace to the utmost of your power, and to bring disturbers of it to condign punishment. This is briefly your duty.'

Members of the Grenada Police Force, in 1951, like others

before them, had been prepared to accept all such responsibilities and they had now to face up to very difficult times. There were under two hundred police to ensure the preservation of peace and good order for over 80,000 people.

There were twelve police stations around the Colony including one at Carriacou. All were connected to headquarters by telephone and all on Grenada were accessible by good motor roads. Headquarters depot and barracks are housed in Fort George, situated high above the town and harbour, with its massive old guns on the battlements still. Entry to the fort was by tunnel through the massive basement wall. Its open parade ground, within the protective walls, and the barrack buildings was all very much what I think a French Foreign Legion fort looked like.

The police headquarters offices and fire brigade station were almost immediately outside the walls. The brigade was manned and operated by the police with the Chief of Police also being Chief Fire Officer.

The Registration and Licensing of motor vehicles was also a police responsibility, as was immigration.

There were nearly 500 miles of motorable roads. A first class road ran entirely round the island as well as across it but hardly any of it to our 'A' class road standard and weight limits were very restricted.

For many years, the Grenada police, like so many other colonial police forces, had been a semi-military force and the only armed service immediately available in defence of the territory. Recruit training had always been on military lines and discipline likewise. It seemed strange seeing constables wearing good conduct stripes on their uniformed forearms. Apart from the small cannon we used for saluting purposes, only small arms were available and training in the handling, care and use of rifles came with the recruit drilling and police training. .303 rifles were available at each police station.

Military rank titles were gradually changing. The rank of sergeant major had given way to inspector but corporals and lance corporals remained at that time as did the rankings of gazetted officers.

171

All gazetted officers were members of the Unified Colonial Police and membership was controlled by the then Secretary of State for the Colonies. It was automatically conferred upon officers recruited by him and, if recommended by the Governors, officers recruited or promoted in the Colonies. The standardised rankings then ranged from Assistant Superintendent to Commissioner. The title of the Chief Police Officer had been varied from time to time but had now come to be Superintendent in the smaller forces and Commissioner in the larger forces.

It was time to leave Trinidad and on 4th April I was one of a small number of passengers, but a full load on a British West Indian Airways Viking aircraft for the comparatively short flight to Grenada. I seat-belted in some small coloured children. Did I put two in the same belt? I am not sure but I am looking at a picture of the aircraft and the children disembarking, as I write. The only airfield in Grenada in 1951 was that one at Pearls on the north east coast, north of Grenville. (082/262 4000 + 1200 x 50).

There was a formality of Customs and Immigration and then the drive in police transport across the island to St. George's. I was met by Brigadier P. J. T. Pickthall M.C. acting as Chief of Police and a situation report was reserved till later while I rather underwent the experience of the drive over the mountain ridges for some fourteen miles The road was narrow, very steep at times and very twisty. As we passed close to Grand Etang, a deep, dark and forbidding looking crater lake, we were nearly 1,800 feet above sea level and soon after we were almost 2,000 feet and the view then is outstandingly beautiful. It was quite something for me to see trees, trees and more trees too after Falklands' wide open spaces.

The St. James Hotel was only a little below the level of the Police Headquarters and nearby. My room had a lovely open view over St. George's, the harbour and the coastline to the south. It would take a little time to become acclimatised again to a tropic existence but the Hong Kong interlude would help in this although that now seemed two life times away. Finding myself being boarded in a hotel, with its variety of diet and after my recent months of lonely existence and where choice of food was limited, both by availabilities and my culinary inabilities, was quite something too and I wondered how long this would last and how long it would be before I was back again with my family in Wales.

Meanwhile, I was concentrating on digesting the up dated situation report. The Governor of the Windward Islands (Brigadier Sir Robert Arundell, K.C.M.G., O.B.E.) in residence in Grenada, had had the major problems in the maintenance of law and order after the eruption of those recent disorders but his political problems had been changing for some time too. He had informed the Legislative Council back in 1949, that certain constitutional changes had been approved by the Imperial Government but would not take effect until September, 1951. These would be wide ranging but to control the new powers to be given to the new elected majority of the Council, the Governor would be allowed to retain his powers 'in the interest of good government and public order' and among other things he would be able to pass any bill that the legislature rejected or to refuse his assent for bills passed by the legislature.

The disorders occurred early in 1951, however, before the proposed constitutional changes were to be effected. The name I had heard, of course, was Eric Gairy. His influence on Grenada was to be felt for many years to come. He had been a Grenadian school teacher before joining the ranks of those seeking work and better living conditions overseas and had himself worked in Aruba in the Netherland Antilles. He was one who returned and tried to improve conditions of the poorer workers.

After an ever increasing number of lesser strikes and despite appeals against it, a general strike had been called for 19th February, 1951. The Governor was away at that time. The Acting Governor had that same day arranged for police reinforcements to come from St. Lucia and asked that an experienced police officer should come from the Trinidad force. H.M.S. *Devonshire* came to Grenada too. Then, three days later, on 22nd February, a State of Emergency had been declared. Gairy was at once detained, at first on H.M.S. *Devonshire,* then on Carriacou. As the situation had then so

173

deteriorated, the Governor hurried back and arrived on 5th March. He had at once convened a meeting of the Executive Council. It was decided to end the State of Emergency and to release both Gairy and another detained trade union leader. There were many who thought this was a mistake but upon his release, Gairy had assured the Governor that the violence which was mainly due to his arrest and detention would cease. For the next two or three weeks Gairy had addressed many meetings and called for peace. Gradually then things had improved. The strike was concluded on 19th March.

It would seem that there had been too much reaction in the early stages of the troubles and this had to some extent precipitated rather than prevented more serious disorder. There were criticisms too of the way in which the police had been used. They had been ordered to concentrate on St. George's so that the country stations were left with insufficient staffs to cope with all the disorder which was island wide. There had been a breakdown in the police communications network and the public had difficulty in calling for police help when it was needed. This was rectified later when new arangements were made.

The post of Superintendent of Police was vacated during the trouble and Brigadier Pickthall, a retired army officer with police experience with the military administration, in Abyssinia, after its release from Italian occupation, and, who staying in Barbados had taken over command of the force on a temporary basis. I was brought as his deputy directly from the Falklands. I was anxious too to fit myself into the scene as quickly as possible and was soon involved in a revision of the administrative arrangements at headquarters as these too were urgently necessary.

On the labour scene, all seemed peaceful enough with all back at work but Eric Gairy continued to call public meetings in all areas. The bigger crowds naturally would assemble in St. George's, on the Market Square. They were held in the evenings when the day's work was done.

I was aware that dusk in the tropics was very brief and throughout the year, the evenings were dark. Lighting up time was at 6 p.m. for six months of the year and at 6.30 p.m. for the other six months. This was one thing I disliked about the tropics. I did miss the long light summer evenings outdoors and the opposite in winter as at home when one would be encouraged to follow indoor pursuits. But I did look forward to sunset with its usually appreciable relief after the heat of the day. We were all early risers and parades would almost always be arranged for the early part of a morning before the sun was too high.

I soon attended at a Market Square meeting and saw Gairy make his appearance. He wore a special suit-like 'tails' with a long red lined black cloak. He carried a Bible under his arm and a white stick. I had quite a shock when he just said, 'Good Night', until I realised he meant this as our 'Good Evening', and of course he at once began to address the gathering. It may have been at another of his meetings that I heard him declare what he and God were going to do for the people. There was no mistaking his hold over the crowd.

The economic and social conditions of the masses in Grenada had been really below acceptable standards for years but it had taken someone with Gairy's qualities to become their voice to demand real improvements. The pity of it all has been that in the following years, his own principles were not up to a standard the people were entitled to expect, although he acquired sufficient power that could have ensured an ever improving future for all Grenadians. He became their first Chief Minister and their first Prime Minister under changing Constitutions.

Conditions seemingly could get worse and worse, and they did although I remember watching years later on television, one of the Miss World contests when Sir Eric Gairy in London was one of the judges. The winner was a very beautiful Grenadian girl and a worthy one too. Then some years later, President Reagan with U.S. power and aided and abetted by some other Caribbean territories, invaded Grenada and took power from those who by force had overpowered Sir Eric Gairy and had themselves abused it. After years of suffering, Grenadians, happily, can now continue under their own steam

175

again with ever improving prospects. Grenada in 1992 continues to be a happy island and an improving tourist attraction. Diana and her husband have visited twice and have been able to tell me so much about it all and show me so many photographs of Grenada today to compare with my own collection and remind us of my stay there forty years ago.

I need not then dwell at length on the political problems of Grenada in my time but I will continue with my story. To help with the crisis of the February-March strike, the Legislature passed four what could be called 'anti-subversive' ordinances, one to deal with public order, another amending Criminal Procedure Ordinance, the third to cover arbitration in Public Utility Undertakings and Public Health Services and the fourth, the Sedition Ordinance. The aim of these ordinances was not only to protect the interests of the employers but to limit the workers' struggle by fettering the leadership of the Trade Union Movement. Gairy had fiercely attacked these new laws time and time again and continued doing so after his release. It was admitted that he had established a remarkable ascendancy over the working class who tended to see him as a heaven sent leader.

At one of the meetings soon after my arrival, Gairy said that if he was sent to prison under the Sedition Ordinance he would look for the graves of those members of the Legislative Council who had passed this law. I felt that the sooner Gairy was brought before the Courts to show him and the people, that he, like all others, was still not above the law, the better it would be for everybody. A small party of St. Lucia police were brought to be available to help in case of need on the day Gairy was to appear at the Magistrate's Court. He had invited the workers to come to St. George's for the occasion. Evidence of the threats was given by the police. Gairy was bound over to keep the peace and all passed peacefully.

After a brief stay at the St. James Hotel, I moved to the Grand Hotel, originally one of Grenada's very beautiful homes, on the outskirts of the town. One of the Slinger family had been the driving spirit behind the erection of Grenada's first 'luxury' hotel to woo tourists in the post war years. He named it 'Santa Maria del Concepcion', the original name given to the island by Columbus. This was situated in a very commanding position overlooking the harbour and the town on the far side and with wonderful views of the surrounding hills and coastline. Dudley Slinger then converted his beautiful old family home into the Grand Hotel to take the overspill from the Santa Maria. I spent some very happy weeks at the Grand. There had been a lack of good live music in the Falklands but here were Dudley Slinger and his wife, each at a grand piano. So then and later we were able to share in some very enjoyable musical evenings. There was good food too but I confess that it was long afterwards that I discovered that 'orange sweet potato' on the menu really meant 'sweet potato with orange flavour juice added to it' ! !

At police headquarters I soon settled in with a staff, all of whom were, naturally, coloured Grenadians as were all members of the force below the rank of Assistant Superintendent. This was quite new to me, although as a boy in the Royal Air Force, I had met, as it were, our station Sergeant Major who was a coloured Jamaican. We held him in the greatest respect — he was a Warrant Officer First Class in rank and in all things first class. So many of us, it seemed to me at that time, knew so little about West Indians or even about the West Indies. I was to find that they were taught far more about Britain than we were ever taught about the Caribbean. Their forbears had relinquished their own African names after the abolition of slavery and had taken European names, sometimes, but not always, associated with their employers. Typical surnames among some of the staff were Nedd, Redhead, Quarless, Francis, Joseph, and Romain and Pierre. By today, we are all more familiar with West Indians in every regard. In the midfifties, we in Britain, were sending teams to the West Indies to recruit labour which was then in short supply here to meet the post war growth and development requirements. When I did arrive back in Wales for my leave, I couldn't think of any of the staff in the context of colour at all, for I could see only the individual, which is as it should be.

I was anxious to see my family again and to bring them

back with me to share in all these new experiences. Brigadier Pickthall too wished to be relieved and Colonel James, a member of the former Palestine Police Force which had ceased to be in 1948, was transferred temporarily in his place. A passage was booked for me on the S.S. *Planter,* a Harrison Line cargo ship. I must have been the only passenger for I have never remembered that there were others. All my visits ashore, in St. Lucia, Martinique and Barbados, I made with members of the crew. We left Grenada on the 21st June, just ten weeks after I had arived there. So much had happened, I was glad to have some time to myself to let things sink in. I was still seeing so much that was new. I sea-bathed in St. Lucia and had a brief meeting with police and a trip on a sugar estate's train and heard of some of the things that had befallen Castries, the capital of St. Lucia during the war years and of the recent devastating fire in Castries. The views of the Pitons seemed unreal. Then there was the Frenchness of Martinique and some detail of the Mt. Pelee disaster when that volcano erupted in 1902, wiping out the town of St. Pierre and all but two of its inhabitants which had numbered some 30,000. Stops in St. Vincent and Dominica (pronounced Domineeca unlike as in Dominican Republic) were brief and I did not go ashore. There was so much that was English in Barbados, at least in Bridgetown, the capital, and it was all so different to the treeclad mountain like Windward Islands. Leaving all the islands behind I felt that I was, at long last, on my way home. We passed through the Azores and I had a good look at Flores. The next land would be home ground and in a few days I saw the first signs of that umbrella of cloud cover that seems to remain in our latitudes whatever the season.

It had been a long time since I sailed with my wife and two daughters from Tilbury and now I was back up the Thames again, this time to the West India Docks to be met by other relatives. I remember the drive down to Dolgellau to join my wife and three daughters with a brother-in-law at the wheel and was almost fearful as we sped up the A5, for mile after mile, at not less than about 50 mph. The Grenada speed limit was 20 and for three years in the Falklands, where I rarely rode in a car, such roads for speeding along were few.

My 180 days Falklands leave plus the few earned in Grenada, began the day I disembarked from the *Planter*. Our own reunion and our reunions with family and friends were wonderful. We attended the 1951 Welsh National Eisteddfod at Llanrwst. There is a very touching welcome by the vast crowd at a set time and day, for all those Welsh people who are at the Eisteddfod but who live and work overseas. They are welcomed by country, in alphabetical order and asked to stand to be seen by all on the vast stage to which they have all been gathered. It is interesting to see where they have all come from. Sometimes solitary individuals from some remote spot and then scores from the U.S.A. for instance. They are called *Y Cymry ar Wasgar* — the Welsh in Dispersion — There'll be a welcome when you come home again to Wales! So the days flew by although we were so looking forward to setting up a new home in Grenada.

To temper our joy, however, we were suddenly faced with a cloud of worry. Sarah, now a two year old, was found to be one of those, in a score of so of girls, who develop some degree of scoliosis, a lateral curvature of the spine. This was not apparent to us. We were told there was nothing that could be done for her at that time so we should carry on with our arrangements to go abroad but we should send them X-Ray pictures every six months and let them see her again at the hospital at Gobowen, near Oswestry when we came home in three years time.

The months indeed flew by and even Christmas came and went. There was now another hiccup and I was recalled and asked to fly out at once. My family would have to travel on their own again. The only relief was that hopefully I would be able to prepare well for their arrival. I flew away in mid-January and they left by sea, to Trinidad, soon afterwards, to arrive in Grenada by air five weeks after my departure.

I flew in a BOAC Constellation on 14th January, 1952, as far as Lisbon where we were served dinner and then on to the Azores, for a late supper in Santa Maria. From a postcard I

179

wrote to Rowena, I see I had a fairly good sleep on the aircraft and breakfast during the ten hours since leaving Santa Maria but with still an hour or so flying before landing in Bermuda after mid-day on 15th January. It was on then to the Bahamas for another brief stop on our way to Jamaica. We were driven to a hotel in Kingston to stay overnight, then flew to Caracas in Venezelua for a last short stop before Trinidad. Here too I had to stay the night of 16th January before continuing the next day to Grenada, as before, in a British West Indies Airways Viking.

Grenada was still peaceful and my recall was purely for administrative reasons. Brigadier Pickthall was back in charge and Lt. Col. James was in St. Lucia. As a former 'civil' police officer, I found it strange to be gazetted a Major and to be so styled. Full dress uniform now included spurs and a sword and so it behove me to learn my sword drill and prepare myself to take charge of ceremonial and other parades. My full dress uniform had not been available before I had gone on leave so I was not able to appear on a special parade during that time but undertook the supervision of the firing of a royal salute. A number of small cannons, unmounted and each weighing about 100 lbs. were laid out on a small grassed area up at the Fort. Well out of sight of the Market Square, I would be out of sight of the parade held there but within hearing of the band. I had to decide on the precise moment I should give the order to fire the first round so that it could be heard immediately, at the Market Square, after they heard the last note of the band's music. There was no question of measuring the distance involved but I had to allow for the fact that the last sound of the band would reach me appreciably later than it would be heard on the parade, that there would be a slight delay before the first cannon actually sounded following my command to fire and the delay before that sound reached the Parade. I estimated I should allow some five seconds in all and as I hummed the National Anthem with the band, I called out 'Fire', as I was about to hum the second 'God Save'. Brigadier Pickthall, an artillery man, told me the first cannon was heard precisely at the right moment and wondered how

180

on earth I had managed it. Beginner's luck I thought. I was very gratified at another parade when I took it myself and made a special point of giving the commands clearly and not in just a loud noise, as one so often hears and to which I had always felt like objecting. A senior civil servant had said it was the first parade he had attended at which he had heard what the commands were. I was trying to be an efficient beginner.

Arrangements were already well in hand to train an auxiliary police reserve — some 200 men were enrolled to form the Grenada Volunteer Constabulary and soon after my return from leave they were brought in from the country areas to have a full time military training, on a fortnight's course, encamped in school buildings at Tanteen, St. George's. Each of the two courses consisted of 100 men plus their officers and instructors. I relived some of my own pre-War RAF days and for the passing out parade thought it would be good for all if some of the drills performed consisted of short sequences of non-command movements. (I had witnessed some RAF trainees at Aberystwyth during the War performing some of these exercises without command daily on the promenade. In 1992 special displays are given by an RAF team when about a thousand movements are carried out without command, once the begin command has been given.) The Governor of the Windward Islands attended to take the salute. The parade was also witnessed by Admiral Fullerton in May 1952.

Before I had gone on leave, we had a detachment of the Royal Welch Fusiliers as a standby force in aid of the civil police, for a short period. Before they returned to Jamaica they attended a large general ceremonial parade on the Market Square but as I was still without my full dress uniform, I did not take part in the actual parade.

All these exercises had helped to restore a state of normality again to the shocked Colony. Only a very few monhts later, some friends who had returned to New York wrote to say that they wished they were still in Grenada's peace and safety rather than in the jungle of their own crime-infested Central Park. We had about that time a case where a tourist walking in the harbour area had her handbag snatched. It had shocked us.

These days, in New York, it seems they tell you not to look up at the skyscrapers for it will be known by all that you are a tourist or visitor ripe for the picking.

Our new home was a bungalow on an elevated site on the ridge dividing the town into two areas — the harbour area and the market square shopping area. This ridge runs to the point on which the Fort is built and the bungalow was right across the road from the entrance to our police headquarters offices and just beyond us was the fire station and beyond that the hospital.

Falmai and the girls flew in from Trinidad on the 23rd February — just five weeks after me. In many ways it was of great help that I had been here before and now again before they arrived.

Our 'cook' was a woman of some years and was most helpful especially in introducing us to many West Indian dishes and practices. Much use was made of charcoal for cooking and it was there, of course that we needed and acquired our first refrigerator and, oh yes, our cook would not open its door until she had first put her cap on. An inspector at the CID office, incidentally, told me, one day, when we were discussing climate and local weather, that he always wore a woollen vest and thereby never took a chill after perspiring. He was the only one I heard to do this though. I was myself to find later that it was more comfortable on hotter days to wear a vest but to be without one on less hot days.

Our new home was ideally situated to ensure we caught any and every cooling breeze and we had the most wonderful view of both halves of the town and the sea and surrounding hills. A short distance further back along our ridge was a road junction from where it was a bit of a climb in our direction and a rise in the other direction and where the main street from one side of town rose up to cross our road and descend steeply to the other half. A level road also connected each half by means of the Sendall Tunnel. It was wide enough for one vehicle only to pass along its 70 yard length and there was a height limit too for it was only about 12 feet high at the top centre of the arched roof. There were inverted 'sleeping

182

policemen' at each end to ensure traffic was virtually stopped before entering. If another vehicle was visible at the other approach, it was pointless to proceed until it had passed through. The tunnel had been built about 1895. It passed directly beneath our house and we could actually see one end of the approach road.

A few yards down the road from our house, we had the Presbyterian Church, St. Andrew's Kirk, popularly known as the Scots' Kirk. Further along, beyong the junction there was the Anglican Church and beyond that a Methodist Church and the Roman Catholic Church and Presentation College. Well over half of the population were Catholics in consequence of the earlier French influence in Grenada. The annual Corpus Cristi procession to the Market Square with all it involved there was very impressive. We worshipped at the Scots' Kirk.

I was less involved in the detail of routine police work, in Grenada, than I had been in my previous police appointments but there were occasions when I would take particular interest in some case. I remember a murder case. A young woman on her way home one evening, had been attacked and her body had been found only a few yards off the road in some bushes. Her torch was found nearby but in two parts. The top, holding the glass cover, had become separated from the main body of the torch, still with its batteries and bulb in place. A finger print was found on the main part, which would have been covered by the top when in place. It looked as if the torch had been in her hand and probably alight when she was attacked and that in the struggle, the torch had been grabbed by the assailant, leaving a print on the part still held in her hand when the top came off. The print matched that of the suspected person. Our finger print man at the CID had easily found the minimum of sixteen comparable points on the part thumb print found on the torch. The judge, unusually, had required the detective to mark up the points on a clear photograph, in the Court, when giving evidence, rather than allowing him to produce a copy of his work as a court exhibit. This was all done. Defence Counsel persisted with his cross examination to such an extent that the poor jury were too confused

183

and returned a not guilty verdict. So I was continuing to find juries unsatisfactory.

We found Grand Anse Beach and its Aquatic Club an ideal place to relax. After my new car, a Triumph Mayflower, arrived, we named her Blodwen, and we had many enjoyable trips finding our way around the island. I felt that the 20 mph speed limit very limiting and I was prone to test the car regularly on a run down to Grand Anse at a higher speed, so that I was sure, if duty called for it, I too could travel at more than 20! During my earlier visits to the beach, I felt very envious when I saw swimmers returning from far out to sea, with beautiful pieces of coral tucked into the edges of their swimming gear. I was told of the lovely reef about 500 yards offshore and that it was almost exposed at low tides. It paralleled the beach until at the north end of Grand Anse it was much nearer the shore. I had never swum such a long distance and had done none at all in the Falkland Islands. The water temperature was now so comfortable that there was never a need to rush a swim and so, in short time, with rests on my back on the way, I found that I too could reach the coral reef and enjoy the sights under water. There were about four fathoms of water between reef and shore at the Aquatic Club end but the water was perfectly clear and the swim out and back a joy.

I found there were no qualified Life Savers in the police. I had qualified for the Bronze Medallion of the Royal Life Saving Society when in the police at Aberystwyth some twenty years earlier and decided to train a bunch of the lads who were prepared to be taught. Brigadier Pickthall backed me and produced a qualified examiner of the Society to test us in fairly quick time. I think there were about twenty constables who qualified for the Bronze Medallion. I was also tested and qualified for the Award of Merit (and later given an examiner's badge for tests to this standard). I found the long swim, I think it was 600 yards, fully clothed was quite strenuous. I also taught the lads the then current method of applying artificial respiration — I think it was Schafer's then.

By this time, Eric Gairy was, shall I say, reasonably well

behaved and I was able to persuade him to come to speak to a gathering of taxi drivers I arranged to be available, in the interests of road safety. Traffic, after the Falklands, was very heavy but the total of motor transport registered, was not in excess of some fifteen hundred vehicles. There were though only three cars to one taxi. With an even lower proportion of cars in the rural areas, taxi drivers were in fierce competition with buses — the smaller ones called jitneys — and driving standards were poor.

My first visit to the Santa Maria Hotel was with the Slingers of the Grand Hotel, before I went on leave. There I met a Cardiff man and felt a bit nearer to Wales. He was what we called a commercial traveller, a representative and was based in Rio de Janeiro and had been married there by our Lampeter-born Ivor Evans, Bishop of the Falklands and South America, south of the Amazon. I had found that the Director of Education was a 'Radio Ham' and he had been in 'touch' recently with someone on Pebble Island in the Falklands — so I really was in the same world, after all, I thought, and getting settled in.

My wife and I, with friends foregathered at the Santa Maria for some very pleasurable musical evenings and with the Slingers, during the hotel's off season. The only visitor of some note I saw there at that time was the film actor John Wayne.

There were too the usual social occasions such as parties at Government House. I am just remembering a ceremonial parade of which I was in charge, when our daughter Diana, with a group of Girl Guides, was also under my command.

Our rifle range was situated at the far end of Queen's Park, on the outskirts of the capital. Lady Arundell, the wife of the Governor came with us once and proved herself to be a first class shot with a .303 Lee Enfield rifle. Brigadier Pickthall and I strove to shoot well too! The Queen's Park was large enough to accommodate some horse racing occasionally and sports days and such like of the various schools and colleges.

Grenada's best cricket ground was also at Queen's Park and as was the case at so many cricket pitches in the West Indies then, the wicket was laid on special matting. There were other pitches too in St. George's. It was at one of these when I was on my first walk around that I stopped to watch my first cricket match in the West Indies. A police team was playing and they were down to the last man in but still needing a lot of runs. It was a long time since I had watched any cricket and longer since I had played. This was worth watching, so I stayed on and on, as the runs mounted. One of them to my great surprise reached his century of runs. It was the first of many centuries though that I was to see scored in the West Indies. I was told of another cricket pitch in St. George's which used to be called 'Old Trafford' where, without matting, the wicket was on a strip of rolled marl which soon deteriorated. The West Indies team had apparently been defeated in Manchester on just such a breaking wicket and this was so remembered in Grenada that this particular one was named 'Old Trafford'. I was told too that many a good batsman was made at 'Old Trafford'.

Carriacou. The day came for me to visit Carriacou with its one police station. This is the largest island in the Grenadines chain, between Grenada and St. Vincent. It lies about 22 miles north of Grenada. I travelled there in one of the schooners operating a regular service for the transport of goods and passengers between St. George's and Hillsborough, Carriacou's main port of entry. Of the islands population of about 7,000, only about 600 live in Hillsborough. The trip along the west coast of Grenada from St. George's was comfortable, sea-wise and interesting. The passage then to Carriacou was not so comfortable, especially as we crossed the channels where eastward currents met westward currents. A notoriously bad spot for this was near Diamond Islet which is commonly known as 'Kick 'em Jenny'. The stern area of our schooner was a convenient spot for some of our not-so-well fellow travellers. The open deck was in use to hold the varied collection of passengers and all manner of goods with even a motor car tied across the deck. A couple of our detectives were also travelling.

Unexpectedly I found there were over 80 miles of roads on the island. These had been built when the French were in occupation and were part of their defence arrangements. The old military fortifications had mostly disappeared. One fort overlooking Hillsborough had been turned into a waterworks but its cannons were now sited on Hospital Hill where the present hospital had been built a few miles north of Hillsborough. The view from here was breathtaking.

The British had taken possession of the island by the 1750s and by the late 1700s, cotton was the principal export and coffee, cocoa and indigo were also grown. Early in the 19th century, a group of shipwrights arrived from Glasgow to build vessels for the planters, to transport the island's produce. Their descendants still practise their trade and many of the fishing boats and inter-island schooners are built there. They use white cedar for the vessels but the keels are made of dogwood, a timber peculiar to Carriacou and which is not found in Grenada. Many Mac names like Macdonald and Macfarlane are still to be found and they are all proud of their Scottish ancestry.

Back in Grenada, I was soon involved in mainly administrative matters. We were about to have a new fire station built at the waterfront on the Carenage and it was our last chance to review the plans and have any improvements incorporated. Up to this time I had only been able to give limited attention to our fire service. Fortunately the demands on the brigade had been minimal for some time but with considerable fire risks especially in the congested area near the waterfront and indeed in the main shopping area of the town, it was essential that our 'Be Prepared' policy should be maintained.

It was now August 1952 and I was offered promotion to take charge of the police force (and fire brigade) of the Colony of St. Vincent. As I had only returned from leave in January, this meant another major upheaval for the family almost before we had settled in properly in Grenada. We had to start our farewells almost immediately. I was very touched by the warmth of feelings expressed by members of the force. I felt I would be leaving lots of friends behind.

Almost on the eve of our departure, my wife and I were expected at a farewell party with friends at the Santa Maria Hotel. Before we could attend there, however, we were having a farewell dinner with Brigadier and Mrs. Pickthall at their

187

home and where H.E. The Governor and Lady Arundell were also guests. It was at quite a late hour the Governor departed for Government House thus permitting us to have ourselves excused to go on to the Santa Maria where our hosts knew we were awaited. We had not been there long when there was a 'Fire Call'. It was a major fire and at 12.45 a.m. many lives were in danger in the maze of dwellings near the junction of Tyrrell and Hughes Streets. I see from the newspaper cutting that 'Major Jenkins who was the first police officer on the scene, arrived from the Santa Maria Hotel in full evening wear [sic]. It was not long before he was a fully drenched fire fighter.' Small business places and dwelling houses and tenements were all crowded together and six of these were completely destroyed and two others badly damaged. 'The Brigade did a good job to bring the fire under control by about 3 a.m. One hundred persons including forty children, were rendered homeless. There were only two minor casualties and the victims were discharged from hospital the very next morning.'

The new fire station would be better equipped and be more conveniently situated than the old one up near Fort George and would have unlimited water supplies at the front door so to speak.

The hustle and bustle of packing and last farewells have been forgotten and the picture I now have of our departure for St. Vincent is in a photograph on board a Canadian Line ship on its regular run through the islands and with us our friends the Isaacs homeward bound to their New York. Many other pictures have been remembered though. On my first visit to one of our police stations on the West or Leeward coast, I saw one cell full of empty coffins. They were ready for use to bury paupers. In another large cell was a very wide wooden bed and at the foot of it, a long heavy beam of wood, hinged at one end and a locking facility at the other and with about twenty inverted U shaped cutouts on the under side. The solid wooden boarded bed would hold ten prisoners. Each would be held on it by the locked beam holding each foot. It should have become a museum piece. I wonder if it did. It had been used to hold prisoners overnight who had been brought from the colony's main prison to work when road making in that area many years earlier. It was so unlike the wooden bed in the police cell in New Quay so far away.

ST. VINCENT

The Colony of St. Vincent comprises the island of St. Vincent and a number of islands stretching southwards towards Grenada. St. Vincent covers about 133 square miles and the Grenadines, as the group of other islands are called, about 20 square miles. St. Vincent is roughly elliptical in shape, with its longer axis approximately north-south. As in Grenada, a backbone of thickly wooded mountains extending along the axis divides the island into Windward and Leeward districts. The chief feature though is the recently very active volcano, Soufriere, which rises to about 4,000 ft.

The St. Vincent climate is healthy. There are two seasons: the dry from January to April and the wet May to December. The annual range of temperature is from about 67°F to 89°F with a maximum seldom over 92°F in the shade. During December to April, the weather is cooler and more pleasant. There is a considerable variation in rainfall as between the mountains and the low lying islands in the Grenadines. The annual rainfall in Kingstown, the capital, on the south west coast is about 100 inches.

The population of the Colony in 1952 was probably about 76,000 but increasing steadily. Kingstown had a population of about 14,000.

St. Vincent was 'discovered' by Columbus on 22nd January, 1498 and named after the Saint whose martyrdom is celebrated on that day. He left the Caribs in undisputed possession, a state which continued until 1627 when St. Vincent was included in a patent given by King Charles I to the Earl of Carlisle. In 1660, England and France agreed that the island should be neutral but 12 years later, King Charles II granted it to Lord Willoughby and it was soon afterwards that the first people of

African origin came to St. Vincent. They were a number of shipwrecked slaves in the Grenadines who came on to St. Vincent. They soon intermarried with the Caribs and before long a new type of inhabitant was found in the 'Black Carib'. The original, 'Yellow Caribs' and the 'Black Caribs', however, were unable to live happily together and the 'Yellow Caribs' invited the French from Martinique, to assist them in getting rid of their Black brothers. They did not succeed, though a few decades later, the relations between the French and the Black Caribs improved and French settlements were made along the Leeward coast in places which still bear French names — Chateaubelair, Petit Bordel, L'Anse Mahaut, etc. They also settled where Kingstown now stands and where the French influence may still be seen in an old fashioned paved street in the middle of the town.

In 1762 St. Vincent had been captured by the British in the struggle which made England mistress of Canada and India!! Then in 1763 European settlers began to arrive in St. Vincent. During the American War of Independence, France declared war on Britain in 1778 and St. Vincent fell into the hands of the French in 1779. It was restored to Britain, however, in 1783 and was never again to pass into foreign hands. The history of St. Vincent and other colonies in the West Indies is well recorded and now most interesting to read. More of us should read more of it.

The English planters later made considerable progress and sugar was one of their chief products. In 1834 slavery was abolished and as in Grenada the former slaves were unwilling to work for low wages and in St. Vincent tried as far as they could to be independent and to aquire lands of their own. Portugese and later East Indians were imported to work on the estates. Both East Indians and Portugese made progress and came to be well respected. There has been some intermingling of the races and St. Vincent is still a land with all races living in harmony together.

So, after a voyage of hours this time and not of days or weeks, we arrived at Kingstown, St. Vincent on 27th August, 1952. The ship had to anchor in the bay for there were no berthing facilities there in those days. We landed at a small jetty and I saw the police headquarters buildings, in a commanding position, on the road running along the waterfront. I saw an archway leading to the rear of the buildings with a guard posted there for security purposes. The town was compressed to a comparatively narrow area between the sea and the encroaching hills and stretched to north and south. Imposing mountains further back, partly encircled the town and bay.

We found our new home was situated on a hillock some half mile to landward of the police buildings which gave us views of the town to the north and south and overlooked the town between us and the sea.

The Acting Chief of Police was Captain A. L. Gentle, a Caucasion Grenadian but he was moved shortly afterwards to the Trinidad Force and during the short period he remained second in command, gave me every assistance, not only on St. Vincent police problems but on much of West Indian matters generally. A recently promoted Assistant Superintendent, Captain Cousins, from the Jamaica Force came to replace him and soon settled in.

I found the Force establishment was very slightly less than Grenada's, as indeed was the population but the area to be policed was more extensive with a number of police stations in the Grenadines. There were two stations on Bequia, the nearest island, some eight miles to the south. There was another on Union Island some thirty miles still further south. We had an auxiliary police force together with an auxiliary fire brigade. A small army cadet unit was another reserve. These with the regular police force was the extent of our immediate defences for, as in Grenada, the police had a dual role of a civil police and a military force. We trained our own forces as in Grenada. Sometime later I attended a special conference, in Barbados, of all the Caribbean Forces including British Guiana on the South American mainland, to consider police training in the Caribbean. Jamaica, Trinidad and British Guiana were large enough to continue with their own training establishments. In the Eastern Caribbean, the smaller forces would send their recruits to be trained in a new training school to be set up in Barbados. I enjoyed the meeting with representatives of all these Caribbean Forces including the Chief of Police of British Honduras (now Belize) in the far west in Central America. Most of us, at a later date, also visited Trinidad to attend a conference on security matters in the area.

Our new home, on the hill, was a large bungalow type building with interesting grounds. On the landward side, it faced the mountains and a large lawn and to seaward, it overlooked the town and the wide bay. There were some large mango trees and orange and lime trees and on the sloping land each side of the lawn there was some cultivated ground. Here we continued growing sweet potatoes and sweet corn. These were planted in the same ground and when the corn was ready we knew the potatoes were also ready. There were some other vegetables and we grew a few bananas. A giant of a Royal Palm tree grew in the middle of the lawn.

Those were the days of the steel bands and the sound of several of these rehearsing would be carried to us from their practice grounds on the outskirts of the town and could indeed be music to our ears. The Police band was standard but small, gave occasional concerts but was adequate for ceremonial purposes.

The constitution of St. Vincent was not very unlike that in Grenada. The Governor of the Windward Islands had his residence in Grenada but would visit of course and stay in Government House on the outskirts of Kingstown. Mr. W. F. Coutts, M.B.E. was our Administrator in St. Vincent and resided at Government House. (He later became Governor General in Uganda.) After the usual calls, social and official, I was properly appointed and gazetted as a Lieutenant Colonel.

The law enforceable in the colony was, in the main, law made by the Colony's legislature together with the Common Law of England. The courts were in two divisions — the Supreme Court and the Magistrates' Court. Each had its criminal jurisdiction and civil jurisdiction as well as probate, divorce and Admiralty jurisdiction. Appeals from the Supreme

Court would lie to the West Indian Court of Appeal and thence to the Privy Council Committee.

The Colony was divided into three Magisterial Districts. The first district consisted of the island of St. Vincent, the second of Bequia and the third consisted of the islands of Union, Mayreau and Canouan. The island of Mustique lies about ten miles to the south east of Bequia but was not as well known then as in recent years when as a privately owned island, it has become the legendary playground for the rich and famous. It has been beautifully developed with many gorgeous holiday homes including one owned by Princess Margaret. In fact all of these islands in the Grenadines have been very popular for years particularly with yachting people. Bequia, is also noted for its fishing boat and inter-island schooner boat building.

I now had to forget much of the U.K., Falkland Islands and Grenada laws and concentrate on St. Vincent's laws. The police had responsibilities with registration and licensing of motor vehicles. I discovered that third party insurance in connection with the use of motor vehicles on public roads had only become compulsory three years earlier in 1949. One advantage of serving in colonies where one was closer to the law makers was that one was able to have some influence in law making. In the U.K. a Chief of Police would have to press his case for an amendment of a law, in many directions and with many people before any proposed change would be found acceptable and be given time to become law. Now I would be in a position to make out a case with the Attorney General or Crown Attorney and other government officials with whom I would be in touch on a daily basis and if urgent action was required and the matter worthy of consideration by the legislature, any delays would be minimal.

I was still very road safety conscious and I see among my memorabilia, a copy of the Saint Vincent Highway Code which I was enabled to issue as the Licensing Authority, with the authority of the Legislative Council on 1st November, 1952. I had only arrived in St. Vincent on 27th August, 1952, and must have seen the need for such a Code. It was printed,.

I see, at the Government Printing Office and issued to the public in 1953.

Much of the Colony's law was of course based on U.K. law but some of the changes or additions thereto were only made long after their introduction may have been recommended to the Colony by the Secretary of State for the Colonies. In the 1950s, capital punishment was still authorised or required by Statute but the minimum age limit had been raised in the U.K. to 18 years. This had not been followed in St. Vincent. We now had a case where a young lad of 16 years had killed a shop owner by striking him on the back of the head with a hand held stone and this was murder and still a capital offence. The Colony's law was changed very quickly so the sentence in due course was one of detention at Her Majesty's Pleasure. It was probably one of the earlier of such sentences of her reign and on Her Majesty's visit to St. Vincent a few years later, she ordered his release. In the meantime though and very soon after his sentence, the lad managed to climb out of the prison in Kingstown. Our recently acquired first police dog showed where he had succeeded in his climb and had taken up the scent again outside the main wall, fortunately though, within a few hundred yards, dog and handler were met by warders and others who were returning with the recaptured prisoner.

The beauty of the St. Vincent Grenadines was quite different from that of St. Vincent island. The beauty of St. Vincent was in many ways much like that of Grenada although I thought St. Vincent had more open views despite its generally even more rugged terrain. While much of St. Vincent was almost inaccessible, there was room to grow a variety of agricultural products. In fact, the island's production was almost entirely agricultural. The chief crops in their order of importance probably, were arrowroot, starch, copra, sea island cotton, peanuts, sweet potatoes and livestock, for export while for local consumption there was sugar, edible oil, and miscellaneous food crops such as maize, pigeon peas, beans, pumpkins, plantain, dasheen, eddoes and yams. There was too a great variety of fruit. It was to St. Vincent that Captain Bligh, of the 'Mutiny on the *Bounty* affair, brought the first breadfruit to the West Indies.

St. Vincent enjoyed a virtual monopoly markets for its main crop arrowroot. Something like 8 million lbs were exported annually. I have good cause to remember an early visit to one of the main arrowroot estates. Some friends had kindly invited us to visit their country home to see the estate and learn something of the growing and preparation of arrowroot. Mr. Forde also wanted us to see their racehorses. He raced them occasionally in Trinidad and sometimes in Grenada. We had enjoyed a most interesting afternoon. As Diana, about fourteen years of age at this time had also done some riding in the Falklands, we were invited to ride two horses along some of the estate roads. They were saddled up and we mounted them. Diana had seemed very much higher than she used to look on her Falkland horses. The horses were fairly frisky and we walked them away leaving the others to await our return. We eventually reached the windward coast public road. I thought we should turn back and the horses seemed to sense this. I managed to keep mine in check but Diana could not restrain hers — she had never needed to pull back on the reins with all her strength in the Falklands — and away her horse took her back on to the estate road. I was afraid to attempt to keep up and held back as much as I could. As we rounded each bend, I feared what I might see. No sight of them, fortunately, until we were back in the estate yard. Diana had already dismounted and was all in one piece. She said she just could not hold her horse back from its fast gallop homeward. I was very thankful that she had been able to hold on. Her mother had merely wondered why I was so much later arriving.

There was only one sugar factory on the island and cane for this was grown both by peasant farmers and the sugar estate. Rum was also produced at the factory's distillery.

St. Vincent at this time, like many other territories, was undergoing, shall I say, political growing pains. With members of the legislative council being elected in equal or greater number than those nominated, the elected members tended to become more vocal than they were formerly. Vocal particularly when addressing supporters or those whom they wished would be their supporters. There was one in St. Vincent who attracted our particular attention and whom we regarded sometimes as a mere nuisance but at other times as a possible cause of real trouble.

I soon discovered we had no one in the Force who could take shorthand notes at our public meeting nor any other means of recording in some detail what was being said. I succeeded in recruiting into the Force a newspaper man from Barbados who was able to write in shorthand. He took notes of a public meeting on 26 November, 1952 and later, with others, gave evidence at the Supreme Court when a member of the Legislative Council was charged with Sedition and with Effecting a Public Mischief. Others gave evidence on a second charge of Sedition in respect of a later speech.

I would refer reports of, shall I say, questionable speeches to the Crown Attorney and secure his advice. It was he who formulated the above charges. My shorthand writer performed clerical duties at police headquarters and received training in general police duties. I remember particularly reading a verbatim report of a meeting he had attended where the same politician spoke and apparently had said that his listeners should never attend a cocktail party at Government House because they would be served drinks 'by someone who would drop "horse-nick" from under their finger nails into your drinks'. The constable's hearing seemed to have been better than his understanding. This, however, never formed part of any charge.

I see from my newspaper cutting of 17 January, 1953 that 'Defence Counsel gives 270 Minutes Address' and 'Tense Crowds Wait During Two Hour Deliberation' and 'One Hundred Dollars Fine and a Two Year Bond Imposed'. They were tense days and I had given orders that a Guard of Honour for the opening of a Legislative Council, instead of being marched away back to barracks, should be stood down and retained as a standby force in the nearby buildings. There was no trouble. Later there was an appeal against the conviction.

To record proceedings at rural meetings I had obtained a tape recorder — in those days these were in 'boxes' about

197

20" x 15" x 8" with tape reels of about 7" diameter. But to be able to use this it had been necessary to get a transformer and batteries carried in our Land Rover and then a long lead for the microphone so it could be taken many yards from the Land Rover into the crowd.

I found another use for the tape recorder. I had not taught or trained any of the St. Vincent Police in Life Saving but I had encouraged them in First Aid including methods of applying artificial respiration. I thought it would be well to standardise the instructions when teaching how it should be done. So we prepared a tape which was played as the instructing accompaniment to the now silent instructor's demonstration of the method being applied to a patient. This ensured that standard instructions were given and that the demonstration was correct and standard too. Later, the Land Rover plus equipment was taken to some of the seaside villages for the instruction of boat people and other members of the public.

Many of the islanders were naturally engaged in the fishing industry. Attempts were still being made with a local salt fish industry in the Grenadines. St. Vincent had a very good variety of fish and it was one of the few places where the pilot whale was hunted. It was known as blackfish with about three hundred caught annually and these would produce some seven thousand gallons of blackfish oil. It was also very good eating.

It had been said that in far too many instances there was a marked reluctance by members of the public to co-operate with or assist the police. I sought to emphasise the civil responsibilities of the police and made a number of broadcasts over the local radio to impress on both members of the public and of the police force that primarily we were there to help the people and not to overawe them with our military capabilities. We could best ensure their safety and well being by co-operating in all matters. These had been well received.

Our family by this time was well settled in. Diana and Rowena were with Guides and Brownies — Diana soon to become St. Vincent's first Queen's Guide. The Guide Commissioner was the wife of our Methodist minister. The Methodists were the strongest of the island's denominations. They were a

198

marvellous couple, both Africans, she a daughter of a one time sergeant major in a police force and he a former sugar estate chemist from British Guiana. My wife and I often remarked that we would like our folk back in Wales to hear him preach.

Memory is a wonderful thing when one is able to relive, almost, the events of days long past. H.M. The Queen had ascended the throne on 6th January, 1952, when we were still on leave in Wales but we were now looking forward to Coronation Day on 2 June 1953. I had already selected one of our Inspectors to represent the St. Vincent Police in the Coronation Procession in London. He was to join members of other colonial police forces under canvas in Hyde Park. London would be full to the seams. He almost collapsed when Newfoundland's cold air met him as he disembarked briefly from the aircraft at Gander on his way to London. Many will remember the London procession in the rain. I remember reading that it was colder in London on that 2nd June than it had been the previous Christmas.

In St. Vincent, we readied ourselves for our own Coronation Day parade. For the Royal Salute we had unmounted an old cannon like those used in Grenada. Lying flat on the ground each piece weighed about a hundredweight. We had rain that day too. It was everybody's parade. I see on the back of a photograph, in my handwriting, that there were 'Behind me on parade for inspection etc. were — Regular Police 40 : Auxiliary Police 30; Cadet Corps 60; Volunteer Fire Brigade 30; Prison Warders 20; Scouts 100; Girl Guides 140; Red Cross 20; Police Band 20.' All went well, very well, well nearly all, for to my embarrassment, some of the cannon would not fire and there was, for me at least, a hideous delay until it was ignored and the next one was lit to fire. (The rain?) There may have been three or four refusals but I resolved it would not happen again. After all, I thought, it was rather a stupid hit and miss affair and as I had seen in Grenada, some recoils could put the gunner's legs at risk. So it was that later I purchased a small starting cannon firing 12 bore blank cartridges and found this to be adequate. It looked like a real cannon but was only about eight inches high and perhaps fifteen inches long overall, as I picture it now and it would not of course be visible on the parades when in use. They were made, I understood for use as starting guns for boat races.

My first visit to Bequia and Union Island was made in a government owned ex-RAF Air Sea Rescue Launch used during the war. Later I was to have several flights in and along the Grenadines in an amphibious aircraft of the British West Indian Airways and also to Barbados and Trinidad. Landings or alightings were on the sea in St. Vincent and the Grenadines. I was allowed to occupy the seat of the second pilot had there been one and made myself generally useful, making fast etc. The aircraft was a Grumman Goose. Our 'airport' also called sometimes a 'seadrome', was a stretch of the sea near Young's Island in the south west and some three miles out of Kingstown and with a minimum of buildings nearby. Some 'red tape' demanded that the airport should have a superintendent. I was appointed in the Government Gazette but never called upon to perform any duties. I would on occasion find a guard of honour there for a governor.

The Aquatic Club was nearby. Diana and I were one day swimming over to Young's Island when we seemed to be subjected to electric shocks. Quite frightened really, I decided the Club was nearer than the island and so retreated quickly. Safely ashore we were assured that the shocks were caused by contact with trailing parts of jellyfish.

St. Vincent had never required as many forts as Grenada needed. Fort Duvernette was in an almost inaccessible position occupying the top of a small island of that name close to Young's Island. French influence was less apparent than in Grenada where the French were in occupation several times.

I once had to make a visit to one of our Grenadine islands on a rather delicate mission. There was no telephone link back to St. Vincent and government officials used radio instead. The frequency though was in a band that could be picked up on ordinary domestic radios. The government officer who would put me in touch with St. Vincent was going to be someone I would need to speak about to his superior officer in St. Vincent. To overcome these complications, I decided to enlist the help of my wife so a message was sent to her asking her to speak to me at that end. We spoke in Welsh and felt what we would say would be reasonably secure. She came back on the air shortly afterwards with the information I sought. A non-translatable personal name had to be used and I did not want even this name to be mentioned. I had to tell my wife that the name of the man she was to take my message to and bring back his answer was the same as that of the toothpaste then in use by our girls. (In those days it was in rather flat round tins.) I had once done the same sort of thing in the Falklands except that there it was done over a many-party telephone line.

It was soon after this that I sought approval to have our own VHF police radio for at this time we had none. Owing to the location of our police stations and the mountainous terrain it was necessary to do some careful checking for the suitable location of repeater stations. I was glad to discover that Pye had one of their experts visiting the Caribbean and it was not long before orders were placed and we could be independent of telephone lines if need be.

On my first visit to the north east of St. Vincent, into the area beyond Georgetown, I went to see some of the visible evidence of past eruptions of Soufriere. The last serious eruption then had been in May 1902, when some 1,500 lives were lost and appalling damage was done over an extensive area. French Martinique had the following day suffered even a worse disaster, as I have already mentioned. The Rabacca Dry River is not only a route for rain water running from Soufriere but has been the natural bed for streams of lava that have run down it from time to time so that its bed is in fact composed of hardened lava. Beyond the river there were thousands of acres of volcanic ash then planted with coconut trees and all these trees were a wonderful sight. They produced something in excess of ten million whole nuts annually. While thousands of whole nuts would be exported, the majority produced copra mostly for export but many tons were processed in St. Vincent in the manufacture of refined oil, soap, stock feed and manure. Much fibre was exported to Trinidad and used in the making of matting etc.

201

Back in Kingstown, Soufriere seemed a long way away. One night though, we were awakened by a severe earthquake. Or it seemed a severe earthquake to us. My wife commendably switched off the main electric switches and we went to see to our girls. Rowena was not in her bed and then we found her, holding a very tall free standing glass cupboard full of rattling glasses and china. We suffered no damage but there was slight structural damage to some buildings in Kingstown including the police headquarters and in rural areas where one church suffered more extensive damage.

Long after we had left St. Vincent and after a lesser eruption of the volcano in 1971, April 1979 saw Soufriere in eruption again. Volcanic activity had begun on the 13th and everyone feared what might yet come. There was a very loud explosion at midnight on the 18th. I have read that the earth shook and the people wondered if the island would break in two. Many of the cruising yachts at Bequia sailed away for fear of an enormous tidal wave which might appear. Ash and stone fell all over St. Vincent and some of the other islands. Georgetown's 20,000 people moved from their homes and sought temporary accommodation on the leeward side of the island. It was an economic tragedy for St. Vincent and the island's most lucrative source of income was ruined.

But back in 1952, we were not in constant fear of the volcano, and a climb up Soufriere was the thing for many visitors to do, I have already made mention of a visit by my old school friend William Ellis. It was good to talk of Aberystwyth and old friends. His home, the Chateau high above the town near Castell Brychan was visible from the Promenade and was often within my view when I lived in Aberystwyth during the earlier war years. Receptions at Government House were routine affairs and the opportunity to meet VIPs visiting the Colony was always appreciated. We met the Archbishop of York for instance and of course visits by H.M. ships were of added interest. We were also visited by ships of the Chilean navy and others. I remember, particularly, three Canadian naval ships sailing into the Bay 'in line astern' I think they say and then coming very smartly into 'line abreast' to face the town as they anchored. Their hospitality too was much appreciated and to me they seemed to be trying to out shipshape the Royal Navy.

I was having my share of fire fighting and I see from an old newspaper cutting that I had a special mention for my activities at one fire in particular. The Brigade though was short of needed equipment and I tried to remedy this and pressed my case by saying we could not afford to be without such equipment. It was not very long after I left that there was quite a disastrous fire at the government's cotton ginnery.

I am remembering an interesting arson case we had to deal with. Fire was detected by one of our night patrols at the Government Treasury. A number of candles had been lit and left standing on heaps of paper and matches. Most of the candles had not yet burned down. The only immediate clue seemed to be the location of the intended conflagration. All documents involving the collection of land taxes would have been destroyed. A land tax collector was already under investigation and he was duly convicted and sentenced to four years imprisonment.

There was as yet no Police Federation in being, as we had in the U.K. One sought to do one's best in the interests of all ranks. For example, I had set up a police welfare association which, before I left St. Vincent about a year later, seemed to be providing answers to many of the men's personal problems. I feel I have to record this incident to show my appreciation of members of the Royal St. Vincent Police for remembering me some twenty two years later. I heard from the then Chief of Police that the association was continuing to be a great success and that on its twenty first anniversary, they wished to send me a gift in appreciation. He had said it was too heavy to send by air mail. It came by Geest Banana Boat to Barry. It was a very beautiful coffee table of a tropical wood (Wamara I think). It was so heavy to move that I had mini castors fitted. This was some twenty one years after I left St. Vincent. And now some twenty years still further on I remember the kind people of St. Vincent.

We had settled very happily there and I enjoyed my duties

and responsibilities tremendously. I had soon become conscious, however, that my prospects of further advancement in St. Vincent, as I was already Chief of Police, were nil, so it was natural I suppose, that I should have been inquisitive about conditions of service in larger colonies when I met representatives of the other Caribbean forces at our Barbados conference. This had been held only some six months after my appointment to St. Vincent. Some months later, the possibility of an appointment for me in British Guiana became apparent and I remembered so much of what I had been told about the place and its police force by my friend Scottie Campbell when together in Hong Kong some eight years earlier. It was all very attractive but it was to be some twelve months of uncertainty before I was offered transfer on promotion to Senior Superintendent of Police in British Guiana. There I was to be in command of the Georgetown Division, the senior division in the colony. I was told it involved the command of about 500 men and that I would probably be required to assist in extensive reorganisation.

I felt it would be to our advantage for me to accept. It would mean though another domestic upheaval and we would find ourselves on the move in less than two years after leaving Grenada. The decision to accept was quickly made and now, after that long wait while the powers that be reviewed the new establishment, in ranks and numbers, of the British Guiana Police in the light of that Colony's constitutional and political problems, I was required to go as soon as possible and the Grumman Goose aircraft was chartered to transport us thither on 21 July, 1954. There were the usual farewells to be made, privately and otherwise in many ways I was sad to leave.

BRITISH GUIANA

British Guiana became Guyana in 1966 on attaining its independence. In 1954 it was still struggling to gain that goal but had just stumbled badly by having a forward Constitution brought into effect in 1953 and then having it suspended before the end of that year. A new and advanced form of Constitution with universal adult suffrage, a two-chamber legislature and with a ministerial system had been lost in a matter of a few months. The circumstances in which the suspension occurred are detailed in the Report of the British Guiana Constitutional Commission 1954 (Cmnd. 9274). I will not attempt to detail the complexities of previous or subsequent Constitutions.

Occasionally Guyana is confused with the West African Ghana. While it may have been due to a 'slip of the tongue', British Guiana had been described as a West Indian island by a senior British government minister (Chuter Ede was it not?) it was of course a British colony on the north coast of South America. I have already mentioned Dutch Guiana (now Surinam) and French Guiana lying to the east of British Guiana and both bordering on Brazil. Venezuela to the west of British Guiana and Brazil were also known at one time as Spanish Guiana and Portugese Guiana respectively.

Native South American Indians of these areas of South America are referred to as Amerindians and Guiana is an Amerindian word meaning 'Land of Waters'. And indeed the Guianas are all exceedingly well watered.

There is such a lot I shall need to know about British Guiana although my immediate responsibilities would cover only a small area of it and not the whole Colony as had been the case in the islands. Compared with the mass of South America, British Guiana seems a very small country but it covers almost as much area as the United Kingdom — some 83,000 sq. miles to U.K.'s 94,000. But with almost 70,000 sq. miles of forest, the Colony's population in 1954 was nearer half a million than the 55 million in the United Kingdom. From south to north, it lies approximately between 2° and 7° north of the Equator.

The Amerindians were soon outnumbered when Europeans began settling in the area. Dutch, French, Portuguese and British settlements were begun from as early as the 16th century in various parts of the Guianas. The British occupied areas from time to time in what are now French Guiana, Surinam and Guyana. That part of the territory which became British Guiana was ceded to Britain in 1814 by the Dutch whose influence is still evident in place names particularly in the coastal area.

The British, like those settlers before them, brought in African slaves and later indentured labour to replace the freed slaves. Portuguese and Chinese workers also came. The Indian newcomers came to be described and known as East Indians. The main ethnic group is now East Indian and outnumber all other groups together. By religious persuasion Hindus and Muslims far outnumber others which include Anglican (Church of West Indies), Roman Catholic, Lutheran, Moravians, Methodists, Baptists and Congregationalists. Missionaries from the United States, mostly, of various sects and persuasions competed for new adherents among the Amerindians in the interior of the country.

About 90% of the population live along the low lying coastal belt which varies in depth from about ten miles in the west to about forty miles in the east but this is only about 5% of the country's total land area. Much of this low coastal belt lies some 3 to 5 feet below sea level at high tide and in consequence needs sea defences for many miles of this coast. On some of the sugar estates, very powerful pumps are often in use to assist in the evacuation of water. Occasionally a sea wall is breached with serious flooding.

A second area, the mountain region, known as the Pakaraima Range, lies along the western boundary of the Colony. The mountains which are covered with forest and savannah, include Mount Roraima, the highest point in the country at about

9,100 ft. The area lying mainly in the east and south, is also forest clad but with acres of savannah. The precipitous terrain of the Mount Roraima area is said to have inspired Conan Doyle's *The Lost World*.

Draining the vast interior of its heavy rainfall are many large rivers which with their tributaries form a vast network of waterways. They are, however, impeded by rapids, cataracts and falls as they drop from the mountain ranges and plateaux to the lower coastal lands. Even so, many of these rivers are the main lines of communication through the forests to the interior and special boats have been developed which can be hauled up the rapids and are yet large enough to carry passengers and goods and baggage. The experienced crews are often assisted by the passengers including pork knockers, balata bleeders and timber grant workers and such like. All the fighting of the rapids which may be needed in either direction has inspired shanties to give unison to the paddles and after years of usage these have now become part of the folk songs of the country.

Pork knockers are the individual gold prospecting diggers, a breed apart who hunt for gold in the interior rivers. Many men from the islands such as St. Vincent and Grenada who came prospecting were known as very hard working pork knockers. The hunt for gold has also been carried out on a larger scale with the use of divers and mechanical diggers. I have seen it recorded that in 1938 gold production was 2,000 bullion ozs. and in 1962 it was 39,728 fine troy ozs. Diamonds are also found.

One of the largest single drop waterfalls in the world is the famous Kaieteur on the Potaro River. It is nearly five times the height of Niagara with a vertical drop of 741 feet and that is followed with a further drop of 80 feet of rapids and falls. The Potaro is a tributary of the Essequibo. Other important rivers are the Demerara, Berbice, Mazaruni, Kaituma and Cuyni. The chief ports are Georgetown (the capital) at the mouth of the Demerara River, New Amsterdam on the Berbice, Springlands on the eastern boundary and with sub-ports at Morawhanna and Kaituma in the north west.

207

For the greater part of the year, British Guiana enjoys a pleasant climate but the summer months are hot. In the coastal areas, the mean temperature is about 80°F. Inland, in the highland forest regions the days are usually hotter and with cooler nights. Two wet seasons and two dry seasons are usual but in the large area of the southern savannah, the Rupununi area has one wet season only; May to September, the rest of the year being very dry. As this open area is used for cattle rearing, this has its advantages and disadvantages for often it is subject to much flooding or drought. Overall it has a far smaller rainfall than Georgetown on the coast. The forest regions have about 140 inches of rain to the savannah's 60 inches.

It was fairly early in the day when the Grumman touched down on the sea at our St. Vincent 'seadrome'. There were the very last farewells and we boarded the plane which had been brought up on to the slipway. Then she returned to the sea, retracted her wheels and, as a flying boat, soon took off. We would be flying southwards some 600 miles to reach British Guiana. The girls were enjoying the trip and in due course we were flying over Venezuela's Orinoco delta and then the northwest district of British Guiana before crossing the wide estuary of the Essequibo and then the Demerara River to land on the runway at Atkinson Field where I had landed a little over three years earlier.

We were met and taken quickly through police immigration and customs and were driven from the old American Base along the road, which more or less followed the right bank of the Demerara River, the 26 miles to Georgetown. The whole area now was very flat after the few hillocks we had seen at the Field. The road was in very poor condition — and the first of many burnt earth roads I was to see in the Colony later. I spotted our second police station — the first was within the airfield's boundaries — at Soesdyke and this was to be the first of so many Dutch names. Soon we could smell the huge sugar factory of the Diamond Estate and then approaching Georgetown we saw more and more of the population and their homes. There were so many signs of poverty around though this could be deceptive. We were seeing mainly the East Indian homes and they are a thrifty people compared with the more happy-go-lucky Africans.

Driving into Georgetown proper though, we could see now how beautiful a city it really was. We saw the public buildings, the Supreme Court and then there was a most beautiful building which was the Town Hall, a wooden building but one would not have thought so. Then a view of St. George's Anglican Cathedral, all in white, which was said to be one of the biggest wooden buildings in the world. Some of the streets we were driven along were unusual in that traffic, moving left and right, as it were on one way streets, was separated by a wide avenue with, in some cases, rows of beautiful flowering trees on each side. Originally the central area was a drainage canal and substantial enough to hold its waters until the next low tide when it would be released into the tidal Demerara. The holding door arrangements are called kokers — another retained Dutch word. They are opened and then closed at each tide, lifted and lowered usually by use of a large sort of steering wheel, reminiscent of old sailing ships, as they allow enough leverage for the job to be done satisfactorily. I was to see that most of Georgetown's main streets had been dealt with in this manner. The excellent 'town planning' by the Dutch had ensured that the streets were straight, parallel east to west and parallel again north to south and with very little interruption. Elsewhere the open canals remained in use but the drainage along the main street areas had long since been converted to piped arrangement.

We were duly installed for our first night at the Woodbine Hotel near the northern edge of the business area and near Government House on the tree-lined Main Street where I had spotted an armed police sentry with his box at the entrance to the driveway.

I had been to sign the Visitor's Book at Government House and had been taken to see the Commissioner of Police, Col. C. H. Ward, by his Deputy T. W. Whittingham whom I had met in Barbados the year before.

The Police Headquarters were in Brickdam near the city centre. The Police Depot was situated at Eve Leary — a mile

209

or so to the north and near the sea wall and promenade. The Depot housed a reserve of police who could form riot squads and Government House guards. Recruits were trained there and as the Force was semi-military as in the other colonies, the armoury with its guard room was there too. The parade ground with its boundary of royal palms with their white-painted trunks at the base, presented a picture of efficiency.

Nearby was the police sports ground with married quarters for some senior officers in the compound. These were two blocks of flats but not of the modern variety. Originally, they were barrack blocks for Dutch troops. Each block was now in four sections or flats. Two on the lower floor and two on the upper floor. Ours was on the upper floor on the left facing the sports ground to the rear and the front facing the sea some 300 yards beyond a very old military cemetery and other Government properties between us and the sea wall. The flats were of timber, mainly greenheart. They were raised on massive greenheart logs so that the floor level of the lower flat was some 5-6 ft. clear of the ground — where we could now park the occasional car — and at the same time ensured they were above any possible flooding. Each flat had a wide open gallery on the sea side, almost the length of the flat. The greenheart pillars extended probably some 45 ft. from ground level. How much in the ground I do not know. The floors of each flat too were of greenheart planking and inside the accommodation, had become highly polished through usage. The internal wooden walls, as in most Georgetown houses, did not reach to the ceilings so as to ensure a freer circulation of air. In our upper flat, the walls were some ten feet high with more than ample space above. In the lower flat, the ceiling was probably about 14 ft. high.

The Assistant Commissioner occupied the flat below ours. He was W. R. Weber, a Guianese of European descent. In the block the other side of the driveway into the compound, the Deputy Commissioner lived in the upper flat nearer ours and the Commissioner occupied the other, while the lower 'flat' extended the length of the building and provided the accommodation for a 'Local Forces Officers' Mess.' This later became the Police Officers' Mess (that is the gazetted officers). A number of bungalows in nearby compounds were allocated to other police officers.

I shall always remember our first night at Eve Leary. We were probably about a third to half a mile from the mouth of the Demerara River and I was amazed to hear what I thought was some sort of outboard motor. At first it was heard so clearly at the rear of the flat and then as suddenly at the front gallery as if seaward bound. It then dawned on me that the boat should have arrived somewhere or at least gone out of hearing long since. Down in the Mess I came to understand the sound had come from nearby frogs not distant boats!

Later, I noticed too that there were occasions when our large fridge door remained open conveniently while at other times, with the same loading, it would close unless held open. Eventually we had to attribute this to the state of the tide. Had I thought of it, I could have checked this by use of a spirit level presumably.

I was still trying to come to terms with the size of the city, the size of the Force and the size of the country (and of our flat). I was surprised at the number of Europeans in Georgetown and that there were a number of European police officers. I was thrilled to hear that in the wet season I would be able to play rugby football again and I played some association football from time to time. In the following year though, at 45 years of age I gave up rugby. I was to watch a lot of marvellous cricket. I played in games such as Officers versus Inspectors but when I was 52 and in the slips, my chest and not my hands dropped three catches, I gave that up also.

As a Senior Superintendent, I was given command of the Georgetown Division. This included the city of Georgetown and the area up to and including Atkinson Field to the south and for some miles along the east coast. The population was about 162,000. The police strength of the Division totalled 518 and of these there were 8 Gazetted Officers, 4 Chief Inspectors, 13 Inspectors, 28 Sergeants, 56 Corporals and 408 Constables. There were also 9 women police on the Division's strength out of a total of 54 for the Force. The very efficient Mounted Police

211

Branch was also under my command. Its establishment was 1 Assistant Superintendent, 2 Sergeants, 7 Corporals, 30 Constables with 40 horses. Their stables, riding school, married quarters and single barracks were all in a special compound, with quartermaster stores and bandroom, on the southern side of the sport ground at Eve Leary.

My divisional offices were located in the police station compound at Brickdam.

For a more complete picture, in 1954, the Police Head-quarters was also located in the same compound, with a staff of just over 300. Police at the depot and Training School at Eve Leary totalled another 200.

In the Georgetown Division we had police stations and each with its own singlemen's quarters at Atkinson Field, Soesdyke and Providence and at Brickdam, Ruimveldt, Alberttown, Kitty and River Station in Georgetown.

Police work in Georgetown was much the same as in the other colonies but I now found that I had more officers to share in the day to day routine work. In this so much larger Force though there were now more senior officers to deal with its widespread responsibilities. The Force's dometsic arrange-ments were still very much on military lines — we still had corporals though sergeant-majors had become inspectors — and I was soon to find that a far too frequent 'orderly room' was necessary. A defaulting constable would be marched in, in approved military style — to answer the charge which might have been preferred against him. Procedures and penalties, at that time, had not reached the standards for police disciplinary procedures reached later which then came to copy some of the more recent U.K. police procedures. On occasion, I found it necessary to award a punishment so much for the original offence, as for the efforts to avoid it. I not infrequently quoted what I used to read on a notice which hung in my Fifth Form room in Aberystwyth and upon which one's gaze had fallen so often. It read, 'Dare to be True — Nothing can need a Lie — The fault that needs it most grows too thereby.'

The Brickdam compound was a very busy place. Police patrol cars and motor cycles were inspected there daily. Some

212

of our traffic men who were driving examiners, brought in the learners for part of their driving tests. These included parking their vehicles in designated areas, marked by cones. Yes, this was included in Guyana over forty years ago. The police too had the responsibility for registration and licensing of motor vehicles as in the other colonies.

After the suspension of the Colony's Constitution in 1953, British Guiana was governed by an interim administration composed entirely of nominated members. The leading politicians who were said to be responsible for the suspension, as the British Government believed there was a danger of communist subversion, were Dr. Cheddi Jagan and Forbes Burnham. They had joined forces in 1950 to form the People's Progressive Party (P.P.P.). This party then a multiracial party, had in 1953, won 18 of the 24 seats for elected members.

The Argyll and Sutherland Highlanders had been brought in to aid the police in preserving the peace in 1953 and were still in the Colony. It was still a time of uncertainty and their presence was a relief to many. The police were able to carry out most of their normal duties although these now also included searches for unlawfully held firearms and explosives. Public meetings were controlled and a permit had to be obtained under the emergency laws even to hold our St. David's Day Party in a private dwelling. We had our alarms and were quick to respond. About three weeks after my arrival, a report came just before midnight indicating that there had been an explosion at the Supreme Court buildings. I was soon there and a search of the building was in progress. No trace of any explosion was seen but the cause of the noise thought to have been an explosion was seen soon after. A portion of very heavy ornamental cast iron roof ridge had somehow, some time become dislodged and was it perhaps a contraction of the metal in the coolness of the night which gave it the impetus to slide down the corrugated iron roof on to the lawn and create such a din? I see I returned home at 1.45 a.m. and much relieved I imagine.

I was familiarising myself with the area and all the police stations in particular. I soon saw the latest riot drill at the Depot — more sophisticated and on a larger scale than I had

had in St. Vincent and Grenada. And my diary tells me I played some tennis the same day. Our paymaster was the Colony champion — I only heard his aces. A few days later I was shooting on the Open Rifle Range at Thomas Lands, near the sea wall on the city's outskirts. This shooting always necessitated temporary closure of the sea wall road which passed beyond our targets. I see a note too that I spoke to the Commissioner who was also up at the Range, (so we probably fired our pistol course as well) about Georgetown's traffic. We also had a well equipped miniature range at the Depot.

I had never before seen so many pedal cycles. Each one had to be licensed and a metal disc for the current year had to be exhibited on the axle of the front wheel. School children's licences were cheaper. There were some very good traffic laws but, in my view, improvements were needed and much improved traffic control called for in Georgetown in particular.

My wife and the girls were settling in happily. Diana and Rowena attended at Bishops, the Government's High School for Girls. Georgetown also had an exceptionally good Catholic Girl's School. Sarah was soon started at Stella Maris, a nearby Catholic Preparatory school for girls with her friend from one of the adjoining flats. It was explained that Sarah was not a Catholic and the Mother Superior asked if she could join them in their prayers. My wife often told the tale against herself afterwards for she found that her immediate answer had been 'Yes, it will not do her any harm'.

At Eve Leary, some convenient land, adjacent to the small military cemetery, had been taken over and a range of buildings had been erected to accommodate the troops in Georgetown instead of at Atkinson Field. The Argyll and Sutherland who earlier had relieved the First Battalion the Royal Welch Fusiliers, who occupied them briefly and were relieved in October 1954 by units of the Black Watch Regiment. Their early morning piping and marching too served to entertain and inspire the confidence of the public. With other senior officers I had attended at the formal 'changing of the guard' at Government House.

My meeting up with Scottie Campbell again was a joy. He

and his wife had three daughters as we had. They were Morag, Fiona and Shuna. We often exchanged visits with them the other side of town — not far from the beautiful Botanic Gardens. On Saturday nights, at one time, it had become the thing to play we were at home and Scottie would produce fish and chips in greaseproof paper wrapped in old English newspapers and with small portions of salt wrapped in bits of blue paper. Some bags of crisps in those days contained such wrapped up salt in blue paper. With the Campbells we often attended a Scots Kirk. We would visit other friends too after the morning service. Asked what we would like to have to drink, we had suggested a cup of tea or coffee would be very nice, instead of a rum and ginger or a strong punch or whatever, at one of our earlier visits. To show what creatures of habit we are, it took but a very few Sundays before most of our friends too were preferring a morning coffee. I was aware that alcohol was such a problem for so many, that I often took a non-alcoholic drink when I might actually have preferred a stronger one. Tomato juice at a cocktail party was often my choice rather than the double whisky or rum I would often hear being asked for. Incidentally, in our Mess, as in many others of course, we had a strict 'No Treating' rule. This was very good for a number of reasons. We would usually forgather there before Saturday lunch and try to relax and it was a good opportunity to meet up with fellow officers whom we would scarcely even see perhaps during the normal working week.

The Force was well equipped with all modern aids — our Force Control/Operations Room, as Emergency Control 44 was our 999 equivalent as well and all incoming requests were recorded on tape. Later, a 999 system replaced the 44. All police cars and most other police transport were fitted for reception and broadcast on VHF and later we had our own Communications Branch where specially trained men maintained the equipment.

A well equipped and efficient fire brigade was a separate section of the Force and was under the command of a Superintendent who was from the U.K. and since the disastrous Georgetown fire in 1945 was a U.K. trained fire officer. I did

215

have an opportunity to help out at one particularly large fire but it was not long afterwards that the brigade ceased to be a police responsibility and became a separate branch of the Government Service. The Georgetown fire resulted from a fire at a fireworks-making factory. Since then fireworks are prohibitated except at displays controlled by the Brigade.

The St. John Ambulance Brigade was well respected in the Colony, as was the Red Cross. I continued my interests in the Brigade and its members were available and very helpful at crowded public gatherings but we had no ambulance service as we know it in the U.K. today. As its Area Commissioner, I was presented to Princess Mary, the Princess Royal, during her visit in 1954.

The Police Force had the services of the British Guiana Militia Band at its disposal. The Band carried out its normal programme of entertaining the public at the three bandstands in Georgetown and as required elsewhere on other occasions. It had a long history and in 1924 had toured England for six months after playing at the Wembley Exhibition of that year. In 1958, by legislation, it became the British Guiana Police Band and its members all became policemen. I spent many pleasureable hours listening to their performances while enjoying the cooling breezes off the sea at Sea Wall Promenade bandstand. They were to become my particular and more immediate responsibility too. The first Guianese bandmaster was appointed soon after my arrival. He was Vincent De Abreu, L.R.A.M., A.R.C.M. and a brother of Superintendent Frank De Abreu whom I had as my second in command in Georgetown. They were Portugese Guianese.

There was also a very good Police Male Voice Choir and I can still hear them sing on L.P. record and tape. I have a record of the Police Band too.

I must mention our auxiliary police services — our first back-up was a Special Constabulary — a voluntary body as we have in the U.K. today. Then a Rural Constabulary into which specially selected men were appointed. It was the oldest auxiliary of the Force as it was formed in 1849. They were employed in serving process, both criminal and civil, in remote parts of the country. They also gave valuable assistance to the regular police in rural districts and villages and in the diamond and gold mining areas. Others were appointed because of the nature of their employment. These were bailiffs, for example and, under the Rivers Navigation Ordinance, where police powers were given to steersmen and bowmen on boats. Those specially selected to give assistance to the regular police were not uniformed except for one or two items, and were paid only for such times as they would have been engaged on some particular duty.

Some Government departments and some large business concerns who wished to have the full-time service of constables were permitted to employ directly their own individuals for duty on their own property only. These selected men would be sworn in as constables and were designated Supernumerary Constables. The Rural Constabulary totalled some 500 and the Supernumerary Constabulary totalled about the 200 mark.

The prison service was naturally a separate department of government. There were prisons in Georgetown and New Amsterdam some 60 miles to the south east of Georgetown at the mouth of the Berbice River. The long term penal settlement was near Bartica, at the confluence of the Mazaruni and Essequibo rivers where they are both very wide and very beautiful. The Superintendent of Prisons had his office at the Georgetown prison. There too was the 'place of execution'. The execution annexe, on the street side, projected from part of the main buildings. It appeared that on the morning of an execution, a crowd invariably gathered and would try to listen for some of the sounds made by the operation of the gallows. We would have been advised on the day before so that I could make such police arrangements as were considered necessary. That portion of the street adjacent to that part of the prison walls would be closed off and kept closed by a small police presence, mounted and on foot, at each end. This would depend on the degree of notoriety of the condemned prisoner. As the hour of 8 o'clock approached all would become very quiet and still. My CID would have been informed too so that they would be available to prepare a report to the coroner.

217

One day I was informed that I was required to act for the Superintendent while he was on a short holiday to Trinidad. Were they aware, I wondered, that I had had charge of the prison on the Falkland Islands? It involved my making visits every day for a few weeks to deal with administrative and any other matters there in addition to my police duties. There was no necessity to visit either of the other prisons except in some emergency and none arose. I did have to visit condemned prisoners daily together with those detained in the sick quarters awaiting trial for murder. There were 11 awaiting execution and 13 in the sick quarters. Having seen my first gallows in Singapore's Changi jail, I was more or less aware of what I would be shown in Georgetown. I feared daily that a fateful warrant of execution would arrive for one or more of the condemned men as I would have an active part to play. I had myself briefed as to what precisely and how all would be done — even shown the bottle of rum, for medicinal purposes for the staff and myself which was always kept in the office safe. Most of the condemned happened to be East Indians and I found several of them had taken to reading the Bible. It was a strange experience to talk to men one knew would be dead in a matter of days or a few weeks at the most. Their cells were in a special block and in turn the prisoners would be moved into the cell nearest to the execution chamber. I was very glad when I was able to hand over to the returned Superintendent before any warrant had reached me.

But, to more cheerful matters, for I see that on 30 March, 1955, I went to the Georgetown Cricket Club at the famous Bourda for a conference about arrangements for the forthcoming visit of the Australian touring team. Three days later I had started those duties at the prison and in the meantime the Second Test Match of that season against the West Indies was being played at Port of Spain in Trinidad. While it was nothing to do with me, as they say, I must give some details of it here for it did whet my appetite for the Third Test to come soon after at our Bourda. It was the First Trinidad Test Match to be played on a turf pitch and it yielded 1,255 runs and only 23 wickets. West Indies included two of the three 'Ws' as Worrell, Weekes and Walcott were referred to in those days, but Worrell did not play until the Third Test with us. The match was drawn, six centuries were scored, three by West Indies and three by the Australians. Walcott scored in both innings and the first of them produced a record then of 242 runs with Weekes for any West Indian wicket against Australia and Walcott became the third West Indian after G. A. Headley and Everton Weekes to score a hundred in both innings of a Test. Sobers had scored 47 and a not out 8. The Australians scored their three centuries in their first innings and declared at 600 for 9. West Indies amassed 655 for 14 wickets before time ran out. There were only 24 extras in all with 5 of them being no balls. Mr. Extra seems to score far more freely these days! !

The Third Test was due to start at Bourda Ground in Georgetown on 26th April and meanwhile I had spoken with Ian Johnson, the Australian captain, and assured him there would be adequate crowd control and no repetition of riotous behaviour that had been experienced earlier. Mounted police were always very useful where crowds gathered and with foot police, were present inside and outside the ground. We had useful radio links and I found that from the special box, in line with the wickets, where radio commentators were operating, I had excellent views of the ground and the roadway behind our stand. That I found it necessary to be there myself daily is understandable. Some of the players not on the field of play would come to join us from time to time to watch the game from this, the best advantage point.

No centuries were scored this time. Australia won by 8 wickets, West Indies scored 182 and 207 but Australia scored 257 and 133 for 2 wickets. The four combined scores included a total of 10 extras only. The highest scores were Weekes with 81 (and a duck!), Walcott 73 and Richie Benaud 68. Ian Johnson took 8 wickets in all, for 86 with his off breaks. This was the first big match of many I was to see from the commentators' box. I need hardly say that the standard of cricket in the senior league in Georgetown was excellent.

Play in the West Indian Inter-Colony matches was of the highest order as might be expected. What did surprise me though, at first, was the almost hero-worship of some of the best English players, be they Test team players or not for they followed our county cricket matches as keenly as if they were their own. But then we have appreciated their wonderful players along the years too. But I have now to declare my cricket innings closed, for long before I was to see Cowdrey and M. K. Smith with their England Test teams at Bourda, there were other things to do.

By July 1955, as conditions in the country were fairly stable and the Force was something back to more normal conditions with improved facilities in equipment, transport and manpower, I was permitted to go on long leave to the U.K. I had a little leave still due to me after my early recall to duty in Grenada from my Falklands leave, some still due to me from both Grenada and St. Vincent and leave earned over the twelve months I had served in British Guiana. It was then about three and a half years since that recall so my leave entitlement amounted to a good six months.

My wife and I were anxious to get home so that Sarah could be seen again by the specialists to whom we had sent X-Ray pictures of her back every six months. Diana would be staying on in the U.K. and was anxious to begin her service in the Women's Royal Naval Service (The Wrens). So on 27th July, 1955, the five of us were flown in a B.G. Airways DC3 (Dakota) to Trinidad where we embarked in the S.S. *Colombie* of the French Line for Southampton. A number of Guianese travelled with us either for work or training, for those were the days when West Indians were being encouraged to come to the U.K. to fill post-War vacancies in our labour force.

It was a very enjoyable voyage for us — the food and service were excellent. I remember two of our waiters were Bretons and I was often trying to find words which were the same in both the Breton and Welsh languages. *Pen Sal* was a headache in both and bacon, for instance, was *cig moch*. One of the junior officers of our Transport and Harbours Department was travelling to England for training with our Southern and other mainline railways. The larger of our two railways in British Guiana was a single line, 60 mile long railway between

Georgetown, along the East coast to Rosignol on the Berbice River, opposite New Amsterdam. I showed him a *Bradshaw's Railway Guide* in the ship's library and later stood awhile in the corridor with him as our train sped along from Southampton to London. It was his first visit to England so I will let you imagine what his feelings were.

It was grand to be back again in Wales and in my wife's home in the hills outside Dolgellau. Diana went to the Wrens and in due time we went to see her back in Wales near Dale in Pembrokeshire. My wife, as a former pupil, was able to get Rowena a place in Dr. Williams' school at Dolgellau and on that first night for her in that boarding school, we were able to signal to her, by arrangement, with the car lights from one of our fields overlooking the town. (She's a grand mother now.) Then began the visits to the Robert Jones and Agnes Hunt Orthopaedic Hospital at Gobowen, Oswestry with Sarah.

Life was now so different to that of a few weeks ago — I wondered would I ever be able to speak on two telephones and cope with an inter-com again at the same time — and dictate several letters or whatever or leave my shorthand notes for my secretary to decipher. So it was that family matters and visits here and there filled the following weeks. One visit, to London, to receive my appointment as an Officer of the Order of St. John of Jerusalem, at the hands of the Duke of Gloucester had been unexpected. Visits to Cardiganshire to meet former colleagues and see friends and relatives, were happy occasions. The time for me to return to British Guiana, which in July, had seemed so long away, was suddenly upon me and the wrench of leaving my family behind me was a dreadful experience. Sarah was to undergo extensive treatment in hospital and her mother was to give some of her own hip bone for Sarah's back. I did not know it at the time but it was going to be some eighteen months before the two of them and Rowena rejoined me in Demerara.

I returned to Georgetown on the S.S. *Arakaka* owned by the Booker Company who had the largest business interests in British Guiana. Their interests were many and included some of the largest sugar estates and, as general importers, had their own retail outlets too. One of the world's leading sugarcane production experts was Dr. Harry Evans from Bethel near Caernarfon and we were so glad to have met him and his wife and daughters soon after we arrived in British Guiana. We spoke Welsh whenever we could. As a hobby he had his own private hydroponic 'garden' and always cooked earth for sterility for other plant production. Harry had served for years in Mauritius after leaving college and entering the colonial service to work at the Sugarcane Production Research Centre. There he had met and married his wife Gladys. She always played the piano for us too at our St. David's Day parties. He had transferred to the College of Tropical Agriculture in Trinidad in 1949 but Bookers had induced him to come into their service in British Guiana where he served them until his eventual retirement. He used to visit East and West Africa and Hawaii to advise on sugarcane production. Later another Welshman, Norman Davies, a botanist, joined Harry's team with Bookers. He turned out to be the son of a St. Dogmael's policeman I knew when I served at Cardigan.

A Welshman who visited us regularly was the Captain of a Harrison Line cargo ship. He was Captain William Edward Williams but known world-wide through the merchant navy as ' 'Ngwasi Williams'. He was a character. He had habitually addressed everyone as ' 'Ngwasi,' be they Welsh, English or whatever. It translates into English as 'my servant' but is best translated freely perhaps, as 'me lad' and in that kinder context when used in its Welsh form to all and sundry. Some twenty years later I visited him at his home near Criccieth Castle. He wrote some three books in Welsh of his seafaring days. I think the third was *O Flaen y Mast* (Before the Mast). I found all most interesting. He had started on another when I last saw him.

I think it was sometime after I resumed duty that the result of the St. Vincent 'Sedition appeal' was published. The appeal was successful though I gathered that Lord Chief Justice Goddard's pronouncements were sometimes far from being acceptable to all in those later years. Now that I am back, in memory in St. Vincent, perhaps I could mention a somewhat unusual murder case which was the concern of the Trinidad police. A German born optician visited St. Vincent regularly in connection with her business. With some other guests one evening, she was at our house on the eve of her return to Trinidad. She was missing in Trinidad within a day or so and as it was said that she had some personal relationship with someone in St. Vincent, enquiry was made in St. Vincent by the Trinidad police. Some days later her body was found in some waterway in Trinidad. It should not have floated for the murderer had disembowelled the corpse. The body was tied with the belt of her husband's dressing gown. He was an East Indian doctor in Trinidad and was convicted of her murder, committed it seemed on the day following her visit with friends to our house.

But let us talk about horses for a minute — on one of my rides with the officer in charge of the Mounted Branch through the outskirts of the city, he suggested I gave my horse its head along the next road. This I did and shortly the horse turned off the road towards one of the houses. One of the troopers lived there and on patrol the horse was well used to turning aside for a short while and some coconut water perhaps?

The Mounted Branch had been formed in 1905 after '. . . some riots — in Georgetown, police had to open fire on several occasions — Militia called out — parties from two warships assisted in restoring order — police casualties: 1 killed, 57 wounded — 105 persons convicted of rioting . . . Result of these riots was the formation of the Mounted Branch . . . 40 horses were purchased from the U.S.A. — training carried out by the Inspector General (Police) and Captain Carroll, Bandmaster of the Militia, late of the 5th Dragoon Guards . . . from its inception the Mounted Branch did its own shoeing, repairs to saddlery and breaking of the mounts . . .' A very high standard was maintained along the years and their displays of riding, tent-pegging and such like were top class and always looked forward to by the public. In 1955 the Branch saddler made me a pair of riding boots. I returned them to the Branch when I ceased to have further use for them. In 1954 Cpl. Baird had ridden his mount in London's Lord Mayor's Parade.

223

No effort was spared to maintain the Force at a high level of efficiency. Occasional attachments of selected men to the Metropolitan Police in London were arranged for mounted police specialist training, advanced level police driving and other subjects. Officers were sent to the U.K. on courses at the police colleges.

An experienced senior police officer came to us too from the Metropolitan Police to help bring our CID up to date in its methods of operation and another senior officer with experience in the U.K. and in Cyprus to reorganise where necessary all our training school arrangements. The latter, Mick Edwards, had started his career in the Montgomeryshire Police.

Traffic control in Georgetown in particular had for some time been a problem. All aspects of motor transport were a police concern and control of all forms of road traffic was our responsibility as well. A Cardiff City Police Inspector, Llewelyn Evans, who had been serving as Deputy Commander of the Police Recruits Training School at Bridgend, had been appointed to serve with us temporarily as Traffic Chief but essentially his job was to produce an operable plan for the better control of Georgetown's traffic. Part of the plan, in the main, was the introduction of a huge one-way system. Unfortunately, the first big day, despite most detailed preparations, including presence of police at all important points, was a disappointment. That part of the plan was just not going to work. Evans had no other chance and returned to the U.K.

Unexpectedly, I found myself the new officer in charge of Traffic, Transport and Communications. I showed how I wished the traffic police to actively control traffic at quite a number of junctions and at particular times, where control by the existing STOP signs was inadequate. I proposed to introduce Georgetown's first traffic lights and these in due time would release our men. I confess to having enjoyed the publicity. The daily papers allowed me to have a 'Traffic Corner' regularly on one of the pages.

One of the schools asked me to write an article for its own special magazine. I had forgotten about this until I came across pages 13 and 14 on an extracted sheet I have found among my papers. Some of what I wrote follows —

'. . . I am not going to attempt to teach Road Safety in one article in a magazine. The Police with the assistance of your teachers are doing so . . . I do not think I need mention the name of Inspector Siebs of the British Guiana Police in this article for his name will be remembered for the excellent work he has done for the safety of school children . . . but I would not allow this article to be published without mention of his name. By the time this article appears in the magazine, I hope that Broad Street school will be helped by its own policeman! A policeman is going to take a very particular interest in each school. He will visit you regularly and help you to keep danger away. He is your friend, your very special friend . . .

When I first came to British Guiana in 1954, Broad Street School was the first one I became interested in from a traffic point of view. Its teachers were very concerned about the safety of the children. I was able to assist them with temporary pedestrian crossings and the town council improved the bridge immediately I suggested it. I have therefore a special interest in you all.

Over a thousand people were injured and thirty nine killed on the roads in British Guiana in 1956. We must not let this happen again. You can help by learning all the rules of the road as soon as you can, obey them always and teach your parents, relatives and friends and make them obey the rules as well. Please be careful children! Be kind and courteous always.'

We did reduce the number of road casualties in 1957 and we did, in fact, have some 300 policemen who became attached to their own individual schools and it so happened that the head of RoSPA, Sir Howard Roberts (Royal Society for Prevention of Accidents) who was on a private visit to the head of the Bookers Organisation, accepted an invitation to address a gathering of our traffic police. He said that our attention in this way to the schools had so impressed him, he was going to tell the police in the U.K. all about it.

A Royal visit by Princess Margaret necessitated a lot of hard work to be done before and during the visit by all police. I had the added burden of preparing the legal orders necessary

225

for publication so that roads and streets could be closed. Deputy Commander Evan Jones of the Metropolitan Police Special Branch came to check with us before the visit. He was a Welshman from Holyhead. Before he left he insisted that I should call to see him when next on leave. This I duly did. I happened to ask him had he met one W. S. Drew, a Welshman, who was with me as a boy in the RAF and later at RAF Henlow. I knew that Drew had done some typing or shorthand for some Scotland Yard detectives who had been to Henlow in connection with the theft of white metal, and had succeeded in getting his discharge to join the Metropolitan Police. He said we would meet him on our way back from lunch to the Yard and this happened in Whitehall before we turned towards the Yard. After nearly thirty years he knew me immediately. (It is now about 35 years since that reunion!). Drew was the Superintendent in charge of the Fingerprint Section at the Yard.

I had taken time to complete a Highway Code to meet British Guiana's needs. It was more comprehensive than my St. Vincent Code. With permission of HMSO I had now included some extracts from the U.K. Highway Code. Our newspapers in Georgetown had kindly printed the whole of it, over a period, in my Traffic Corner and had given publicity beforehand so that each issue of the paper could be followed. I pressurised Government for its publication in booklet form and free issue but without success. Financial considerations were the only problem and these remained.

I must mention the buses. Long distance buses in particular were carefully controlled as to what could be carried in them and on the roof, for example. These laws were enforced by the police and our approval was required for time tables and one of the conditions required that drivers should report on arrival at specified police stations en route. This was to ensure that speeding between them was hardly worthwhile!

It was a wonderful day when my wife, Sarah and Rowena were able to rejoin me. Ronnie Weber (the Assistant Commissioner Administration), who had lived beneath us in the huge flats, and I were now occupying adjacent bungalows. We overlooked the Police Depot across the road from us and were still quite close to our previous accommodation but now in our own corner plot. Sarah in her orthopaedic support soon became acclimatised and resumed her schooling. Rowena resumed at Bishops as she had not wished to remain at Dolgellau.

We had become settled into another church by this time — Smith's Congregational Church. The minister with his wife were English and had come to B.G. with their daughters after serving for some time in Samoa. I was pleased to see that two members of our Police Male Voice Choir were also in the church choir. I can still enjoy Thomas' tenor voice on my LP record and cassette. The services were very well attended and on Sundays all in their Sunday best. We did get used to it but it was a lovely sight to see perhaps an entire family — well, at least about three or four of them — all on one bicycle, in Sunday best — riding by up to the Sea Wall 'to catch the breeze'.

While there was a lot of unemployment in the country as there was in most of the West Indian colonies, some seasonal labour had been available for some years in the United States. By this time though, many people of all classes were trying to emigrate. Immigration into Canada was allowed on various conditions and at one time, one of the conditions was that the immigrant had to undertake to do domestic work for twelve months after arrival in that country. Their abilities in this field were tested in Georgetown. We lost several general domestics in this way to Canada and including our washerwoman. They were tested at the Carnegie Institute and the Principal was one of three sisters of a wonderful African family. Their only brother, Bryn, was a legal draftsman in the Attorney General's Department. Our Doreen had been asked who had taught her to dust the top edge of the door, amongst other things and so it was Miss Pollard herself who told my wife how we would be losing our Doreen. In several years Doreen, a very buxom African had served us well.

As 'the troubles' persisted and independence was approaching, though in consequence, not yet imminent, more and evermore Guianese were leaving the country. A number of our European officers were moved on transfer to other colonies. They included

Superintendent Rex Jones who was married to Eleanor, an Aberdyfi lass.

Time passed and I was again due for leave in May 1958. It was a short tour for Falmai and the girls and this time we were to travel on the S.S. *Willemstad* of the Dutch Steamship Company. Our first port of call was Paramaribo in Dutch Guiana or Surinam as it is now called. The ship was thus able to unload and prepare for the return voyage to Holland. After calling in Trinidad we should have to disembark at Plymouth ourselves but this would be very convenient for us as we had booked a holiday cottage for a while to be near Diana who was now serving at Culdrose. My new Vauxhall Victor was to be handed over to me at Plymouth and I would in due course take it with me overseas free of purchase tax. I would also gain some small advantage by importing an used car and not a new one when I got back to British Guiana.

We found the Dutch practice of using a fork with the knife when eating bread and butter or toast with jams or marmalades or whatever was far easier and more comfortable than our way of knife only. I recommend it to you. Or do you?

Have you ever seen or read about Trinidad's pitch lake? The pitch with which to tarmacadam our roads may well have come from there. Trinidad's pitch lake is almost one of the world's wonders. I do not remember the details but it is of very many acres in extent — it seems to maintain the same level despite the fact that pitch has been carried from it for very many years. Its surface was generally fairly firm so that vehicles could be driven on it. Small surface pools were presumably of some acidy fluid for copper coins could be instantly made to look like new when dipped in it and all visitors seemed to try this out just like we did in school laboratories. Barrels full of pitch travelled on a non-stop conveyor system to be loaded directly into waiting ships at the jetty. On occasion the huge heavy machines used for cutting and extracting the pitch were wont to sink gradually under their own weight and could not then be lifted out. The best that could be done was to salvage what they could of the upper parts by cutting them off with oxy-acetylene cutters.

The voyage was a holiday in itself really. The approaches to the English Channel were quite rough but we eventually made it carefully into Plymouth. The new car was there on time and we were soon on our way west into Cornwall and to our holiday cottage near Helston and the R.N. Air Station at Culdrose where we could spend some time with Diana as she was now stationed there.

I was privileged to watch a flying display from the control tower gallery at Culdrose. The display included a low fly past by the strange looking Vulcan bomber not long then in general service. (I never thought that a bomber of this type would drop bombs on the Falklands and that in 1993 the very last Vulcan would be offered on sale to the highest bidder).

We saw quite a lot of Cornwall before driving to North Wales and the remaining weeks of leave soon passed. We were back again in British Guiana by mid-November so missed most of the winter. Our return voyage was from Avonmouth and Diana met us at Bristol Railway Station to see us off. She gave us a miniature old fashioned Welsh settle which still plays the tune of 'Land of My Fathers' when the lid is lifted.

Back in British Guiana we were soon back into our routines but I was now to be engaged on special duties at Police Headquarters.

I had been looking forward for some time to seeing the famous Kaieteur Falls. The Countess Mountbatten of Burma came to the Colony in connection with the work of the St. John Ambulance Association in 1958. I was one of a party of five to accompany her to see the Falls. We travelled in the Grumman Goose for otherwise it would have taken days of strenuous travel even to get there, although the Falls are only about 240 miles from Georgetown.

The trip into the Interior was very interesting though we flew over miles and miles of forest, for we had views of vast rivers and rapids and of the mountains ahead of us. We were soon over the Falls and what a breathtaking view it was! We flew upstream though to 'land' on the river without delay — we taxied to the left bank, were made fast, as if we were the boat we were — and climbed ashore. We then faced a rather

229

hot walk for about half a mile through the wooded bank of the river though we were able to follow a well used footpath. The Countess had a shoe problem as we walked along but our gallant pilot, Mr. Wilson, a New Zealander, was immediately to the rescue. He tied the shoe firmly in place again on her foot with his large white handkerchief and all was well for the rest of our walk. The river which looked to be about 200 yards wide, ran along on our right and a little ahead we saw where it suddenly disappeared. The sound of crashing water now seemed to penetrate everything. As we neared the edge, we saw the water descending in sheets like vast, white curtains and these were being met by clouds of spray rising from way down below, more than 700 ft. — over 200 yards!

We moved to a point along the cliff top and could see how the water, over countless years, had cut through the rock to leave a long valley way below, not to be compared with the Grand Canyon in the United States but a similar case of wearing away the rock to create a gorge or canyon. The river below proceeded in a series of small rapids too but height was so deceptive and the rapids could not have been as small as they appeared. Some of the rock layers at the top where they were in the process of being worn away, overhung the Falls. It was a little nerve wracking to walk out on to one of these projections and really feel above the Falls when at the same time one was completely drowned in a torrent of non-stop sound. Water constantly moving is always fascinating to watch but now it all seemed to have a hypnotic effect on me.

We then went some short distance beyond the Falls for some better photographic views. We then met a lone 'walker' with his pack heading for the deeper Interior. He was soon put at his ease with the Countess and both sat on the cliff top chatting away. So, after more photo taking, we reluctantly wended our way back to the Goose. But the best was still to come. We taxied into midstream and headed down river towards the Falls. We were quickly airborne and almost as quickly right over the Falls and then the thrill of circling and circling the big drop and on our part, more attempts at picture taking. I regret to say that an 8 mm cine camera I had had pushed into my hands by Mick Edwards (Training School) just before we left Georgetown but with negligible instructions, stopped operating almost immediately although I had taken pictures for a minute or two when we were disembarking. But I still have the few miserable feet of developed film. It was very kind of Mick.

The Countess enjoyed the trip immensely and didn't we all? She kindly autographed some of my still photos later and some four years afterwards, I was able to give a set of those showing the Countess, with the Falls in the background, to Earl Mountbatten after meeting him on his visit to the Colony in 1962. His wife, Edwina, had died in 1960, only two years after her own visit. Earl Mountbatten had visited the Colony as Chief of the Defence Staff and came to see us at Police Headquarters during our troubles of that year. He was callously murdered while holidaying in Ireland during his retirement.

I was required to act as Assistant Commissioner (Crime) for some months and found I was being kept as busy as ever. We were suddenly faced one day with a case of kidnapping — the first, it was thought, in British Guiana although we had all manner of crimes to deal with. The phone calls for ransom money were anticipated and intercepted so I was naturally delighted when within some three hours, we recovered the young boy unharmed; he was the son of one of the medical staff of a hospital run by a Roman Catholic organisation.

Tempting financial rewards were available to any person who assisted in the discovery and destruction of illicit stills and securing the conviction of the operators. The stills were used to produce rum or 'bush rum' as it was generally known. The stills were usually hidden away in the depths of sugar cane growing areas and therefore needed to be conveniently portable. Catching the operators was often a difficult and even a very dangerous task.

An unusual case of fraud was detected and dealt with. An Indian 'business man' imported quite large stocks of a very cheap paint. He imported large numbers of plain tins of a size and shape as used by one of our more expensive U.K. paint manufacturers. He sold his cheap paint in tins which appeared like tins of the best paint and at top prices. He then tried to

231

wriggle out of it by bribery. A trap was set, for the Detective Assistant Superintendent met him by arrangement but was equipped with microphone attached to his wrist and a hidden recorder. The business man was put out of business for quite a long while.

Armed hold ups were not an unheard of thing but at one stage it was the practice for an armed police escort to be provided as a back-up for a party from a sugar estate with its own escort when collecting its large payroll cash from the Georgetown bank. A sugar estate's factory, administrative buildings and workers' houses were usually quite a distance from the public coast road and at the end of its own private road. An estate van with its driver, pay clerk and armed escort had turned on to such a private road and was followed at some distance by a police Landrover with a Constable armed with one of our standard .303 rifles. The estate van was brought to a stop when the driver saw the road obstructed ahead by large branches. The man with the pay bag got out of the van and started running back — he was shot down by a gunman who now showed himself behind the obstruction and with that the police Landrover arrived from around a slight bend which had until then obscured its approach. The Landrover was braked sharply to a stop, the Constable in the front seat aimed his rifle through the open door top and fired one round. The gunman fell. The single round had penetrated the centre of his forehead, killing the man instantly. The Constable's quick reaction may well have saved several lives.

In December 1959, I was promoted Assistant Commissioner (Administration). This gave me more opportunity of seeing the country than previously. The most remote station from Headquarters was at Lethem nearly 400 miles away on the border with Brazil in the south, although the colony stretched much further south. It was the administrative centre for a vast area of savannah and mountain area. One of the products of the savannah was beef and cattle, for beef would be driven for miles to the abattoir at Lethem. Overland travel between Georgetown and Lethem would be both arduous and time consuming, so the use of air transport had become general. My first trip was in a Dakota aircraft and with stops en route at a number of landing strips which were adequate for a Dakota. Passengers and stores were unloaded and at one stop, we took on board a number of bales of balata. This is a sort of rubber and is harvested like rubber, by cutting into the bark of the tree and collecting the latex as it bleeds. As I first saw it, it was in the solidified form and tied up in bales which could be manhandled into the aircraft. We carried no beef out on my return trip but all beef was flown out by air and the Dakota conveyed most of it to Trinidad.

Lethem was the nearest I got to seeing one of the largest freshwater fish to be found anywhere. This is the arapaima. They are said to grow to a length of about twelve feet. They are found in some of the rivers and creeks in the Rupununi and over the border in Brazil. The flesh is said to be good eating and can be sun dried for eating later.

Another large water creature which I did see, was the manatee, but that was in Georgetown's Botanic Gardens. If one whistled, any old tune I imagine, the manatee would appear at the edge of the water in a convenient pool at one end of a long stretch of water in a sort of canal there. My daughters and I fed it with grass several times. An alligator frequented this pool too, though I never saw it.

The manatee is closely related to the dugong, a marine mammal, found mostly in the Indian Ocean and as far east again as Australia. Both are herbivorous with the dugong living on seaweed. The manatee grows to a length of about twelve feet, looking somewhat like an overweight seal. It has a tail shaped rather like a shovel and with some sort of nails on its flippers giving it the appearance of having arms and hands. It has been said that the mermaid story originated years ago after sailors had seen the dugong suckling its young at its breast, above the water level. I also heard the story that when a female dugong was caught, the catcher had to provide a certificate that he had 'not taken advantage of her'. The manatee was called a 'water-mama' by many in B.G. I remember several manatee were caught in Berbice and brought specially to Georgetown to help clear some of the canals of excess weeds. Nowadays,

233

through colour television, the manatee and dugong can be seen on screens in our homes.

An even less lovable inhabitant of some of the rivers is the cannibal fish, otherwise known as the pirae, pirai or piranha. The tales told of these fish are countless and some of them may be true. I was taken one day in a speedboat up the Abary River to do some fishing and in the hope that I would be able to catch a prize specimen. The object was to acquire a skull with its formidable teeth as a bit of a show piece. I kept the larger of two I did catch but was unsuccessful in my attempt to preserve just the skull. One was supposed to bury it in the ground and let nature leave just the bare bone. It didn't work for me so I have no example of the skull of 'Pygocentrus niger' to show anyone.

I have often been amazed to read how casual visitors to a country have succeeded in seeing so many creatures, be they birds or animals that most of the 'locals' hardly, if ever, see. I saw but very few and most of those were in Georgetown's zoo. Perhaps I ought to list some of the fauna — deer and monkeys of many kinds, ocelot, jaguar, puma, opossum, anteater, tapir, armadillo, porcupine, squirrel, labba, racoon, otter, wild dog, fox and bats including vampire bats. There is an abundance of amphibians and reptiles, including, cayman, anaconda, marine and river turtles, including then the manatee, lizards, gecko, iguana, many kinds of toads and frogs, several types of boa, rattlesnake and electric eel. There are over 700 species of resident and migrant birds. They include toucans of many kinds, eagles, storks, cranes, herons, scarlet ibis, vultures, quail, parrots, teal, humming birds, finches, orioles, umbrella birds, bell birds and calf birds. Two of particular interest are the oil bird which lives in remote caves and the rare hoatzin, unique to British Guiana and which has claws on its wings when young.

In B.G., the hoatzin (Opisthocomus hoazin) is known as Canje pheasant. On a visit to New Amsterdam, I was able to join some friends who took me with them by boat to see some of these birds, which are only to be found in this part of the world and mainly on the banks of the Canje River. We were lucky and saw quite a number. I had thought they would be rather ugly looking birds but I saw why they were called pheasants — they had their own beauty and were about the size of pheasants. We saw no chicks but we were told that they were able to climb about in the bushes and on thin branches by gripping with their legs and using the claws on their wings — the only birds capable of using the wings in this way. The grown birds do not have the use of the claws.

It is time that I give a brief report on the changing political situation in British Guiana. After the suspension of the Constitution in 1953, an interim government was formed without elected members. This continued until an election was held in 1957. In the meantime, though, the main leaders of the P.P.P. (People's Progressive Party) which had been out of power since the 1953 suspension, Dr. Jagan and Mr. L. F. S. Burnham, had so drifted apart that Burnham formed his own party in 1955. It became the People's National Congress (P.N.C.).

In the 1957 elections, Dr. Jagan secured the majority of the elective seats so his P.P.P. was again the largest political party in the Legislative Council but this time, its powers to govern were far more limited. Some progress was made though and in 1960 it was agreed that British Guiana should again advance to virtually full internal self government in 1961 and in a two chamber Legislature.

The elections under the new Constitution were held in August 1961 and the P.P.P. was again in the lead with 20 of the 35 seats. Burnham's P.N.C. gained 11 seats and the remaining 4 were won by a new party called the United Force.

Many Africans followed Burnham out of the P.P.P. but he had support too from numbers of East Indians who left Jagan. There were Africans who remained with Jagan but it was evident that the split was mainly on racial lines and this was to cause a lot of trouble later. Dr. Jagan was now Premier. Under a Minister of Home Affairs, the police were not made to feel unduly uncomfortable but as the country's problems were economical, the P.P.P. was too busily engaged in trying to obtain finance from anywhere and everywhere overseas, to

235

engage in activities which seemed to have promised lots of trouble to many in British Guiana.

These problems were not being resolved and business people and others began taking their money and often themselves as well out of the country. Strict currency restrictions were then imposed.

To have their security arrangements in good shape, some of the larger businesses authorised to employ supernumerary Constables, were filling all vacant posts. Brief courses of instruction were also being provided for all such cosntables who had not yet received training. I arranged to visit one company in the Interior to swear in a number of its existing staff in the office of Constable. This I could do as an ex-officio Justice of the Peace.

The Canadian operated manganese mines at Matthews Ridge in the North West District, were some 200 miles from George-town and perhaps some 80 miles from the coast at Mabaruma. I had been flown in the Grumman Goose to the Kaituma River and had travelled by police launch up river before meeting company transport for the rest of the journey. The mines were tucked away in the middle of the forest but were connected by a railway on which the manganese ore was transported, with Port Kaituma. We met one of the large cargo ships which had just left Port Kaituma with its load of ore on its way to Canada. The river seemed not so very much wider than the ship at that point but with the laden ship well down in the water, it was certainly very deep though. There were signs near bends where the ships were having to brush against the jungle covered river banks. The ship was still about 65 miles upstream.

As the manager's guest, I was having a most enjoyable little break away from the rush and scurry of Georgetown and police headquarters. The silence of the short tropical evening in this jungle retreat, with all its mod cons and home comforts, was broken only by the squawk of flocks of parrots, homing for the night. Then suddenly, my host asked me to listen and I heard a train just arriving at a platform with sounds of people and banging of doors. I got up, questioningly, as I didn't think they carried passengers on their little line — nor that the railway was so near the manager's house. Then the train was driving off and I went to a side window to see if I could see it. There was nothing. Then all was revealed. He had played one of the then new fangled stereo records with its very special effects sounds and with well separated speakers, very effectively.

Too soon, it was time to return to Georgetown. They drove me to the nearest pick up point on a river where the Grumman would collect me. Here I saw that a stretch of the river had been cleared of floating debris between two rafts drawn right across the river. These would keep canoes, ballyhoos and other vessels from encroaching into the prepared 'landing' strip.

While I waited, I was told of the presence of a camoodi (anaconda) on the river bank a short distance upstream. I was excited for I had in my hands a .22 rifle which I had brought with me from Georgetown in the hope that I might see something in the wild animal line to shoot. Here, at almost the last moment, was a chance. I was assured it would still be there and of course they would take me in their canoe — such a narrow, shallow one! We were soon near the spot and as the canoe was edged nearer to the bank, I thought I could see a massive thing, all coiled up and nearly all submerged. I looked for its head, for a shot anywhere else would be quite useless. I could not quite see it but luckily calculated precisely where it ought to be and fired one round. There was massive squirming and I was sure I had found its head. In a moment or so, I saw it, so fired again. It was obvious it was neither going to go away nor drag me into the water. It was far too heavy to lift into the canoe, so we tied a rope to it and towed it back with us to the landing. Pictures and measurements were taken and someone suggested they would skin it and send the skin on to me. Minutes later, almost, the Goose had arrived and I was on my way back to Georgetown. The landing and take off on the comparatively narrow river seemed to be no problem.

A few days later the skin was duly delivered to me in Georgetown. The number two man at Georgetown's museum undertook to cure it for me. The anaconda had measured

17 ft. 6 ins. long on the landing without being stretched straight out.

In September 1961, Falmai and I with Rowena and Sarah sailed in another Dutch ship, the *Oranjestad,* for my long leave in Wales. The curing of the skin had not been successful for it soon then started to show signs of decay in parts. I offered it to the Zoology Department of the University College of Wales in Aberystwyth and they were very grateful when I delivered it to them. And now, over thirty years on, I have the memory and pictures.

We were going to spend this leave in a seaside flat at Borth, near Aberystwyth. It became time for Sarah to submit to more surgery on her back at the Gobowen hospital and there she met again some of the girls with similar back problems she had known there earlier. It was a difficult winter for all of us. Rowena was travelling daily to Aberystwyth to the College of Further Education. Falmai and I were visiting Sarah. Diana was still in Malta at that time but joined us at the end of the year and her service in the W.R.N.S. to await her wedding day. She and David A. Prothero were married at the parish church in Borth on 5th February, 1962. As a Fleet Air Arm pilot, David had also served latterly in Malta but was now to become an air traffic controller with the Civil Aviation Authority as it now is. They called to see Sarah at the hospital on their way to start their new life together.

My wife and I had to arrange other accommodation in Bow Street where she could receive Sarah from hospital after my return alone to duty. Sarah was severely restricted for months in plaster casts but later resumed her schooling at St. Padarn's Convent School at Aberystwyth as a day pupil but later as a boarder. In 1963 though, she became a boarder at the St. Helen's and St. Katherine's School at Abingdon.

I was recalled to duty before the expiry of yet another leave as serious rioting had occurred in British Guiana. I was back there on 23rd February. From that date too, I was the Deputy Commissioner.

Falmai had a fearsome burden to bear without me for before she would be able to rejoin me, it would be September and

Sarah's problems were going to be major ones. Rowena was anxious to do social work in the U.K. and joined the staff of Dr. Barnardo's training in London and Llandudno.

The rioting in Georgetown on 16th Febraury, 1962, had resulted in the death by shooting of one police officer, Supt. Derek McLeod and the wounding by shooting of Senior Supt. James Phoenix and four other policemen. All this at one incident. Phoenix who was hit soon after McLeod fell, had nevertheless stood his ground and even returned fire but was shot a second time and had to be taken away to hospital. The riot sqaud had used tear gas but a total of only 18 rounds were fired to contain the mob who were kept from attacking the P.P.P. headquarters until the arrival of an army unit when its appearance soon caused the mob to give up and disperse. Later, other army patrols had to open fire on several occasions, killing two and wounding four after the usual warnings to looters who were now rampant as business premises were attacked and set on fire. Huge areas of the city's business section were burning. Some shots were fired by the rioters even at fire brigade units whose efforts to contain the fires were hampered by the lack of water supplies in the mains for there was no power, through strikes, to circulate the city's water supplies.

56 business premises were destroyed by fire and 87 damaged and of which 66 were also looted.

In all, 39 police were injured plus one fatally and over 40 rioters injured including two killed. The cost in dead and injured could have been considerably more.

H.M.S. *Troubridge* and H.M.S. *Wizard* arrived that day and some security platoons came ashore to assist the police. On the following day H.M.S. *Urchin* also arrived.

When I arrived a week later, Georgetown seemed quiet after what must have been a dreadful day. The fires had been brought under control by midnight and finally put out on the Saturday morning. I found that much of the streets had been cleared and many areas of badly burned properties cordoned off with police patrols posted.

Police efforts to trace the person or persons who had fired

239

on the police and the firemen were unsuccessful and though the bullet which killed Derek was recovered at the post mortem examination, it was 'lost', and could not therefore, have been traced back to a specific rifle.

Phoenix had made a good recovery and after his retirement some two years later, went to the Anglican Theological College in Barbados to prepare for a new career in the Church.

The Secretary of State for the Colonies appointed a Commission of Inquiry into the Disturbances, in May, and the Report was published by HMSO in 1962 (Colonial No. 354). They concluded that the disturbances were not the result of a deliberate plan to overthrow by force the country's government and that the police had performed their extremely difficult task to the best of their ability; the army had come promptly to their assistance when requested and handled the situation firmly and effectively with minimum use of force.

As Deputy Commissioner, I did all I could to support Ronnie Weber who had been appointed Commissioner in 1959. He had joined the British Guiana Police Force as a sub-inspector in 1928. There was a short period of relative calm but we knew there was yet more trouble to come.

It was about this time that we enlarged our Dog Section. An experienced dog handler from the Kent Police Force came to us and in due course we had set up proper kennels, acquired about a dozen Alsatian dogs and trained our men to handle them. It was a great day when at our Annual Display with the Mounted Branch we also put on a special display by the dogs and their handlers. Our original one Alsatian dog did not like our riot/emergency policemen at the Depot and occasionally a lot of fun had been had by many — other policemen! But from now on it was serious business and calls for the assistance of the handlers and dogs became routine.

H.R.H. Prince Philip Duke of Edinburgh had visited the Colony shortly before the disorders. He was then visiting a number of South American countries and he was now again in British Guiana but in transit only. His Excellency the Governor met him at the private airfield at Mackenzie informally and introduced me. (I had been on leave in U.K.

during the official visit). Prince Philip was a guest of the Canadians at their Mackenzie Bauxite Complex overnight before resuming his tour. A request had been made that our police patrols that night should wear soft shoes instead of regulation boots for Prince Philip was a very light sleeper. I remembered many years earlier when on a night beat, meeting a doctor walking to a night call out. I had said, 'Oh, it's you doctor? Your job is not all honey either?' He replied, 'Honey be damned — all bloody pickles!'

In September 1962, my wife was able to rejoin me for Sarah was in boarding school. Later, she would be 'cared for' by Mr. and Mrs. Sanger-Davies who, in retirement, went to live near Banbury. Joe (V.J.) Sanger-Davies was Principal of Queen's College for Boys in British Guiana and his wife, Nancy, had taught at Sarah's junior school in Georgetown. They had been our near neighbours on Camp Road. They had served in West Africa before coming to British Guiana. They had very kindly pressed us to let Sarah be taught at the school in Abingdon so as to be within their reach.

At our home, Cox House, on Camp Road, we were on the southern edge of the police mounted branch/bandroom/QMS complex but it was the Sanger-Davies's who could hear the band and our police male voice choir at practice. We grew an interesting variety of tomatoes in our small garden and had our own bananas and some coconut trees. One of the troopers would pick nuts as required. There were plenty of flowers and colourful bushes. Our own Alsation was a wonderful creature and the cat would rush to meet me, from tree top or wherever. She drank her tea from my saucer while standing on her hind legs, fully stretched, to reach the saucer on the small occasional table. We would be visited by a colourful bird, near an open window. This was a kiskadee (We often replied in Welsh 'Cysga dithau hefyd' for kiskadee sounded like 'cysga di' meaning 'You go to sleep', so our answer was, 'You go to sleep too!) Others said Kiskadee equalled Qu'est ceq'il dit? However it was a pretty bird with a pretty call.

The Premier, Dr. Jagan, went to London at year's end for an important conference for another election was approaching with a new Constitution leading up to Independence. I went to meet him at Atkinson Field when he flew back. We really did not guess at how much trouble there was still ahead for us. With units of the Army still with us and with visits by various ships of the Royal Navy, we felt we could contain any sudden major outburst of trouble.

There was a short period when I acted as Commissioner. There was a short period too when Ronnie Weber was still with us on the eve of his retirement and our new Commissioner, unusually, was present as well and already in process of taking over. I presumed I was now too near my own retirement age and could better serve as a Deputy and the Force, thereby, have a new Commissioner from outside, as an extra rather than that we should continue in such difficult times with a series of promotions and in effect, only replace an experienced Ronnie Weber with someone in the lowest rank. Ronnie was the first Deputy in British Guiana to be promoted to Commissioner but after Independence, of course, this would become the rule. So I consoled myself, although by this time, after a long and hard stint overseas, I was looking forward to making our home once again in the U.K. and to be nearer our daughters.

In normal times, our police did not carry firearms in the course of general duties but, unfortunately, it became necessary that they should do so. For quite some time, men going out on patrols and ordinary beat duties had to carry their .303 rifles, usually slung on shoulders. Occasionally, but rarely, accidents occurred. An overzealous young constable, against all rules, fired a shot with his rifle after an escaping thief down a busy main street. Fortunately, no one was hit. As and when hand-guns could be procured, the rifles were replaced by .38 revolvers. Each riot squad though still had its rifle party as well as its tear gas and baton sections.

Some more rioting and looting occurred in April 1963. But this time it was condemned by the leaders of the opposition parties and they could not be accused of incitement. The trouble originated as an industrial dispute between employers and employees at the Rice Marketing Board. British Guiana exported over 90,000 tons of rice in 1961 and the annual production had increased tremendously over several recent years. There were two trade unions immediately involved in the rice business and had been fighting each other for some time. One of the consequences was that in April some of the workers claimed they were being locked out and many had gathered outside the gates of the Board's headquarters in Georgetown and where ships could be loaded directly from its main rice stocks. A Russian ship was alongside loading rice for Cuba. Mrs. Janet Jagan, wife of the Premier, arrived with a passenger in her car which was driven by an East Indian to where the Russian ship was tied up. A number of parcels were taken aboard the ship but were not accepted by the captain, so they were returned to the car. The crowd outside the north gate saw parcels being taken from the ship to the car and at once loudly called for the parcels to be searched. The police did so and the parcels were put back in the car. This did not satisfy the crowd who now jumped the gate and attacked the car and its occupants.

Mrs. Jagan was believed by many to be a confirmed communist and so to be influencing her husband, the Premier. Police reinforcements had to be sent for and meanwhile the crowd started stoning the Board's premises and overturned and set fire to the car of the president of the 'other' trade union. The crowd was again brought under control but later in the evening when the Russian ship resumed loading, they became yet more hostile and attacked the police also burning a police motor cycle. With yet more police reinforcements the crowd was driven away from the area but now that they were more scattered, several small groups started attacking shops and looting. Some properties were also set on fire. Before order was restored that night one man had been shot dead and more than 24 injured with some 50 arrests made.

It was suspected that firearms were being brought by the Russian ships calling for rice to Cuba and this was undoubtedly the reason the crowd had demanded the parcels be searched. In fact, though, the outgoing parcels — not incoming — were being sent to certain P.P.P. members undergoing training in Cuba and contained only personal clothing, toilet requisites and books. The captain had refused to take the parcels until the agent had given him permission to do so.

It was about this time that I procured a box of divining rods which could be used as metal detectors and so enable us to search more easily for firearms in bags of rice stored in large quantities. The detectors were tried out by the army to search for three separately hidden revolvers on the banks of a canal. They were found but what other successes if any, there were later, I do not know. Failure to find anything in rice bags may have given the searchers a degree of satisfaction too. Following the rioting, many searches were made at suspect properties for gunpowder bombs and gasoline bombs such as were used in attacks against shops and in one instance found on a person attending a political meeting.

In July 1963, Sarah came to join us for the school summer holidays. We were delighted that she had been able to fly out to us unaccompanied. We were able to go with friends on a picnic cruise some forty miles up the Demerara River where there were beautiful sandy beaches and wooded sandy hillocks. Eating ripe mangoes in the approved manner while in the river bathing was as enjoyable as usual. We met some friends water skiing there and Sarah and I enjoyed the ride in their speedboat but refused the offer to a first attempt to ski. So it was that life was proceeding in a normal fashion too.

Along the years, the police force had attracted far more African than East Indian recruits. We were now being asked by Government (Dr. Jagan's) for racial breakdown of the general force and its special constabulary and riot squads. I see that at that time when there were about 300,000 East Indians in the general population, there were only about 200,000 Africans. In the police, however, there were only about 300 East Indians to 1,200 African. Incidentally the Europeans were now down to 5 officers only, to 42 others. We had 9 Amerindian constables but these were usually employed on duties in the Interior only. There were only some five each of Portuguese and Chinese races. Police of mixed race totalled 88.

It was understandable that Dr. Jagan and his P.P.P. should imagine that as the majority of the police were of African descent, most of them might lean to the P.N.C. rather than the P.P.P. In the police, though, we felt that whatever their personal feelings might have been, the Africans and the East Indians in the Force, continued to carry out their duties fearlessly and without bias.

All too soon, unfortunately, they were all to be tested to the utmost. Hitherto most of our troubles and disorders had been confined to Georgetown but now they were spreading to the country areas as well. Labour troubles in both rice and sugar industries developed and were added to by rivalry between opposing trade union leaders.

A negro walking in company with an East Indian 'was approached by 9 unknown East Indian men and told he was a strike breaker. They began to lash him with sticks about his head and body. He was taken to Government medical officer, Skeldon.' This was typical of some of the reports in the earlier stages. But then came the report of a far more serious incident — 'information received at 5.10 p.m. that a bomb was thrown into the Enmore school children's bus . . . About 9 children injured. Supt. Barrow and party left for the scene. Bus generally conveys the children of senior staff at Enmore (a Sugar estate) to and from school. Further report later.'

Throughout the period of the troubles, I would be supplied with a copy of all reports coming in to Headquarters.

A 13 year old boy named Godfrey Texiera died that night of his injuries and the next day, another report said — 'Residents of the area are very annoyed and are blaming the G.A.W.U. (one of the trade unions) and the P.P.P. They termed this as barbarism at its highest, as the children involved are in no way connected with the sugar dispute. They are of the opinion that the Governor should take action now as this act will result in civil war in the near future. Continuing, they said that if the injured children were of African descent, the war would have started last night. Some of them are of the opinion that the reaction to this incident would be terrible, as the Premier's children may also be injured shortly.'

Placards with pickets outside P.P.P. headquarters in Georgetown the following morning, read — 'P.P.P. Cowards Attack

Inocent Children — 12 children. They should be yours. Jagan
were you born with a conscience. Jagan asked for Troops Use
Them. Janet Are you Mother or Murderess? Communists
murdered little Godfrey.'

Next day, there were yet more pickets with more placards.
Reports from all parts of the coastal area of attacks on
properties, sugar cane, other crops including coconut plantations
and individuals continued to come in. Many searches were
carried out by police and occasionally some weapon, ammunition
or explosives were found. Numerous unexploded bombs checked
by the army proved to be hoax bombs.

Two notices fixed to a tamarind tree at Blairmont read —
'No negro to enter Nos. 1, 2 and 3 Settlement. Death, death,
We intend to kill any negro that enters'.

An explosives magazine at Monkey Jump Stone Quarry, up
the Essequibo River, was broken into and 500 lbs gelignite,
2 coils of fuse wire and 1,600 plain detonators and 400 electric
generators were stolen. In consequence of this, it was decided
that we should limit the number of magazines in use at all
quarries and mines and ensure proper guarding of those selected
to continue. Explosives would only be drawn from these by
other quarry operators as and when actually required.

I decided I would examine all of the stores myself so that
the necessary arrangements could be made. The army kindly
provided the ideal transport for me. I would be taken to each
quarry and mine in one of the army's helicopters. As I had
not travelled in a helicopter before, it was quite a day for me.
More importantly, however, I was able to accomplish in that
one day, what could otherwise have taken me perhaps up to
a fortnight, as all the stores were located in out of the way
places in the Interior. Later, substantial quantities of the missing
explosives and detonators were found hidden near the Monkey
Jump quarry magazine. Hidden, presumably, to be collected
later.

As the weeks and months went by, the attacks on property
and person became ever more severe. One man came in the
early morning to a police station with his throat cut and could
not speak. He had been attacked from behind and held and

unable to see whether his attackers were African or East Indian. His head was forced back and the front of his neck cut across. Shots were fired at houses and at individuals. Houses were now being set on fire by night and as the occupants dashed out, they were frequently being shot at from the darkness.

A bomb was set in a large passenger launch on its way to Mackenzie from Georgetown. Bombs were thrown into cinemas patronised mainly by one racial group.

In an attempt to reduce the degree of violence, we decided to suspend all gun licences of people in the coastal areas and call in, temporarily, all their weapons for safe keeping. This was a really major operation and I have often wondered since, how and when the firearms were restored to their owners. As the guns were being surrendered at all the various police stations, they had to be adequately tagged and recorded. In British Guiana, shotguns were treated in the same way as rifled firearms for licensing purposes and when first registered would be stamped with a number. All the surrendered firearms would then be brought under armed escort to the police depot in Georgetown. Here I had arranged for suitable wooden stands to hold them and these in due course just about filled our miniature rifle range accommodation. I do not remember what the total figure was for weapons surrendered but it was of several thousand.

Dr. Jagan's wife, Senator Janet Jagan, had held the Home Affairs portfolio following two other members of the P.P.P. but we had encountered no problem. There was continuing interest, of course, in the radical imbalance in the Force but this was the same in the civil service generally and had not come about with intent. More East Indians lived in the country areas while Africans generally favoured town life and the jobs occurred mostly in towns. In the professions, there appeared to be a far more even mix of the races. Hitherto British Guiana had been known as the 'Land of Six Races', all living harmoniously together.

For several years, there had been a continuing exodus of many people whose services would be sorely missed by the country in its early years of the now so near independence.

The British government spared no effort in preparing the ground to ensure the approaching election would be properly conducted and fair.

We tried to live a normal life too, although our house like other police quarters, continued to have an armed guard. Our Sarah joined us again for her 1964 summer school vacation. Rowena, in London, had just joined the Metropolitan Police. Diana and David had our first grandchild to show us, but we didn't know then that one day, Ellen was to take me for my first flight in a glider nor that she was to become a commercial pilot and fly holiday jets for a commercial airline. She flies other aircraft too. Meanwhile her Dad is still helping to ensure our controlled airways are safe.

Back in British Guiana, the long awaited Election Day arrives and for the first time, Burnham's People's National Congress secures the majority it has so wanted. The P.P.P. has to stand aside. Dr. C. Jagan is replaced by L. F. S. Burnham, Q.C. as Premier.

The year's end approaches and for the time being, at least, the troubles decrease.

I have earned another lot of leave and I am anxious as I approach the end of what has to be my last tour of duty as a colonial police officer in H.M. Overseas Civil Service, to beat it back, on a long leg, to the north east and retirement to Wales where, hopefully, peace will constantly prevail.

I shall miss the many friends and colleagues in British Guiana. Twenty nine years later, as I write this, my quarter clock still chimes beautifully and I remember my last Mess night. I can put on my record and tape at any time and hear again the police choir and band.

It became a bit of rush and scurry to get home for Christmas. Falmai and I flew from Atkinson Field, where we had our last farewells, firstly to Curacao in the Netherlands West Indies to overnight then on to a brief stop in New York and on in the joy of being on our way to see our children. Our friends Nancy and Joe Sanger-Davies were to be our hosts for a short while. Falmai was going to lend a hand as Nancy was to have a hip replacement — rather a job in those days — but they had

248

thoughtfully arranged for our entire family to be with us for Christmas and we managed to get to The Homestead, Shotteswel, Banbury, some three days before Christmas.

We missed the warmth of the tropics that winter of 1964-65 but we revelled in the warmth of welcome home and the thought that we would no longer have to be away again, from kith and kin, on three year tours.

In our few weeks in England then we started to get to know Banbury of course, and Oxford and the Cotswolds. A visit to the theatre at Stratford on Avon was a must but Wales was calling.

HOME FOR GOOD

We were fortunate in finding a house to buy, within our means, at Fairbourne, on the coast, on the south side of the Mawddach estuary, opposite Barmouth in what was then Merionethshire. We moved into it in early 1965. Then, once well settled, it was time for me to look for a job. I soon found it was not going to be easy, for even in those days, who would want to be employing a man of 55? I was offered employment though, very quickly, in a garage office but at a ridiculously low wage. While I felt I had to be prepared to lower my sights considerably, I had to refuse this first chance.

I had found it to be a strange experience to discard not just the uniform but the 'built in' responsibilities of a police officer when I went to Hong Kong. At that time though, I had still been in government service and under War Office control but now I was suddenly out on my own permanently.

In February, I had received a letter from Anthony Greenwood, the then recently Secretary of State for the Colonies, which read — 'Dear Mr. Jenkins, Having learned that you have retired from public service overseas, I should like you to know of my gratitude for your work for the Governments and peoples of Hong Kong, Falkland Islands, Grenada, St. Vincent and British Guiana since your first appointment in 1946. I send you my best wishes for the future. Yours sincerely . . .' It was nice to receive it but it did indicate that quite a chapter had just been closed and an entirely new one lay ahead.

A second chance of a job came, as the Golf Club at Aberdovey needed a Secretary/Treasurer. I managed to get the appointment. As Aberdovey is some sixteen road miles from Fairbourne, it was necessary to lunch away from home and as the season was getting into full swing, my hours lengthened, though more through my own fault than any demands by the Club. I tried to improve my golf and enjoyed my efforts. My best effort was a drive via two hard frozen bunkers on to a green, for my side against a captain's side. It is nevertheless a good winter links and recommended. A blind one-shot hole, beyond a very steep sandhill, has the novelty of a long periscope to ensure an unobstructed green.

I needed a better paid job and I needed to see more of Falmai now that I was 'retired', and not less than I was able to when I was so much busier actually overseas. Sarah at school in Abingdon was still a long way away too. Rowena had agreed to become the wife of a police officer and would resign her own appointment. Our daughters were growing up. As someone said to us, we were not losing daughters but gaining sons and Philip was soon afterwards one of us. London was further than Abingdon — Diana and family were up Preston and Manchester way.

In early November 1965, Falmai and I were invited to attend for interview for the joint posts of Matron and Warden of a Working Boys' Hostel for the city of Oxford's Children's Department. I felt we could cope with a family of 9 working boys for we would have a full time cook, a domestic cleaner and adequate relief staff. However, it was not to be, for the Committee and Children's Officer invited us to apply for appointment as Warden and Matron of their new Rehabilitation Centre. The centre was being set up under the Children and Young Persons Act 1963 and in the premises already acquired and converted there were five self-contained flats for families and adequate accommodation for the Warden and his wife.

It was intended that for the benefit of the children, the families would be those who had been evicted for non-payment of rent, or those where the parents had neglected their children. The warden and matron would co-operate with the child care staff and be responsible to the Children's Officer. It was hoped to re-establish the families back in council houses. The scope for good works seemed boundless.

251

We were asked if we would go to Marple in Cheshire to see the work at a Recuperative Centre there and also visit an Elizabethan Fry Home in York. Our stay at Marple was for a fortnight. We found that our Oxford Rehabilitation Centre would be operating in quite different circumstances though with the same aims. Falmai and I thought we would really enjoy tackling the job ahead together and we did.

One of 'our' families, as an example, consisted of the father just being released from prison for stealing from his electricity meter — mother and baby from the homeless family unit — and two other children from their 'incare' children's hostel. All brought together again and we wanted to help them and organise them gently into a properly ordered family once more. But I must leave them now. So much I could write about.

Falmai's appointment had been a temporary one — for one year — on medical grounds. Much to our dismay, it was not to be extended, as we had expected it might be and we were very sorry to be leaving our families.

We did carry on for several months though while the council sorted out their staffing problems. This gave us the opportunity, meanwhile, to look for other employment. We were thinking now mostly in terms of joint posts and where accommodation would be provided. We also wanted to be as near as we could to Sarah and Rowena in the south east. We had to turn down one good joint post in Nottingham because we would not be able to take our time off together! There were cases where I had been invited for interview by local authorities and it had become obvious immediately that the local candidate was already in waiting and that others had been called only to show compliance with the rule that all posts were to be advertised. In another case which I felt was unusual, I had been called only to show compliance with the rule that all posts were to be advertised. In another case I had been invited to attend for an interview for a job as a race relations officer — the other candidates attending were an Englishman, a West Indian African and a Pakistani. While we were awaiting around, the African became tangled with one of the council officials and I, with what I hoped was my best police type approach and comprehensive race relations experience, soon restored peace if not harmony! The Pakistani was appointed. In Pakistan surely he should have been appointed but I felt it was the host country who should provide an officer to fill such an important job. But, maybe after all, this was a case of a job for the local man too.

But back now to a joint post. My wife and I agreed to run a small hostel for specially selected offenders in Slough. A large private house in a residential area had been purchased by a special Slough and District Hostels Association Ltd., and we would be in at the beginning and see to its adaptation and preparation to receive our ex-prisoners. It sounded very interesting. More immediately it had been decided that I should visit and see for myself what was happening in other places. My first visit was scheduled for the day after Falmai and I had moved in. I attended a conference for Chairmen and Wardens of After Care Hostels at the Women's Voluntary Service Headquarters in London. It was chaired by Lady Reading, the head of the W.R.V.S.

It was also arranged for me to attend a Langley House Trust hostel at Cheltenham for a fortnight. I went there but found it too overladen with staff, I returned to Slough after about ten days as it really was pointless my staying any longer. N.A.C.R.O. — The National Association for the Care and Resettlement of Offenders — had arranged that visit and later arranged a series of brief visits in London to some small hostels run by various organisations and to a Social Service Unit at St. Martin-in-the-Fields and the Blackfriars Settlement. Later, I also visited H.M. Prison Wormwood Scrubs — a rather frightening sort of place compared with my Port Stanley prison — I thought! I listened in to a committee considering applications for parole and how some prisoners were being eased back into the community by short stays at hostels in the first instance.

In the meantime, in Slough, it seemed that most of the residents in our area were loud in their protests against our proposed hostel. I do not know who it was who now discovered after several months, that the house deeds contained a covenant which restricted its use for all time to a private dwelling only.

So July had become November 1967, and we were on the move once more.

We went to stay briefly with Diana and David at Hale Barns as David was now air traffic controlling at Manchester Airport. Rowena's first child was our scond grand-daughter, Samantha Sian. Sarah had finished at St. Helen's and would be taking up an appointment at the Tate Gallery.

In my search, earlier, for employment, I had registered with the Overseas Services Resettlement Bureau. One interesting offer I considered was to attend for an interview for a post as a Temporary Executive Officer to join a Welsh Office team in London to assist in making arrangements for the Investiture of the Prince of Wales. Much as I would have liked to accept, I had to refuse as I could not afford to go to London to work for the salary on offer. We went instead to Slough for those five months.

For a few weeks, while at Hale Barns, I tasted a dole queue in Altrincham and that was a strange experience too. But suddenly the Overseas Services Resettlement Bureau came up with another vacant post for me to consider. A farm secretary was required near Wrexham, '. . . on a large estate, with its own Anglican chapel . . . would occupy a modern three bed-roomed house with garage and private garden . . .' I went for the interview by arrangement together with my wife and we were led through a disinfecting footbath on to the farm premises, for we were in a Foot and Mouth control area.

The estate owner who had met us explained he was working the home farm himself and living in the big house and we would be occupying what was previously the manager's house. Everything bar the 'wages' was most attractive. But the house and free milk and occasional other perks were worth a lot too and I had no hesitation in accepting. My employer was chair-man of the local bench and various other bodies including the Police Standing Joint Committee, so we had much in common.

I had much to learn about modern farming and it was all delightful, with no crime or criminals, no rioting and no problem families to worry about. There were several 'enterprises' as they are called — a dairy herd, potato, wheat and barley crops and a pig fattening piggery. A lot of the land was being reinstated after some years of open cast coal mining. It was interesting to witness the development of the land, with access roads and a large pond was created. There was some shooting and I rode occasionally to exercise one or two horses being looked after by a groom at the original stables, near the old mansion which had been demolished during the war.

We sold our house at Fairbourne and for the time being made our home in the house provided. We were enjoying our stay and the change of seasons on the farm. Our daughters came to stay in turn and we enjoyed being back again in Wales and able to visit relatives and friends.

On the day of the Investiture of the Prince of Wales at Caernarfon, he was being driven in his car after the event along many miles of roads and through many towns and villages of Wales, to be seen by the people. He would be passing our house and we waited but only a short while until he was passing. We were there with our other farm workers and some of their families and waved. I wondered what might have been had I gone to that post in London and I thought of the day a royal salute was fired in the Falkland Islands to salute his birth.

I was conscious of the fact that we were living in a 'tied' house and that we should be prepared, after all, to seek yet another home some day. It was this, I think, which gave us an excuse to see a lot of North Wales when house hunting again though not yet seriously. We did miss the sea, so tended to visit coastal areas after our other so far away islands.

After three years, 'on the farm', we found a bungalow overlooking the sea at Dyffryn Ardudwy, a few miles south of Harlech. It also overlooked the airfield at Llanbedr which reminded me of the time, some thirty years earlier, when I had had a little — a very little — to do with its conversion from a sandy waste to a much needed airfield. Diana's David had flown for a short while at RAF Llanbedr — so he would be seeing it again too.

The estate agent who was trying to sell the bungalow pressed us hard to buy but refused to ask the owner if she would accept the price we were prepared to pay. I decided later to call on the owner/occupier and make the offer directly to her. She was glad to accept and so we acquired a home of our own again and moved in. It was now 1970. On our first Sunday at 'Westfield' we went to the nearby chapel, where Falmai and I met another couple who were long time members there. Both were known to us, separately, from childhood days. So we soon settled in and met others too, mostly known to Falmai and her family.

Jobs were still hard to come by but I was fortunate, as I was willing not to be too demanding, for the manager of a large holiday Caravan Park engaged me to start as one of his senior clerks. Most of the work involved letting of the caravans for the holiday seasons, usually by the week. Some of the caravans were owned by the company owning the park but mostly they were privately owned and rent paying. Where we undertook bookings for them we took a percentage.

While it had the advantage of not being far from 'Westfield', the job became a little more demanding than I had expected. So much overtime was needed just when I needed more time to spend enjoying our 'retirement' with my wife that I began to feel that I should start looking for yet another job. It was beginning to look as if the three year tour of duty was following me or was it a three year itch to be on the move? Matters were delayed a while as I was asked if I would go to manage another park the owners were hoping to buy in Anglesey. But it was not to be for the deal fell through.

I then decided I no longer wanted to work at weekends and public holidays, so resumed my search for a different job and almost overnight as it were, I found I was running an estate agent's branch in Barmouth. The proprietor operated his main office in Dolgellau, with some staff and I worked alone in Barmouth. There was another small part time branch office in Harlech.

I had never imagined that I should be trying to sell houses other than my own — but here I was. My duties also included payment of wages, PAYE, VAT and some other exercises for the business. Variety they said was the spice of life. I was certainly having the variety. An occasional auction sale — a shut shop hour or so to allow me to go out to measure up a property and prepare a description of property to be offered for sale and its suggested valuation. I was remembering my own experience and always gave a would be seller a chance to refuse an offer lower than the asking price. Good for the seller and a quick sale should be good for the business though the commission may be slightly less.

I was visited one day by Maldwyn Lloyd Jones of my Falkland days. That was a pleasant surprise. He had heard that I was to be found there and during his short visit, we tried to fill in the twenty two year gap since we last met. Several years after this visit, I was telling a former Cardiganshire police colleague of mine of my meeting with the Bishop of the Falklands and his Lampeter connections. My friend had known him well for they were in the Navy together briefly at the end of the First World War and showed me a cutting from the local newspaper, reporting the Bishop's visit to Lampeter in 1956 when he was home to attend a Lambeth Conference.

It was of advantage on occasion to have an enquiring mind. I had been measuring up some land to be offered for sale in Dyffryn Ardudwy village. There was something that did not quite match up with the deeds of the property. My figures were correct and the tape seemed to be genuine. I decided to seek a sight of a six-inch O.S. map. Part of a contour line on the map had been translated as a boundary on the plan of the land in the deeds prepared years earlier.

We had sold our bungalow in 1973 to buy a very substantial stone-built semi-detached house in Barmouth. It was so very much more convenient for Falmai and myself to be in Barmouth. The nearby bowling green beckoned and I was managing an occasional game of golf.

Time passed and in 1976, nearly a year after my sixty-fifth birthday, I thought I should retire. Reducing sales in the property market had by this time necessitated a reduction in our opening hours so I had no hesitation in calling it a day and to take up my now but very slightly improved retirement pension. I was allowed one based only on the few years I had worked in this country after returning from overseas. I had not been told in 1948 when working in H.M.'s Colonial Service that I would not be granted an Old Age Pension unless I paid my share of the 'stamps'. I was deemed to have earned £7.32 a week with a total of £3.78 for Falmai. Since she was sixty, my wife's graduated pension had been paid to her monthly — 20p @ 5p per week.

We continued to enjoy Barmouth for two more years but the house was too big. Itchy feet won the day and Anglesey called and the chance of a bungalow again and with glorious views was offering. So we sold our house in Barmouth in 1978 and moved to Anglesey. We could see the sea some five miles away and Holyhead and Rhosneigr and RAF Valley from our sitting room. We looked forward to meeting new people and making new friends as we had done so often before. Old friends too came avisiting — some we had known in British Guiana and Harold Bennett too from the Falklands.

Falmai who had not been well for quite some time was glad of the convenience of our bungalow. I became a member and later chairman of the Community Council (formerly the Parish Council) and my wife persuaded me to undertake the duties of Treasurer of our congregational church. I had many flights as a social member of the local flying club.

Our daughter Rowena and Philip acquired a small property some ten minutes drive from us in 1983 and in 1986 left London when Philip, latterly a Detective Chief Inspector in the Metropolitan Police, retired, to start up their herb nursery. Pigs, chickens, ducks, geese even peacocks and sheep have kept them busy too. Their two daughters and son with Diana's Ellen, make up our four grandchildren.

Diana and David have lived for some years at Flackwell Heath near High Wycombe, with Ellen nearby. David still in Airways Control at West Drayton Air Traffic Control Centre, probably helps Ellen too, for she continues as an airline pilot with a commercial airline.

Sarah lived for some years in London before moving to New York. Among other things, she has reviewed books for publishers and has worked as a copy editor. In 1985 she submitted herself

258

to some modern surgery, in Minneapolis, and came home to see us some three inches taller.

Falmai, my partner on that long, long, often tough beat, for over fifty three years, died suddenly and unexpectedly in hospital in January 1989. Sarah came home briefly for her mother's funeral and came again, as promised, a few months later for my birthday. In the meantime, however, she had decided she would then remain in this country. She was too late for the 1989 entry to the University College at Bangor but she had been assured of admission in 1990. She went up to London to look up old friends and perhaps suitable employment but it was not to be and she died there suddenly and only ten months after her mother. They had suffered a lot together and separately.

I continue to live in this Anglesey bungalow alone but Rowena and Philip are near and so helpful.

I keep an eye open for every bit of news I can get from all parts of my long beat. Guyana has had a particularly hard time for many years. I was glad to learn the other day that after twenty eight years of opposing the P.N.C., Dr. Jagan has at last succeeded in regaining power and I hope that in today's world political climate, he will be able to help Guyana into a more prosperous and happier future.

St. Vincent and Grenada I hope will continue to prosper and may their hurricanes and earthquakes be few.

The Falklands have been changed almost out of all recognition I think and Harold Bennett's voice and the *Penguin News* he sends me, keep me in touch.

I would almost be afraid to enter Hong Kong's maze of tall buildings — today perhaps, they are even more unappealing when one thinks of the City of London's Bishopsgate. But Hong Kong Chinese will I am sure continue to thrive.

On my Cardiganshire beat today, I find much still the same outwardly. The roads are little, if any, wider, in most places, though admittedly busier. I see many reminders of days gone by but so many friends are now missing. Aberaeron's Gorwel still looks out to sea, sixty years on, so I have seen quite a few far horizons since I was a young lodger there. And it was in

259

Aberaeron, at a place with another view, that some months ago, I was at last persuaded to sit down with pad and pen to try to write of these my other days.

THE END